THE **LEXINGTON** SIX

THE
LEXINGTON
SIX

Lesbian and Gay Resistance in 1970s America

JOSEPHINE DONOVAN

UNIVERSITY OF MASSACHUSETTS PRESS
Amherst and Boston

ISBN 978-1-62534-544-8 (paper); 543-1 (hardcover)

Designed by Deste Roosa
Set in Electra and Helvetica Neue
Printed and bound by Books International, Inc.

Cover design by Deste Roosa
Cover photo by Mark Neil Paster, *Kentucky Six*,
from the front cover of *Gay Community News*, March 22, 1975.
Courtesy of the photographer.

Library of Congress Cataloging-in-Publication Data
Names: Donovan, Josephine, 1941– author.
Title: The Lexington Six : lesbian and gay resistance in 1970s America /
Josephine Donovan.
Description: Amherst : University of Massachusetts Press, [2020] | Includes
bibliographical references and index. |
Identifiers: LCCN 2020019277 | ISBN 9781625345431 (hardcover) | ISBN
9781625345448 (paperback) | ISBN 9781613767894 (ebook) | ISBN
9781613767900 (ebook)
Subjects: LCSH: Power, Katherine Ann. | Saxe, Susan. |
Gays—Kentucky—Lexington—Case studies. | Fugitives from
justice—Kentucky—Lexington—Case studies. | Civil
rights—Kentucky—Lexington—Case studies. | Gay
rights—Kentucky—Lexington—Case studies.
Classification: LCC HQ76.3.U52 L4936 2020 | DDC 306.76/60976947—dc23
LC record available at https://lccn.loc.gov/2020019277

British Library Cataloguing-in-Publication Data
A catalog record for this book is available from the British Library.

When [they] threatened to . . . arrest me . . . I made up my mind
that I would run the risk, having law and justice with me,
rather than take part in your injustice.
For the strong arm of that oppressive power
did not frighten me into doing wrong.

—Socrates
Plato, Apology 32

CONTENTS

Author's Note | ix

The Story | xi

AUTHOR'S NOTE

At the time of the Lexington Six events, I was an assistant professor in the Honors Program at the University of Kentucky and active in feminist activities on campus. In that capacity I knew some of the participants and was peripherally involved in some of the events covered in this book. In an afterword I explain the details of that involvement. Occasionally, in the course of the narrative I mention my first-person experience of an event, but in most of the text I write in the third person and attempt to relate events objectively and factually, offering opinions and interpretations, as necessary, based on the evidence presented, as well as on my firsthand knowledge. I often use the participants' first names because this is the way they referred to one another, and because it helps to establish the familiar sense of community that characterized the political resistance movements of what has been called the long 1960s.

THE STORY

On September 23, 1970, a group of antiwar activists who called themselves the Revolutionary Action Force robbed a bank in Brighton, Massachusetts, a section of Boston. Among the five gang members who participated in the robbery were two young, white, college-educated women. The other gang members were three white men, ex-convicts on parole. One of them in the course of the robbery shot and killed a police officer on the scene. The three men were soon apprehended, but the two women escaped, becoming fugitives for several years—four and a half in the case of one of the women, twenty-three in the case of the other. The Federal Bureau of Investigation (FBI) put them both on their "Ten Most Wanted" list.

The two women first traveled in disguise around the Northeast, settling for an extended stay in the Hartford, Connecticut, area in 1972. In the spring of 1974, they moved on to rural Kentucky, where they helped some friends they had met in Connecticut build a house. During their time as wayfaring fugitives the two women became lovers and came to fervently embrace a newly discovered feminism.

In early May 1974, the lesbian couple arrived in Lexington, Kentucky, where they sought out similarly identified women in its feminist community. They soon moved into a large house where several other young women, most of them lesbians, lived as a collective, and they found jobs in the city, one as a cook in a health-food restaurant adjacent to the University of Kentucky campus and the other as a telephone receptionist.

Meanwhile, as the two had long since been indicted for the bank robberies (including one earlier to the Brighton job) and murder, their photos and descriptions had been placed on "Wanted by the FBI" posters, which were circulated throughout the country.

The two women left Lexington rather abruptly and without much explanation to their friends in late summer (in the case of one) and early fall (in the case of the other) of 1974. Not long after, in early January 1975, the FBI, having been alerted to sightings of these women in Lexington, began preliminary investigations. By the middle of the month, this inquiry had exploded into a full-blown dragnet. Scores of members of the feminist, lesbian, and gay communities were contacted by the FBI during this period. At first, the questions posed by the FBI agents seemed to focus on finding the whereabouts of the two fugitives, but as the interrogations continued, the questions broadened to include questions about the lesbian community in general—who was in it, who was involved with whom, who were friends with whom, the tenor of their political beliefs, and the nature of their lifestyles and "sexual preferences."

Several of those thus interrogated refused to cooperate with the FBI and would not answer their questions. Of those, four lesbians and one gay man received subpoenas to appear on February 3, 1975, before a federal grand jury in Lexington. Another lesbian was also later subpoenaed. The week before, on January 28, 1975, in a parallel case in Connecticut, two lesbians who had similarly refused to answer FBI questions had been summoned before a federal grand jury in New Haven and had refused to answer essentially the same questions in the grand jury room. They were then held in contempt of court and sent to prison on March 5.

Three days later, the Lexington Six, as they came to be known, similarly refused to answer questions posed in the grand jury hearings and were likewise held in contempt of court on March 8, ironically International Women's Day. They were handcuffed, put in chains, and sent off in pairs to Kentucky county jails scattered about the state.

The term of the Connecticut grand jury expired at the end of March so those two women were released. (In grand jury civil contempt cases the prison sentence terminates at the end of the grand jury session, which generally runs eighteen months.) However, the Connecticut women were soon re-subpoenaed under a newly empaneled grand jury, held in contempt again on June 6, 1975, and sent again to prison—this time for six and a half months.

In the Kentucky case, two of the Lexington Six—one of the lesbians and the gay man—finding after several days the jail conditions intolerable, agreed to cooperate with the grand jury, to "purge" themselves of contempt, which occasioned their release. Three others, having spent over two months in jail, on learning that their plea for bail had been denied and their appeal to the federal circuit court indefinitely delayed, agreed to testify before the grand jury and were thus also released, the contempt decree abrogated.

One intrepid young woman, however, continued to refuse to cooperate with the FBI-controlled grand jury and thus was confined in Kentucky county jails for another twelve months, the remainder of the grand jury's term, winning release finally on May 4, 1976.

As a spontaneous refusal to allow government officials to intrude into their private lives, relationships, and community, the resistance of the Lexington lesbian and gay feminists recalls the celebrated Stonewall uprising in New York. Like the Stonewall action, the defiant stand of the Lexington Six initiated and inspired a nationwide resistance movement of mostly women against FBI and grand jury harassment, which lasted for years and spread to numerous other minority communities, including Native American, Chicano/a, and Puerto Rican.

Why then did these six young people—Gail Cohee, Debbie Hands, Carey Junkin, Jill Raymond, Nancy Scott,* and Marla Seymour—put up such prolonged and determined resistance, at great personal sacrifice, to what Socrates called "the strong arm of that oppressive power"?

This is their story.

---

* Pseudonym, used throughout.

THE **LEXINGTON** SIX

CHAPTER ONE

Lena and May in Lexington

One afternoon in late fall 1974, Letty Ritter, a sometime student at the University of Kentucky, happened to be in the Lexington Post Office with a friend she called her "drug buddy," Alan Johnson.* As they idly flipped through a binder of the FBI's "Wanted" posters, they noticed that two of the sought fugitives bore a certain resemblance to two women who had recently roomed in the house Letty shared with several other women on 341 Lexington Avenue. One in particular, identified on the poster as "Katherine Ann Power—5', 150 pounds, light brown hair, hazel eyes, wears glasses"—struck Letty as resembling a woman she had known as May Kelly. But no, she thought, that's silly, that can't be May. Then she noticed a second poster—of a "Susan Edith Saxe—5'4"–5", 160 pounds," with "dark brown hair," also wearing glasses and with "an identifying black spot in her left eye"—and her suspicions grew. Letty still wasn't sure, though. After all, the woman they'd known as Lena Paley had blonde hair (though it was likely bleached) and didn't look exactly like the FBI poster photo. Nevertheless, the more she thought about it, the more she was shocked to realize that her two former housemates were likely the fugitives on the FBI's "Ten Most Wanted" list, wanted for "Interstate Flight, Murder;

---

* Pseudonym, used throughout.

1

Theft of Government Property; Bank Robbery," the posters read. At the bottom of the poster Letty couldn't help but notice a further alarming warning: "Both may be armed and should be considered very dangerous." Signed: J. Edgar Hoover. (J. Edgar Hoover, longtime director of the FBI, was dead by then, but the agency hadn't updated the poster.) Yes, Letty finally decided, Lena and May were indeed Saxe and Power.

Nevertheless, Letty hesitated about what to do with her discovery. Because she was a heavy drug user, smoking marijuana every day and "dropping acid" (LSD) two or three times a week (Ritter 1987) — both of which were illegal with heavy prison sentences for anyone convicted of using, she was afraid of contacting the police or FBI lest they do a house search and turn up drugs or other evidence of drug use, sending her to prison. Alan Johnson, however, told her he doubted the FBI would go after them over a small amount of pot. In the end, Johnson decided it was his "civic duty" to report their suspicion to the FBI and so, pressured by his "straight-laced" girlfriend, Johnson called the FBI on January 6, 1975, at the bureau office in Cincinnati where Johnson lived (Ritter 1987; FBI, January 13, 1975).

Meanwhile, Letty began doing research on Saxe and Power and the Brighton bank robbery by checking through newspapers in the university library. She learned that the policeman who had been killed during the robbery, Walter A. Schroeder, had several kids, which upset her quite a bit. "I felt sorry," she later recollected, in trying to explain why she eventually cooperated with the FBI and grand jury, "for the policeman" (Ritter 1987).

Moreover, as she thought back on her experience with Lena and May, she realized she hadn't really liked them, having had a few straightforward confrontations with Lena especially, whom she found too "bossy" and "militant," constantly harping on political issues. One time, for example, they'd gotten into it over whether Letty's cat should be allowed on a counter, and it was clear to Letty that Lena and May didn't approve of her heavy drug use. Letty, who wasn't particularly political at the time, found herself trying to avoid the two as much as possible. Thus, since she "didn't even like them," when the time came to decide whether to testify or face contempt, she "couldn't see going to jail for them" (Ritter 1987).

On November 12, 1974, at about the same time that the FBI posters caught the attention of Ritter and Johnson, another person, Barry Bleich, a filmmaker connected to Kentucky Educational Television, also happened to notice the poster photos and likewise recognized the two fugitives, especially Saxe, whom he had seen at the health food restaurant Alfalfa where he and she had worked (Kundert 1986; Peterson 1975a). The next day Bleich mentioned his discovery to several friends but decided not to contact the FBI. "They were not criminals to me," he later told a reporter, Bill Peterson of the Louisville *Courier-Journal*. "They were just young radicals like we all were at the time. They got caught up in Kent State and the injustice of the war and went out and robbed a bank" (Peterson 1975a).

Somehow the rumors, which by December 1974 were swirling around the Lexington radical community, that Lena and May had been "most wanted" fugitives, reached the ears of a reporter, John B. Wood, at the *Boston Globe*—probably thanks to Alan Johnson, who notified the *Globe* through a friend. According to FBI records, on January 7, 1975, a *Globe* reporter contacted the Kentucky FBI, asking for information (FBI, January 13, 1975). Wood then headed for Lexington, determined to find out if Saxe and Power had indeed spent part of the preceding year in Lexington. On January 12, 1975, Wood published in the *Boston Sunday Globe* the results of numerous interviews he conducted in Lexington during the preceding week: "Were Susan Saxe and Kathy Power Living in Kentucky?" Wood interviewed Bleich; Letty Ritter; Marla Seymour, later one of the Lexington Six; Betty Rudnick, who was chair of the Nursing Program at UK; and some forty, mostly unnamed, others in the course of his week's stay in Lexington (Wood 1975a).

Wood gleaned from these sources that Saxe and Power had arrived in Lexington on bicycles in early June 1974 (some of these minor details proved to be inaccurate) and had lived for approximately six weeks in a house called the "Lexington Avenue Women's Collective"—the house where Letty, Marla, and several others lived—and later for a few weeks in another apartment nearby.

By the time of Wood's interviewing (roughly January 7–11), most of those who had known Lena and May well were convinced that these two women were indeed Saxe and Power. Marla Seymour, however, portentously declined to identify the two as such. When pressed by the reporter as to why, she replied, "Because this is America." Although she didn't elaborate at the time, with those words Marla, almost by instinct it seems, laid down the first line of the Lexington Six defense. This is America. This is not Nazi Germany or any other totalitarian regime where enforced loyalty to the state supersedes all other loyalties—to friends, to family, to lovers. On the contrary.

As rumors continued circulating about the true identity of Lena and May, one of their former housemates in the "Lexington Avenue Women's Collective," Nancy Scott, who had since moved to Louisville, went to the local post office, along with her lover Laura Clark,* to check for herself. "I looked at Lena's picture, and I knew it was her," she reported. "It wasn't a good picture, but it was her. Then I turned the page, and right in the middle of the Post Office, I yelled 'May!' I freaked out." Bleich offered the *Globe* reporter an even more positive identification; he said he had noticed a distinctive black spot in Lena's left eye, which is specified on the FBI poster as a distinguishing mark. "We used to sit across the counter from each other and talk. I remember looking at that spot . . . and wondering what it was" (Wood 1975a).

Curiously, despite what was by then a general awareness in the Lexington women's community that the women they had known as Lena and May were probably Saxe and Power, none of the people John Wood interviewed for his article had as yet been visited by the FBI. Those visits began shortly after the appearance of the *Globe* piece. So it appears that it was the article, more than the information called in to the FBI by Johnson and Ritter, that triggered the FBI investigation in Lexington. Indeed, an FBI agent later acknowledged that the *Globe* article had regalvanized the hunt for Saxe and Power, which by January 1975 had "run out of gas." Until the *Globe* investigation in Lexington, the agent admitted, the FBI hadn't received a single bit of information about the two since the time of the Brighton bank robbery in 1970, a fact acknowledged by FBI director Clarence Kelly in a teletype on January 16, 1975. The FBI didn't even know if they were still alive. But, the agent revealed, "the Lexington clue started it all. . . . The hunt jumped into high gear" (Jones 1975).

---

* Pseudonym.

Kathy Power and Susan Saxe had met in the late 1960s at Brandeis University in Waltham, Massachusetts, where they both were students. Saxe graduated *magna cum laude*—a literature major—in 1970, and Power, a sociology major, was set to graduate the following year. Both were active in the movement against the escalating Vietnam War. Like many activist protestors of the day, they were appalled at the atrocities—such as that at My Lai on March 16, 1968, where several hundred unarmed Vietnamese civilians were slaughtered by American troops—being reported almost daily in the news. The first notice of the My Lai massacre reached the American public on November 13, 1969, when the *St. Louis Post-Dispatch* published a series of articles by Seymour Hersh. The *Boston Globe* featured the Hersh exposé of the massacre the same day on its front page—where Saxe and Power likely learned of the atrocity (Brandeis being within the Boston news compass). In addition, like other antiwar activists, Saxe and Power thought the war was unjust and ill-conceived to begin with.

Also at Brandeis at the time was a charismatic, twenty-five-year-old ex-convict, Stanley Ray Bond, on parole from a nearby state prison in Walpole on an experimental prison-release program. Bond, who had been a heli-copter pilot in Vietnam, shared Saxe's and Power's opposition to the war, and he and Power became romantically involved. She later said they had been "soulmates" (Franks 1994, 50) because of their shared political vision.

Up to the time of meeting Bond, Power's activism had been focused on a National Student Strike Information Center at Brandeis set up after the Kent State massacre on May 4, 1970, in which four unarmed antiwar protestors were shot and killed by Ohio National Guardsmen, triggering massive nationwide student protests, demonstrations, and strikes. But during the summer of 1970, she, Bond, Saxe, and two other ex-convicts who had been released to Northeastern University in Boston under a similar parole program—Robert Joseph Valeri, then twenty-one, and William Morrill Gilday, forty-one—formed the Revolutionary Action Force gang, whose purpose apparently was to rob banks to fund the antiwar movement—a sort of "Robin Hood" concept of robbing the wealthy for a just cause, in this case the cause of obstructing the war. In particular, they had in mind a plan to buy "thermite to weld military trains to their tracks." As the three men had considerable experience in robbing banks—all had been in prison for armed or attempted armed robbery, Bond being said to have committed twenty-five heists within a three-month period in 1968 (Franks 1994, 50, 49)—their expertise could be put to good use. During the summer Bond taught the women how to use weapons, and they read up on how to rob banks and what weapons to use in the *Mini-Manual of the Urban Guerrilla*, an underground publication. Thus fortified, the gang proceeded to purchase weapons, steal cars, and rob banks in Los Angeles; Evanston, Illinois; and finally at the Bell Savings and Loan in Philadelphia on September 1, 1970. Three weeks later, on September 20, the gang stole guns and ammunition as well as files from a National Guard Armory in Newburyport, Massachusetts. In these cases, Power was not involved in the actual entering and robbery but rather drove the getaway car, while Saxe and the men, armed, carried out the actual robbery operation.

Three days after the Newburyport job, on September 23, 1970, the gang targeted a branch of the State Street Bank and Trust Company on 300 Western Avenue in Brighton, Massachusetts, a section of Boston. Saxe and two of the men, Valeri and Bond, entered the bank. Gilday took a lookout position in a car just outside the bank, while Power was in a getaway vehicle several blocks from the scene. Saxe, in a red wig and purple dress, carried a .30-caliber semi-automatic rifle (Franks 1994, 51), then commonly used by the military in Vietnam. After retrieving several thousand dollars, the three—Bond, Saxe, and Valeri—successfully drove away to where Power was parked, jumped into her car, and made their escape. Gilday, however, who had remained at the scene, shot police officer Walter Schroeder, who died in a hospital the next day.

Power was deeply shocked by Schroeder's death: "It was like a world shattering," she later told reporter Lucinda Franks. "It was a sharp, intense pain. . . . There was this overwhelming sense of wrongness, this wasn't supposed to be about taking lives—this was about stopping the taking of lives" (Franks 1994, 51). Power remained haunted by Schroeder's death. Bond, in a somewhat fatuous gesture, decided to send $4,000 from the robbery stash to Schroeder's widow.

After the robbery Saxe, Power, and Bond met up in Philadelphia on September 24. Then Bond and Power, now with dyed short hair, drove south to Atlanta where they separated permanently. Power then flew to St. Louis where in the baggage-claim area of the St. Louis airport a suitcase Bond had given Power exploded due to a cocked shotgun inside. Kathy was not hurt (a couple of baggage handlers were injured, though), but since her ownership of the suitcase was easily determinable, she made a hasty exit from the airport, bought a wig and new clothes at a local department store, and headed for the bus station. She managed to get out of St. Louis without being discovered and made her way to Detroit, where she met up again with Saxe. From that point on, they traveled together, aided by members of the antiwar underground who helped them get fake IDs.

Stanley Bond was arrested shortly thereafter on September 27, 1970, in Grand Junction, Colorado. He was killed by a homemade bomb on May 24, 1972, in Walpole Prison in Massachusetts, where he was serving a life sentence. William Gilday was captured in New Hampshire the day after Bond. He was sentenced to the death penalty, later reduced to life without parole. Robert Valeri had been arrested right after the robbery on September 23 in Somerville, Massachusetts.

For the next year or so after the robbery Saxe and Power traveled from place to place in the Northeast, never staying anywhere more than four months. It was during this time that they became lovers. (Saxe already thought of herself as a lesbian.) On International Women's Day, March 8, 1971, Power and Saxe issued a public letter to Bernadine Dohrn, a leader of the Weather Underground, a radical antiwar group, in response to Dohrn's "New Morning—Changing Weather" communiqué, issued in December 1970. The Power-Saxe letter was published as "Underground in America" in the feminist journal *off our backs* on April 15, 1971. In the letter, which has an exuberant—even euphoric—tone, the two seemed eager to make the point that one can live well and joyfully underground as a fugitive: "We laugh with you, knowing what it means to be underground in Amerika—not hiding in a cellar or living tightassed straight lives disguised as good little middle class Nazis, but just being ourselves with new names and faces, singing, dancing, blowing dope and making love and revolution." Part of their "revolutionary duty," they wrote, is "to prove to the people that it is possible to live underground in Amerika. . . . We can not only evade the pigs, but have a good time doing it. . . . In short, we are alive and well" (Power and Saxe 1971).

Dohrn's communiqué had announced a new strategy for the Weather Underground, forged in the wake of a disastrous March 1970 townhouse explosion in Manhattan in which three activists were killed. "The townhouse forever destroyed our belief that armed struggle is the only real revolutionary struggle"; henceforth, organizing, "armed propaganda," and working together with other radical groups will be equally important. The townhouse operation Dohrn characterized as a "military error," reflecting "technical inexperience" (Berger 2006, 109).

In response to the Dohrn message, Power and Saxe acknowledged that their Brighton bank robbery was likewise a "military error," a "fuck-up," a "political mistake," which "forced us into hiding." They did not, however, renounce the use of violence, regret the death of Officer Schroeder, or repent of their actions. Like most radical antiwar manifestos of the day, Power and Saxe's letter is filled with rage and indignation about the war and the apparent indifference of the American public—clearly their prime moral animus. During the Christmas 1970 bombing of North Vietnam, they found themselves appalled "as [they] walked through the streets watching people do their Christmas shopping and wondering why rocks weren't flying through the windows of all those big stores with their hypocritical nativity scenes" (Power and Saxe 1971).

In the spring of 1972, Saxe and Power obtained valid Social Security numbers and moved to Torrington in western Connecticut as Lena Paley and May Kelly. They remained deeply bonded emotionally and increasingly committed to radical socialist feminism. During the next two years they lived in the Hartford area where they worked in a health food store owned by Dick and Pat Ensling and openly participated in the alternative feminist community there, frequenting a lesbian bar, the Warehouse, and becoming involved in a consciousness-raising group that included Ellen Grusse, who later with her partner Terri Turgeon refused to cooperate with the FBI and grand jury regarding Saxe and Power in a case that paralleled that of the Lexington Six.

In April 1974, Saxe and Power left Connecticut rather abruptly, traveling by Greyhound bus, to join the Enslings, who had moved to the Stanford, Kentucky, area, about fifty miles south of Lexington. There they helped the Enslings build a house on a rural farm site. While in Stanford, the two occasionally rode into Lexington to have their hair redyed—an important part of their disguise (Power n.d.). When the housing job was complete in early May, Saxe and Power moved to Lexington, bringing with them their high-speed bikes, which they had used to navigate in rural Kentucky. Once in Lexington they sought out the lesbian community and soon found Marla Seymour, a twenty-two-year-old former University of Kentucky student, one of the few out lesbians on campus. Seymour, who worked in a donut shop, had given many talks on lesbian and gay issues and was one of the few women active in the Gay Liberation Front, the only lesbian-gay organization in town. Accordingly, as Marla was well known as a local lesbian leader, Saxe and Power—as Lena Paley and May Kelly—looked her up as someone who could help them integrate into the community.

In their first get-together at a pizza parlor near campus, the two new arrivals told Marla they were lesbians traveling the country who had decided to stopover for a while in Lexington. They didn't mention anything about their fugitive "most wanted" status. Nor did they in subsequent months ever reveal to anyone in Lexington their true identities. The talk in the pizza parlor devolved into a heavy political discussion—as it always seemed to with Lena and May, many have reported. Marla was impressed by the depth, astuteness, and radicalism of their political thinking. They told her they were getting into separatism—a vein of lesbian feminism that advocated women cutting off completely from men, both personally and politically. This position appealed to Marla, and it became the focus of many heated discussions that summer among Lena, May, and other lesbian feminists in the Lexington community.

Marla decided she liked the two well enough to invite them to stay in the house she shared with several others at 341 Lexington Avenue, the so-called Lexington Avenue Women's Collective. At the time Marla was living there on the second floor with her lover, Gail Cohee, then twenty-one and a UK student active in feminist political activities. Also sharing the five-bedroom house with them were, on the first floor, Letty Ritter and Nancy Scott, another UK student. As one of the upstairs bedrooms in the house was vacant, Marla thought it might work for Lena and May, who soon moved in. When asked later about her unquestioning acceptance of two strangers, however compatible they may have seemed, Marla said that at the time there was a general feeling of lesbian-feminist community bonding, an unspoken code of solidarity that lesbians should support and trust one another, helping out when needed (Seymour 1987a). Marla felt this connection with Lena and May, lesbian "strays" who had wandered into town and need a pad to crash in—to use the lingo of the day. In the radical counterculture of the 1960s and 1970s, this kind of casual linking-up with others in "the community" was far from unusual; indeed, it was a norm, part of the ethos.

Once installed in the Lexington Avenue collective, Lena and May soon became the center of an informal discussion group that included Jill Raymond, a twenty-three-year-old UK student who lived nearby; Nancy Scott; Sally Kundert; and Debbie Hands, as well as other feminists in the vicinity. A sign posted at the collective's entrance on the bannister of the stairs leading to the second floor signaled the separatist stance of the occupants:

> *Attention all XY (male) chromosomes and other mutants. You are now leaving friendly territory and entering Amazon. (Peterson 1975a; Wood 1975a)*

The sign usefully reflects the mood and attitude typical of lesbian feminists at the time. They knew they were a hopelessly menial and powerless minority whose thoughts and positions counted for nothing, and so, knowing how brazen statements such as the above would be taken in the "mainstream" world, they were issued as much in a mood of campy humor as in a serious political vein. Nevertheless, ironically, the powers-that-be of that mainstream world—namely the FBI and judicial authorities—apparently took this and similar Amazon bravado seriously, much more so than did lesbian feminists themselves. How seriously, the Lexington community was soon to learn.

Several days after Lena and May moved into the collective, a blazing shootout occurred in Los Angeles between the police and a radical bank-robbing gang that called itself the Symbionese Liberation Army (SLA). Four hundred and ten officers attacked the house where the SLA members were hiding; they used five thousand rounds of ammunition and eighty-three tear gas cannisters (Burton-Rose 2010b, 119). Six SLA members were killed, among them a lesbian couple, Camilla Hall and Patricia Soltysik. The whole conflagration was shown nationally live in real time on television.

Several of the women at the Lexington Avenue collective—including Lena, May, Marla Seymour, and Gail Cohee, as well as a visitor from Connecticut, Ellen Grusse, who had been part of Lena and May's circle in Hartford—gathered around the TV set that evening to watch the horrifying drama unfold. When they realized the SLA lesbian couple—Hall and Soltysik—had been killed, "a weird sense of ambivalence grew in the room," Kathy Power later reported:

> *These were women like all of us and not like us at all, it seemed. . . . They were lovers; they were freedom fighters; they were violent outlaws. They were horrifying; they were fascinating. I stayed silent. No one knew of Susan and my secret story as fugitives and formerly violent revolutionaries ourselves.*
>
> *Throughout the coverage Susan cried, wailing, "that could have been us." No one really understood what disturbed her or what she meant. I recall a certain coldness, trying to manage Susan's feelings for the sake of our safety. (Power n.d.)*

Perhaps the others were so focused on what has been called the "Compton massacre" exploding before them on the TV screen that they didn't notice Lena's strange reaction. "It was hideous," Marla later recalled, "and very frightening to see" (Seymour 1987b).

All did not run smoothly that summer of 1974 at the Lexington Avenue collective once Lena and May moved in. Letty Ritter, for one, found Lena in particular overbearing and, as noted, spent her time avoiding her as much as possible. On the other hand, Marla found herself somewhat in awe of Lena's brash outspokenness and pride in being an out lesbian. From Lena, Marla later said, she was exposed not only to a lot of new political ideas but also, more personally, she learned "to carry myself with less fear about what people think." Because they seemed so much more politically sophisticated than she, Marla at first felt like "a political moron" in discussions with them but "finally learned I could argue with them . . . effectively" (Seymour 1987a), and that was a sort of personal triumph.

Lena did seem to have a magnetic effect on some of the women who knew her. Discussions with her and May, which often took place over beer on the front porch of the Lexington Avenue house long into the summer night, were "intoxicating," Jill Raymond later recalled. The intellectual "give and take" made her "feel I had something to contribute" (Raymond 1987a). Like Marla, Jill felt empowered as she learned she could hold her own with these sophisticated Eastern politicos. "I never felt put down or looked down on," she later wrote, "because Kentucky wasn't Brandeis" (email to author, March 19, 2018). Letty, who did not share the others' enthusiasm for Lena and May, felt her housemates—especially Marla and Nancy—were too bedazzled by the two; indeed, she thought, "they idolized them" (Ritter 1987).

One of the main topics of their heated political discussions was the question of the use of violence to further antiwar, anti-imperialist campaigns—whether that struggle should be "armed" or nonviolent. The SLA deaths in Los Angeles were on their minds as they questioned the effectiveness of guerrilla actions, such as robbing banks or the Weather Underground tactic of setting off symbolic bombs. For Jill these discussions were entirely theoretical. She felt that "the SLA people were nuts" and their actions pointless, but she noticed that Lena and May seemed to identify with the two lesbian lovers who were killed in the SLA conflagration. In the study group Lena and May formed, the women read Marxist texts such as Mao Zedong's "Little Red Book" and writings by Marx himself, but the discussions remained more like bull sessions than serious plans of action. "I felt like our conversations over beer were like a spirited jousting match in the best sense," Jill reminisced. Lena and May were not entirely consistent, Jill realized; they called themselves separatists but identified to some extent with the SLA women who were involved in mixed-group actions. And, much later, after she was captured, Susan Saxe, the erstwhile Lena, seemed to repudiate a separatist position in her defense of the use of armed actions in the antiwar movement. But what impressed Jill, despite their inconsistencies, was how Lena and May "were driven by passion for revolutionary change" (email to author, March 19, 2018).

In addition to their heavy political discussions, Lena, May, Jill, and other lesbians in the group would occasionally go out dancing at the Living Room, a gay and lesbian bar in downtown Lexington (later renamed the Montparnasse). On August 8, 1974, they watched television together as President Richard Nixon resigned under threat of impeachment. To celebrate this momentous event, Jill Raymond recalled, several of "the gang of us" went out for "a night of dinner and beer" (email to author, February 13, 2018).

While Kentucky was (and is) a deeply conservative state, Lexington itself harbored a longstanding radical left-wing community attached to the university. During the late 1960s, as the Vietnam War escalated, it was the site of numerous protest demonstrations, and a Lexington Peace Council—some of whose members were later active in the Lexington Six defense committee—became an active organizing center for antiwar activities.

As in the antiwar movement nationally, the Lexington activists ranged from those who embraced violence as a necessary tactic to pacifists, such as in the American Friends Service Committee, who insisted on nonviolent protest. Some of the Lexington radicals saw themselves as socialists. By the early 1970s, some of the women socialists in Lexington became socialist feminists, seeing class and economic conditions as essential components of women's oppression. They formed a study group they called the "Red Star Sisters"—the nomenclature another example of inflammatory brazenness issued half-humorously, half-defiantly, knowing full well the mainstream public would likely be freaked out by such a title, hearing it as the "Women's Maoist Group" or some other scary label (Sutherland 1986). In fact, the group did read writings by Mao and other Marxists and adopted some classic Marxist practices, such as having "criticism/self-criticism" sessions. But the group's atmospherics was often one of jovial banter that belied the ferocity of its name. Jill Raymond, one of the Lexington Six, was a member of the Red Star Sisters.

The most massive antiwar eruption in Lexington occurred after the U.S. invasion of Cambodia in May 1970, along with hundreds of other protest marches throughout the country, one of which at Kent State University in Ohio turned deadly on May 4. Following the Kent State killings of antiwar protestors, a blocks-long protest march was held at the University of Kentucky on the evening of May 6. Late that night, as the demonstration was winding down, the campus ROTC building was set on fire. Shortly thereafter, a young woman, Sue Ann Salmon, who happened to be walking home from a 7-Eleven store carrying a bottle of ginger ale, was arrested for arson (the ginger ale presumed by the police to be a Molotov cocktail). Sue Ann, who later became an active member of the Lexington Six defense committee, spent a night in jail before the police realized they had made a ludicrous mistake. The perpetrator of the ROTC arson was never found.

Tensions remained high at UK when the following day Governor Louis B. Nunn, saying he was determined to get all those "woolly boogers" on campus, ordered the Kentucky National Guard onto the university grounds. The guardsmen were armed with loaded and bayonetted weapons. A curfew order was issued, and those who defied it were tear-gassed and run off campus. Within a couple of days the campus was shut down, final exams effectively canceled, and the school year was over. Great and long-lasting hostility had been engendered, however, between the police, university authorities, government, and judiciary on the one hand, and the protest community on the other. That enmity—the sense that government authorities are out to get you if you take a nonconformist political position—remained a constant in the Lexington radical community, as it did in the antiwar movement throughout the country. And, although none of the Lexington Six were yet on campus for the 1970 uprising, such feelings of being under siege were palpable in the lesbian-gay community of Lexington in 1975 when the FBI arrived on the scene in pursuit of Saxe and Power.

Members of the lesbian-gay community had additional reason to feel persecuted in Lexington in the early 1970s. As one gay member of the community remarked, at the time "we kind of expected to be harassed as gays and lesbians" (Taylor 1987). In November 1972, the president of the University of Kentucky, Otis A. Singletary, turned down a request by the Gay Liberation Front (GLF), submitted the previous year, to be recognized as a student organization. A second application led to a suit and countersuit filed in January 1973 with the U.S. district court. On October 10, 1973, the district court judge, Bernard T. Moynahan Jr.—later the judge in the Lexington Six case—dismissed the claims of the Gay Liberation Front that such a denial was a violation of its First Amendment rights to assembly and speech. *Otis A. Singletary v. Peter Taylor* was appealed to the Sixth Circuit Court of Appeals, sitting in Cincinnati, which denied the appeal on May 9, 1974, saying the university's denial of gay and lesbian students' right to assemble as a bona fide student organization did not constitute a violation of the First Amendment.

This seemingly illogical decision was a demoralizing blow to the gay and lesbian community. "Everybody" began to feel "like the U.S. government was rapidly turning into a police state," one of the plaintiffs in the case, Peter Taylor, remembered (1987). It was clear the law was not on their side. In fact, homosexuality was a crime in Kentucky, as in other states, in 1974. (Ironically, it was in 1974 that the state revised its penal code to include lesbians under its sodomy law specifications; see Morrison 2001, 1165.) The penalty for even consensual gay or lesbian sexual activity was a year in prison and a five hundred dollar fine. It wasn't until 1992 in *Commonwealth of Kentucky v. Jeffrey Wasson* that the Kentucky Supreme Court struck down the state's sodomy law, and 2003 in *Lawrence v. Texas* that the U.S. Supreme Court finally determined that laws criminalizing homosexuality were unconstitutional nationwide.

As a despised minority, gay men in Lexington were especially targeted, routinely subjected to physical violence. Carey Junkin, a leader of the gay community on campus, later one of the Lexington Six, was on one occasion beaten up on campus and, as one activist recollected, "this was condoned." The feeling was "he asked for it." Street harassment was common; men were physically attacked in the parking lot outside the Montparnasse, on at least one occasion with a baseball bat (Hackney 1989). One evening a gay activist was arrested while sitting outside on a porch stoop with a male friend. As no one could pay the bail, he sat in jail a few days until he finally feigned a suicide attempt, hoping thereby to be sent to a mental institution where he thought he had a chance of gaining his release. There, however, he was put on Thorazine, which laid him low until finally a family member found out what was happening and had him released (Taylor 1987).

Homosexuality had been especially stigmatized in this country during the so-called Lavender Scare, a pogrom paralleling the "Red Scare" of the McCarthy era — the 1950s — when somehow in the minds of the authorities, homosexuality became associated with communism, so gays and lesbians — then referred to as "perverts" — were by definition considered security risks (Johnson 2004, 114–15). In 1951, the FBI under J. Edgar Hoover initiated a "Sex Deviates Program" collecting thousands of files on people suspected of such so-designated behavior (Weiner 2012, 214). (Those files were systematically destroyed in 1977 [Johnson 2004, 238 n.6].) In 1953, President Dwight Eisenhower issued an executive order officially banning lesbians and gays from serving in the federal government, and homosexuals were barred from immigrating (Weiner 2012, 214; Hobson 2016, 106). Earlier, as commander of Allied forces in post–World War II Europe, then-General Eisenhower decided to purge the Women's Army Auxiliary Corps of lesbians. When he asked his secretary—the intrepid Nell "Johnnie" Phelps—to draw up a list of known lesbians, she replied, in an act of personal resistance, "I'll be happy to do this . . . but you have to know that the first name on the list will be mine" (Sears 2001, 342 n.19). Eisenhower then canceled the order. Unfortunately, there were no Johnnie Phelpses around in 1953 to restrain President Eisenhower when he issued Executive Order no. 10450.

An embarrassingly ignorant exchange recorded between J. Edgar Hoover and then-President Lyndon Johnson in October 1964 gives an idea of how prejudiced authorities were against gays and lesbians well into the 1960s:

> JOHNSON: "I swear I can't recognize 'em,"
> HOOVER: "It's a thing that you just can't tell sometimes. . . . There are some . . . who walk kinda funny . . . [so] you might kinda think might be a little bit off or maybe queer." (Weiner 2012, 249)

Police routinely harassed gays and lesbians throughout the country, raiding gay bars and arresting customers. Finally, in a celebrated revolt on the night of June 27–28, 1969, in New York City, patrons at the Stonewall Inn bar rebelled against such harassment and fought back against the police. This iconic moment is now seen as a turning point in gay-lesbian movement history. Resistance groups, such as the Gay Liberation Front in Lexington, began to form all over the country.

Meanwhile, a "second wave" women's movement was beginning to sweep the country as well. By the late 1960s, radical feminist publications such as *Notes from the First Year* (1968), *Notes from the Second Year* (1970), and *Notes from the Third Year* (1971), began appearing. Many of the key ideas of second-wave feminism, such as the "personal is political"—that power relations extend to the bedroom, that the oppression of women is the root evil in society, and that women should form their own political liberation movement—are found therein. "Feminism," Boston feminist Roxanne

Dunbar declared in 1968, "must be asserted by women . . . as the basis of revolutionary social change" (1970, 48). In "Sexual Politics: A Manifesto for Revolution" (1968), which also appeared in *Notes from the Second Year*, Kate Millett declared, "When one group rules another, the relationship between the two is political. . . . All historical civilizations are patriarchies: their ideology is male supremacy. . . . Government is upheld by power, which is upheld through consent . . . or imposed by violence. . . . There may be a resort to the latter at any moment when consent is withdrawn — rape, attack, sequestration, beatings" (1970, 111). Millett's characterization would prove oddly prophetic of the political situation faced by the Lexington Six in 1975. Their consent withdrawn, severe reprisals ensued.

In 1971, the first major statement of second-wave lesbian feminist theory, "The Woman Identified Woman," appeared. Issued by a New York collective called the "Radicalesbians," a group that formed in the wake of the Stonewall uprising, it provided this famous definition: "A lesbian is the rage of all women condensed to the point of explosion. She is the woman who . . . acts in accordance with her inner compulsion to be a more complete and freer human being than her society cares to allow her." The authors urged women to refuse to be "male-identified," which meant defining themselves in terms of men's needs and ego-driven priorities. Instead, one should be "woman identified": "Only women can give to each other a new sense of self. That identity we have to develop with reference to ourselves, and not in relation to men" (Radicalesbians 1971, 81, 83).

Another article in the same journal that undoubtedly had a huge effect on lesbian (or would-be lesbian) feminists of the day was "Loving Another Woman" by Anne Koedt, which described the "coming out" experience in terms many could readily identify with: "All of a sudden . . . I was flooded with a tremendous attraction for her. And I wanted to tell her I wanted to sleep with her. . . . At the same time I was totally bewildered" (1971, 26).

Other influential works that began theorizing lesbianism in feminist terms were Sidney Abbott and Barbara Love's *Sappho Was a Right-On Woman* (1972), Del Martin and Phyllis Lyon's *Lesbian Woman* (1972), and Jill Johnston's *Lesbian Nation* (1973), which effectively argued for a separatist lesbian political movement. "In Amerika They Call Us Dykes" was issued in 1973 by a "Boston Gay Collective," a group of nine lesbians, as part of *Our Bodies, Ourselves*, an enormously popular feminist health manual, which eventually sold millions of copies. And novels like Rita Mae Brown's *Rubyfruit Jungle* (1973) and Isabel Miller's *Patience and Sarah* (1969) helped make the political personal. As with many second-wave feminists, numerous political lesbians had been active in the civil rights and antiwar movements of the 1960s. LGBT historian Lillian Faderman notes, "The fervor they'd once put into ending racism or the war in Vietnam, they now put into lesbian feminism" (Faderman 2015, 240).

With the ideas of the gathering women's movement flooding the country, women in the Lexington community—as elsewhere—began examining their own lives in terms of these newly articulated feminist insights. Those who were married began to consider how restrictive some of that institution's prescribed roles were. Those who were unmarried questioned why intimacy was only allowed in marriage between a man and a woman. Many began seeking new kinds of intimate relationships. Works popular in the counterculture like Herbert Marcuse's *Eros and Civilization* (1955) and Norman O. Brown's *Love's Body* (1966) proposed that eroticism had been constrictively channeled into genital hetero sex and that it should be freed up, diffused, and expressed in other ways, what Marcuse, following Freud, famously called "polymorphous perversity" (Marcuse 1962 [1955], 44).

New York radical feminist Shulamith Firestone applied some of these ideas to women's restricted hetero situation in *The Dialectic of Sex* (1970), another seminal second-wave source. "All animal needs," she complained, "for love and warmth are channeled into genital sex; people must never touch others of the same sex, and may touch those of the opposite sex only when preparing for a genital sexual encounter." But, she maintained, it is not a matter of eliminating love or eroticism. On the contrary, "No one wants to get rid of [eroticism]. Life would be a drab and routine affair without [it]. That's just the point. Why has all joy and excitement been concentrated, driven into one narrow, difficult-to-find alley of human experience? . . . When we demand the elimination of eroticism, we mean not the elimination of sexual joy and excitement but its rediffusion over . . . the spectrum of our lives" (Firestone 1971 [1970], 147, 155).

Under the influence of some of these ideas, women in the Lexington feminist community began experimenting with new ways of relating to others—especially to other women. At first, these new ways were not, in many cases, sexual or intended to be sexual. Rather, it was a matter of trying to extend intense, loving, and erotic experience beyond the narrow confines of heterosexual marriage. The women in the Red Star Sisters began, for example, experimenting with alternative living arrangements, such as cooking together, having meals together, even sleeping together nonsexually. Collectives formed, such as the one on Lexington Avenue where Lena and May lived. Another was a group that lived in a large house they called "Off Hand Manor" at 1625 Nicholasville Avenue—later the initial site of the Lexington Six defense committee.

So there was in the Lexington community of the time a spirit of personal exploration of new ways of living and relating. Inevitably, perhaps, the new closeness, trust, and intimacy women had begun feeling toward one another led in some cases to physical intimacy and lesbian love. As Jill Raymond later remarked, all of a sudden it seemed everyone "began to fall in love with each other" (Raymond 1987a). "It was a time," one member of the community recalled, "when one wasn't sure whether someone was a lesbian or not" (Sutherland 1986). Thus many women in the community were in 1974 awakening to a new lesbian identity, in various stages of transition. This was the case with several of the Lexington Six.

The second-wave feminist movement had therefore arrived in full force by the early 1970s in Lexington, Kentucky, and was affecting women in deeply personal ways. The ideas of the movement were in energetic circulation, being widely discussed and personally enacted. On September 22, 1971, Gloria Steinem and Florynce Kennedy, leading national feminists, gave a talk to a standing-room-only crowd at UK. Among their proposals was one for a women's studies program. Such a proposal was formulated on campus shortly thereafter but, as with the GLF's quest for academic legitimacy, was rejected unanimously by the Academic Affairs Committee on March 15, 1973. The courses continued, however, as electives, and several of the Lexington Six women took them.

Other feminist projects took hold. A Rape Crisis Center was set up; a Lexington Women's Yellow Pages was published, which listed organizations providing trustworthy services for women; a Lexington Women's Center was established; a Lexington Free Clinic provided counseling by volunteers for gays and lesbians as well as pregnancy, birth control, and abortion information; a Kentucky Women's Political Caucus became active; and the university had a Council on Women's Concerns, of which Gail Cohee, one of the Lexington Six, served as chairperson in 1974.

On March 4, 1973, the Kentucky Women's Political Caucus held a conference on the UK campus. Among the fifty or so in attendance were Jill Raymond, Gail Cohee, Mary Dunn, Margaret Wendelsdorf, and Barbara Sutherland, the latter three of whom were Red Star Sisters and later on connected with the Lexington Six defense committee. Also in attendance at the conference was Anne Braden of Louisville, a nationally known civil rights activist.

The Lexington feminist community was thus a vibrant, energized group of a hundred or so when Saxe and Power arrived in the early summer of 1974. By the end of June, Saxe, alias Lena Paley, had been hired as a cook in the health food restaurant Alfalfa. Saxe was by all accounts an innovative and health-conscious chef. Power also had culinary talents, having won a Betty Crocker cooking prize in her youth. Occasionally, Saxe would fix special meals for the collective on Lexington Avenue where she and Power resided. On July 11, Kathy Power, as May Kelly, obtained work at Broughton's Farm Dairy as a receptionist. By this time Saxe had dyed her hair carrot red, which puzzled some of her newfound friends, given her by then militant feminism, but most wrote it off as a consistent eccentricity. Saxe occasionally called herself "Lena Luna" and implied that aspects of her identity were a campy self-invention.

After about six weeks at the Lexington Avenue Women's Collective, Lena and May moved to another apartment at 367 South Broadway where one of their neighbors was Carey Junkin, then president of the GLF and later one of the Lexington Six. Many who knew them commented on the evident love Lena and May felt for one another. Even Letty Ritter, who was otherwise critical of the two, noted it approvingly: "You could see the affection they had for one another" (Ritter 1987). On one occasion while they were still in the collective, May went out for an evening apart from Lena and was late coming back. According to Ritter, Lena became very upset and began crying on the porch waiting for May to return. It seems Saxe feared Power had been apprehended—always a looming concern.

Power left Lexington not long thereafter—in early to mid-August of that year—to return to Hartford to help a friend, Carol Romano,[*] who had been diagnosed with breast cancer (Franks 1994, 53; Power, email to author, September 29, 2018). Carol was a member of the feminist circle in Hartford that had included Lena, May, and others. She was a trusted friend, so trusted that she was the only one of the group to whom Kathy and Susan had revealed their true identity (Power, email to author, September 29, 2018).

Carol apparently shared this information with her ex-husband, Jim.[†] As Carol recovered from her breast cancer surgery, she began to seem increasingly hostile to Kathy, accusing her and Susan of betraying the women's movement by allying themselves with the (male) left, seeing them as "part of the Left conspiracy to make a revolution that once again left women behind" (Power n.d.). In this it seems Carol may have been influenced by Jane Alpert's "Mother Right" article (see below), which appeared in August 1973 and argued that feminists should dissociate from the male-dominated New Left.

As Carol became increasingly hostile, Kathy sensed that that her friend might be about to turn her in—a feeling ratified by an urgent phone call from another friend, Ellen Grusse, who suspected as much. So, Kathy immediately left Hartford. Power later recounted, "After about six weeks, I began to get very hostile vibes from this woman, and my instincts told me to get out. It was excruciatingly painful" to feel thus betrayed. According to *New Yorker* reporter Lucinda Franks, the FBI "swooped down" on the Hartford community only hours after Power's departure (Franks 1994, 53), thought to be as a result of Carol's or Jim's informing the FBI of her presence.

According to FBI records, however, this assumption is not correct. Carol and Jim appear not to have informed on Kathy in the fall of 1974 but did so in late January 1975, when contacted by FBI agents, who had located them through the Lexington phone records of Saxe and Power obtained in the Lexington investigation (FBI, January 29, 1975). In a series of interviews in

---

[*]   Pseudonym, used throughout.
[†]   Pseudonym, used throughout.

early February 1975, Carol and Jim told the FBI that they had been close friends with Saxe and Power but when they learned in April 1974 about the women's connection to the Brighton bank robbery, the couple broke off the friendship and told the two "they wanted them out of town or they would turn them in" (FBI. February 5, 1975). Saxe and Power then left for Kentucky. Carol and Jim verified that Kathy Power had returned to Hartford in August 1974 to help Carol with her surgery. But at this time they developed a theory that Saxe and Power had revealed their identity in order to compromise Carol and Jim as accessories after the fact. To check out this theory, Jim, who had a key to the apartment where Kathy was staying, stole letters between her and Susan (FBI, February 5, 1975). These letters were tendered to the bureau. The names found in the letters were then forwarded to the FBI in Lexington (FBI, February 7, 1975), and letters of this kind were later used to identify Susan Saxe after her arrest. The FBI was suspicious of Carol and Jim, however, given that they had known about the identity and whereabouts of "most wanted" fugitives for almost a year. The FBI director ordered the Hartford agents to put "all-out pressure" on them and to threaten the two with a charge of harboring fugitives until "full cooperation [is] obtained" (FBI, February 5, 1975).

In any event, because of the hostility that had developed or redeveloped between Kathy and Carol in mid-fall 1974, Kathy left Hartford and alerted Susan Saxe, who was still in Lexington, that she feared the FBI was hot on their trail. Saxe abruptly left Lexington shortly thereafter. The two met up again for a few days in late October somewhere in the Northeast. During this meeting they decided to split up over the issue of how openly they should participate in political activities. Saxe felt frustrated at not being fully able to do so, but Power felt such a step would be suicidal; she sensed it invited capture. As it turned out, Power was right.

Meanwhile, back in Lexington, several women who knew the two women well and had grown fond of them were shocked and devastated by their sudden departure. Strong emotional bonds had formed among the women, forged by their shared lesbian-feminist political vision, as well as personal camaraderie. "She didn't even come say good-bye," Marla Seymour later lamented, referring to May (1987a). Of those who knew

Lena and May well, Jill Raymond had gotten perhaps the closest to the two, especially to May. On the eve of May's departure from Lexington, she and Jill spent the night together in Jill's apartment (Raymond, email to author, February 13, 2018). So May's sudden departure was especially "hard to take," Jill recounted (Raymond 1987a). In fact, except for one phone call a few weeks later, Jill wasn't to see or hear from Kathy Power again for nearly twenty years.

Lena's departure was also abrupt. She told her friends her mother had had a heart attack but gave no details as to where her mother was or when or if she would be returning to Lexington. Nor would she give them a forwarding address, which struck her friends as especially harsh. In explaining her sudden leave-taking, Lena told her Lexington friends that relationships are existential, implying it was best not to get tied down to any one place or to other people. Her friends were somewhat mollified by this explanation, because it fit in with the somewhat freewheeling aura that surrounded the vagabonding duo, and because they themselves were seeking new ways of relating to others that would allow for more personal freedom and independence. Still, their seemingly casual departure hurt. When Lena said goodbye to Marla, she gave her a gift—a book of poems—saying, "Believe me, we'll see each other again" (Seymour 1987a). Lena also left behind in the Lexington Avenue house an "objet-trouvé" sculpture she had made of a purple toy rabbit inside a small crate, entitled "The Introduction of the Absurd into the Mainstream of Lesbian Culture"—signed "Lena Luna (c. 1974)" (Wood 1975a).

Several weeks after May's departure, Jill Raymond received a collect call from her from Hartford. May said she was calling from a payphone in a gay bar called The Warehouse. According to FBI records, this call was made on September 23, 1974. A bartender recalled to the FBI that he had seen Saxe and Power there in the fall of 1974 (FBI, January 23, 1975b). Sometime later, when the FBI search intensified in Connecticut and Lexington, the bureau discovered (or fabricated) another Warehouse phone call. A teletype report, dated February 25, 1975, issued by the New Haven FBI office and sent to the Louisville office, which was overseeing the Lexington case, includes the following notation:

Pursuant to a subpoena duces tecum it was determined that a collect call was made to the telephone of JILL RAYMOND, Lexington, Kentucky from telephone 728–9006 on April 12, 1974 for a period of 48 minutes. It was determined that this phone was listed to a pay telephone at Delchard Warehouse, Inc., 61 Woodbine St., Hartford, Connecticut. (FBI Report, February 25, 1975)

The FBI has the date of this call as April 12, 1974, which Jill maintains is incorrect: "I had no prior knowledge of anybody up there [Connecticut] . . . before they showed up in Lex" (Raymond, email to author, December 19, 2017). Kathy Power recently confirmed Jill's statement: "That April 1974 date is most definitely wrong. I never knew Jill before we moved to Lexington in May 1974" (Power, email to author, October 1, 2018). Kathy did call Jill from Hartford sometime in September or early October 1974, the day she left Hartford for good—a phone call both remember (Power, email to author, September 29, 2018; Raymond, email to author, February 13, 2018)—and which, as noted, the FBI also had record of.

So the April date is either an FBI error or a "dirty trick," something we know from the COINTELPRO papers (see below) that the FBI was quite capable of: in this case, tampering with evidence. If they did so, that is, changed the date, it could be that they were trying to implicate Raymond on a charge of harboring fugitives. The April 1974 date would imply that Jill had known Saxe and Power before they arrived in Lexington—assuming the call was from them—and thus that she might have been willingly harboring them. The FBI teletype is stamped FUG SUP, their code for harboring fugitives. As it turned out, the New Haven authorities, which issued this report, were more focused on the harboring fugitives issue than the government officials in Lexington, although that became an issue in the appeals litigation. It is also worth noting that in this report the FBI also got the "Warehouse" reference wrong, mistaking the gay bar in Hartford for an actual warehouse. However faulty the evidence it contained, the February 25, 1975, FBI report nevertheless appears to have played a significant role in the federal judiciary's decision to prosecute the case of the Lexington Six.

CHAPTER TWO

FBI Dragnet

Sally Kundert was a radical activist who had just moved to Lexington in the fall of 1974. She was looking for a place to live, and when she learned that Lena and May were leaving, she was happy to move into their vacated apartment in a house at 367 South Broadway after their abrupt departure. She was startled to discover, however, that they had left nearly everything behind—kitchen utensils, bedding, even food, which seemed odd. Sally had known Lena and May briefly as sister participants in a feminist book discussion study group in the fall of 1974 (Kundert, phone interview with author, April 19, 2018).

On the evening of January 12, 1975, the day the *Globe* article by John Wood appeared, Kundert heard a knock on the front door of her house at 454 South Ashland. She had just moved there from the apartment on Broadway. It was the FBI. At first, Sally thought the two men, who were dressed in coats and ties, were renters being shown the apartment by the accompanying landlord.

"You're wanted for murder," one of the two agents—probably Wayne McDonald and John Gill, special agents who conducted most of the Lexington interviews—announced to Sally. "The house is surrounded" (Kundert 1986). They apparently thought she was Kathy Power, one of the fugitives they sought. The agents told her that a "lot of people" had identified her as May Kelly. "They said Marla Seymour had identified me as May Kelley, but I learned later that they had not talked to Marla at that time" (Gatz, February 19, 1975). The FBI had likely been informed by Letty Ritter or others that Lena and May lived at 367 South Broadway, which was where Sally had lived temporarily. Sally realized retrospectively — putting two and two together — that she had been under surveillance for weeks (Kundert, phone interview with author, April 19, 2018).

Kundert, who hadn't heard any of the rumors circulating about Saxe and Power, was completely shocked and mystified as the FBI agents pushed their way into her apartment that January evening, searching the closets, overturning everything, and demanding to take fingerprints. Producing the FBI's wanted posters of Saxe and Power, they said they were after a "woman wanted for murder and interstate flight, one of the SDS Weather people," Kundert recalled (1986). Saxe and Power were not members of the Weather Underground, but two of the others on the FBI's "Ten Most Wanted" list of the day were Weather women — Kathy Boudin and Cathy Wilkerson, members of the "Proud Eagle Tribe," a "women's brigade" (Burrough 2015, 150), which may have fueled apparent FBI suspicion of a women's terrorist network.

The FBI was at that time also involved in a massive hunt for Patty Hearst, another woman turned urban guerrilla, as well as Pat Swinton and the recently captured Jane Alpert, antiwar fugitives long underground who were wanted for bombings and bank robberies. Hearst had been kidnapped by the Symbionese Liberation Army (SLA) on February 4, 1974, and had apparently joined in with her abductors as part of their bank-robbing gang. She had not been at the scene of the shootout on May 17, 1974, however, and thus still remained on the loose at the time the FBI moved into Lexington in early 1975, having failed to "uncover . . . a single significant lead" in the search for Hearst (Burrough 2015, 335).

The FBI under J. Edgar Hoover had initiated a so-called COINTELPRO program in 1956. Its purpose, Hoover explained to then-President Eisenhower, was to infiltrate and subvert groups it considered subversive, originally the Communist Party, using illegal means such as "'surreptitious entry' . . . safecracking, mail interception, telephone surveillance, microphone plants, trash inspection, infiltration, IRS investigations" (Davis 1997, 5). Many of these techniques were later used on the Lexington Six.

In the spring of 1968, as antiwar demonstrations increased, an FBI project called COINTELPRO NEW LEFT was put into operation to target the antiwar movement (Churchill and VanderWall 1990, 177). The program intensified in early 1970 after the townhouse explosion on West Eleventh Street in Manhattan in which several Weathermen were killed but from which Kathy Boudin and Cathy Wilkerson escaped alive and undetected. The intensified COINTELPRO activity, called the Huston plan, was promoted by William Sullivan, head of the FBI's Domestic Intelligence Division. President Richard Nixon approved the plan, and while Hoover himself disapproved of it, the policy in its essentials—namely, to use illegal surveillance and break-ins on "dissidents" (Weiner 2012, 291)—was carried out.

The FBI also routinely planted false news and informed relatives and employers if a person had any socially damning characteristics, such as drug use or being a suspected homosexual. A May 29, 1968, FBI memo notes how agents "neutralized" a member of a communist youth organization by publicizing his homosexuality, recommending the effectiveness of using anonymous letters to out a gay person's identity to his parents (Davis 1997, 51).

On March 8, 1971, a group of antiwar activists calling itself the "Citizens Committee to Investigate the FBI" managed to break and enter an FBI office in Media, Pennsylvania (Medsger 2014, 113). They were able to remove boxes of FBI files—a thousand or so documents in all—which revealed the COINTELPRO operation. The antiwar burglars gave this information to a reporter, Betty Medsger, at the *Washington Post*, who published it on March 24, 1971, in an article entitled "Stolen Documents Describe FBI Surveillance Activities" (see Medsger 2014 for a full account). Despite these revelations, although they eventually led to an accounting for the FBI, the program continued unabated through 1975 when a Senate Select Committee to Study Governmental Operations under Senator Frank Church (often referred to as the Church Committee) began hearings on illegal FBI activities. But by then it was too late for the Lexington Six.

Despite being unprepared—"I didn't know a damn thing about my rights," Sally Kundert said, acknowledging that she knew nothing about the FBI or grand juries when the FBI showed up at her door that evening in mid-January—she nevertheless told the agents she didn't want to talk to them. "I said I didn't know anything" (1986). After the FBI agents left her premises, Sally called her friends Marla Seymour and Gail Cohee to let them know what had happened. She wished someone had told her beforehand about the FBI search for the Boston fugitives so she could have been better prepared, and she resolved to spread the word herself through the community as quickly as possible. Kundert then consulted a lawyer who told her she didn't have to answer FBI questions. While true, the FBI can turn to a federal district attorney, who can bring the recalcitrant before a federal grand jury. Refusing to answer the same questions the FBI had posed before a grand jury can result in having a judge hold one in contempt of court, the accompanying penalty for which is time in jail or prison. In this way, a person can thus be compelled to answer FBI questions. With Marla and Gail notified, Sally Kundert collapsed: "I had a pint of Scotch, straight," she recalled (1986). The next day she was late for work and fired from her job.

Sally had not seen the last of the FBI, however, despite the obvious realization, quickly ascertained by fingerprints, that she was not Kathy Power. Shortly after this initial encounter, Sally's mother, a schoolteacher in a Minneapolis suburb, was accosted by an FBI agent in the school lunchroom. He took it on himself to publicly inform her in the crowded lunchroom that her daughter was unmarried and pregnant. One has to wonder what the purpose of this interrogatory was; it surely had nothing to do with Saxe and Power. Sally thinks it was simply an example of the FBI's campaign to "harass and intimidate." Indeed, some months later, when Sally was on her way to a baby shower, nine months pregnant, the FBI came back again for further questioning (Kundert, phone interview with author, April 19. 2018).

Within a few days after Sally Kundert's encounter with the FBI in mid-January, dozens more in the Lexington community were visited by bureau agents. A massive dragnet had begun. One of the first to be interrogated was Letty Ritter, possibly before the Kundert interview but shortly after Alan Johnson informed the FBI of their suspicions that Lena and May were the sought fugitives on the "most wanted" list. Letty reported that the FBI agents first contacted her by accosting her on the sidewalk in front of her house one afternoon: "two guys in three-piece suits." The questioning was done in the agents' car and it continued every day, it seemed, for a month or so. At first Letty was inclined to cooperate and she answered their questions "as honestly as I could." "I didn't see anything wrong with answering their questions at first," she said (Ritter 1987). But, as she hadn't known who Lena and May were at the time of their residence and had no idea where they were, it seemed that any pertinent information she could have given the FBI was limited and might not have required weeks of repeated questioning.

So, when the agents kept coming back day after day and asking "questions that had nothing to do with Lena and May," Ritter became annoyed. The agents were primarily asking her for information not about the fugitives but about the lesbian-feminist community. She concluded as much: "I think they were quite interested in the lesbian community." It soon also became clear that despite her efforts to conceal her drug addiction, the agents knew about it and were using that knowledge as a club to keep her cooperating. One of the reasons they met at first in the FBI agents' car was that Letty didn't want them searching the house and finding drugs. Nevertheless, she would often return home to find them sitting in her living room waiting for her. (It is unclear whether the agents broke in or if the door had been left unlocked.) In any event, her drug use was probably fairly obvious at the time; as she admitted, "I was stoned and out of my head all the time" (Ritter 1987).

The constant FBI attention became oppressive. "They never left me alone. They kept coming back. They were aggressive, forceful men and they intimidated me." Like Sally Kundert, Letty had never had dealings with the FBI before and thought you had to cooperate with them. But as the interrogations dragged on and the agents kept asking irrelevant, personal questions about specific lesbians, Letty came to feel she had been "duped by the FBI." "They abused me. They wouldn't leave. They intimidated me." And because of her drug use, "I was very vulnerable" (Ritter 1987).

Shortly thereafter, Marla Seymour and Gail Cohee, now moved out of the Lexington Avenue collective to another apartment nearby, heard that dreaded FBI knock on the door. As Marla later recalled, "a knock in those days was like, this is it." Marla answered the door but the agents asked for Gail. So Marla went to get Gail, who was watching TV. By then, although they knew little about their constitutional rights or about the grand jury system, they knew, having been alerted by Sally Kundert, that they didn't have to talk to the FBI. As indicated by her cryptic comment to the *Globe* reporter—"This is America"—Marla already had, however, an instinctive inclination not to cooperate. The FBI agents tried to persuade them to do so. "If you talk now," they said, "you'll get it over with. It'll just take a few minutes" (Seymour 1987a). Marla and Gail refused to do so unless in the presence of their attorney. But that did not satisfy the FBI.

As Ritter's experience showed, however, the interviews did not just take a few minutes. Rather, as the agents returned, and as they fanned out among community members, it became clear that their primary interest was in the lesbian aspect of the case, asking numerous questions about peoples' "sexual preference" and that of their friends and acquaintances. It was this line of questioning that especially provoked Marla at the time, "more than anything else." Marla didn't want to help the FBI gather information about the women's community—her community. Indeed, she felt outrage at the agents' persistent questions about her sexuality and other private matters (Seymour 1987b). That outrage fueled her resistance to the FBI intrusion into their personal lives. "This is America," after all.

At about the same time Marla, Gail, and others were being interrogated, Carey Junkin, then a nineteen-year-old first-year student at the university and president of the Gay Coalition (the renamed Gay Liberation Front), received a late-night phone call from Special Agent Wayne McDonald. By then, Junkin had "heard the FBI was going around . . . asking all sorts of nosy questions." Carey told McDonald he didn't want to talk to him on the phone. Carey had lived in the same building on 367 South Broadway as Lena and May but barely knew them beyond saying an occasional hello in the hall. After McDonald's phone call, Carey consulted with some of the others who had been visited by the FBI. Feeling solidarity with them, he "decided not to cooperate." By the time McDonald called the second time, "I'd made up my mind I wasn't going to talk to them," he reported. "It seemed like they were trying to destroy our community." But McDonald didn't take no for an answer. He and another agent soon showed up at Carey's door. "You have to talk to us," they said, but Carey "slammed the door in their face" (Junkin 1987).

Although she later became the principal actor in the Lexington Six case, Jill Raymond was one of the last to be contacted by the FBI. Sometime in mid-January, "two men in suits came to my door," she recalled (Raymond 1987b). Jill had by then heard the rumors circulating since November about Saxe and Power. When she first studied their FBI poster photos, however, she didn't think they were of the friends she had known as Lena and May. She talked it over with Marla and Gail and others who had known the two fugitives, but "we didn't know for sure" (Raymond 1987a). She recalled,

> There was a lot of doubt about those posters. After all, Susan Saxe and Kathy Power had been underground for five years, and the pictures were from high school. I myself said, "Oh, it can't be." The Lena and May we had known in Lexington were not preaching the wisdom of robbing banks or shooting policemen. They weren't preaching the immediate violent overthrow of everything by any means necessary. In fact, we found them thoughtful, astute, careful, and caring people who, if they were the people who robbed this bank in 1970, had made a mistake.

When, therefore, she finally realized that Paley and Kelly were in fact Saxe and Power, it "was like a bomb dropping" (Raymond 1989, 293).

So, when Jill saw "two men in suits" approaching her house that January day, having been forewarned by Sally Kundert and others in the community, she knew it was the FBI. Jill had long been active in the antiwar movement. She had worked for a People's Party candidate, Benjamin Spock, in 1972 and had participated in various antiwar demonstrations and actions. Indeed, the FBI already had a rather innocuous one-page file on her, dated July 26, 1972, from the Louisville office. The memo listed her as active in the University of Kentucky Student Mobilization Committee (SMC), an antiwar group, but as "she has not exhibited a propensity for violence," the "case is being placed in a pending inactive status" to be reviewed in six months to determine whether "the subject should be recommended for inclusion in ADEX" (FBI, July 26, 1972). ADEX was an "Administrative Index" kept by the FBI, as authorized by President Nixon's attorney general John Mitchell; it was a list of "radicals with a potential for sabotage, as well as the leaders and functionaries of left-wing organizations." Originally called the Security Index, the list was used extensively during the height of the Cold War Red Scare when it was expanded to include over 25,000 names (Deutsch 1984, 1177 n.82).

The July 26, 1972, FBI report on Jill Raymond, though recommended for inactive status, was nonetheless forwarded the same day to the U.S. Secret Service by then–acting director of the FBI L. Patrick Gray as a "Security Matter": because of "membership in the Student Mobilization Committee To End The War In Vietnam," "Jill Patricia Raymond" was considered "potentially dangerous because of background, emotional instability or activity in groups engaged in activities inimical to the U.S."—a form designation (FBI, July 26, 1972). An enclosed information sheet gave Jill's birth date, April 22, 1952; noted that she had brown hair and brown eyes and was 5'1", 115 pounds. It also gave her address; Ohio driver's license number; Social Security number; and the facts that she had participated in two "peaceful demonstrations" in 1971, ran the meetings of SMC from September 1971 through April 1972, and attended a meeting of the Young Socialist Alliance on March 28, 1972. The SMC, the memo stipulated, "is controlled by the Socialist Workers Party (SWP) and its youth affiliate, Young Socialist Alliance." The SWP had long been a central target of the FBI's COINTELPRO program (Medsger 2014, 306–9). (Under Executive Order no. 10450, issued by Dwight Eisenhower in 1950—the same order that banned gays and lesbians from the government—SWP was designated a threat to "Internal Security.") Although COINTELPRO NEW LEFT had been officially terminated in April 1971, following the Media, Pennsylvania, burglary revelations (Churchill and VanderWall 1990, 229), it is clear from the 1972 Jill Raymond file that surveillance of the New Left was still fully operative. Indeed, it was understood within the bureau that, following Hoover's April 29, 1971, memo on the subject, while the "acronym" should be "dropped," "the activities" would be "continued . . . 'with tight procedures to insure absolute secrecy'" (Churchill and VanderWall 1990, 333 n.8).

By 1975, antiwar activists were well aware that the FBI had long since designated the movement as "anti-U.S."—one of the COINTELPRO terms—and targeted it for intensive surveillance and harassment. So, as Jill acknowledged, when the agents showed up at her door, she had "long since looked at agencies like the FBI and CIA as very sinister, very untrustworthy, frightening intelligence organizations. . . . So I was really disinclined to do any talking to FBI agents" (Raymond 1989, 294).

"We'd like to ask you about these two girls," the agents told her, producing the wanted posters of Saxe and Power. "You know what we're talking about." Jill replied, "I'm sorry. I just don't have anything to say to you. Here's my attorney's name and phone number" (1989, 295).

The week's lapse between Sally Kundert's encounter with the FBI and Jill's had given her a chance to collect herself, and she was better prepared to resist the agents' questioning when they first approached her. They soon returned, however, on January 22 for a second round. This time they put on more pressure, at one point evoking the children of Officer Schroeder, who was killed in the Brighton bank robbery: "If somebody had murdered your father," they asked, "wouldn't you want everybody to cooperate?" Since Jill's father was dead—a painful reality for her—this argument was not persuasive. She shook her head. They then asked her to describe her political beliefs, veering into questions like, "If you were going to describe your political philosophy in one word, would it start with an 's'?" (Raymond 1989, 295), suggesting the political nature of their quest. (Needless to say, it should not be the business of the government to track one's political philosophy.) Jill demurred. Finally, "as they were walking away," she recalled, "they said, 'well, you may find yourself sitting outside the door of a grand jury room then'" (Raymond 1987b). This improper, veiled threat shows the FBI clearly saw the grand jury as a way of forcing people to talk to them.

By the third week of January and into March, scores of people in the Lexington community, including several at Susan Saxe's former workplace, the Alfalfa Restaurant, were interrogated by the FBI. On February 5, for example, Agent McDonald questioned an Alfalfa employee, Meredith Moore, in her apartment. During the course of their conversation, the agent asked Moore if she thought anyone in Lexington had known that Lena and May were wanted fugitives. Meredith said, no, she didn't think anyone knew who they were. Robert Benedict, who was in the apartment at the time, concurred. Moore and Benedict then asked Agent McDonald whether he thought anyone in Lexington had known who they were (and had thus been knowingly harboring fugitives), and "he said no, he was sure that no one here in Lexington know [sic] who they were when they were here." While McDonald later denied under oath having made this statement, it would seem to be corroborated by the fact that no indictments were ever issued for the crime of harboring fugitives (Transcript 1975, DE 46–47, 504, 471–73). Indeed, in a later interview with the Enslings (the couple at whose Stanford, Kentucky, farm Saxe and Power had stayed in late spring 1974), the FBI was told that "as far as [the Enslings] knew," Saxe and Power "had no pre-arranged contacts" in Lexington (FBI, March 6, 1975), thus precluding any harboring possibility, an issue that became central in the appeals contentions.

In addition to the Enslings, who provided considerable information (FBI, January 22, 1975), the FBI interrogated numerous others, including employers and landlords of Lena and May. The bureau also obtained phone records and fingerprint and handwriting samples of the two, which confirmed their identities.

Although many of those visited by the FBI cooperated, having little to reveal, some didn't, including Nancy Scott, who had lived in the Lexington Avenue Women's Collective, and Debbie Hands, who had been in a feminist study group with the others. These two, along with Jill Raymond, Marla Seymour, Gail Cohee, and Carey Junkin—all lesbians or gay—formed the Lexington Six. Now thoroughly alarmed and on alert, members of this community of resisters gathered one evening to plan strategy. The meeting was organized by Marla and Jill and included others who had lived in the Lexington Avenue collective, namely Letty Ritter. At the meeting the consensus was that "nobody was going to talk to the FBI." Letty was surprised at how adamant Nancy Scott, who had previously seemed the most conventional of the group, was about taking a stand. She was "dead set against talking to them." However, Letty herself, keeping her silence, thought, "I'm not going to go to jail for those two women" (Ritter 1987).

At about the same time, following Jill's suggestion, the group who planned to resist—the Lexington Six—met with a civil liberties lawyer, Robert Sedler, then an assistant professor at the University of Kentucky Law School and well known locally for taking on liberal cases. In his meeting with the group in his office at the law school, Sedler asked each of them individually if she or he knew where Saxe and Power were. Each said no.

He then asked whether any of them had known the true identities of Lena and May when they lived in Lexington, and each said no. Sedler was struck by the fact that the FBI agents had threatened some of them with federal grand jury subpoenas if they failed to answer agents' questions. Sedler was aware that the Nixon administration had been "using the grand jury process to get information from political dissidents," he later recounted (Sedler 1986), and he began to see the outlines of a case of "grand jury abuse" as he talked to the group. So he agreed to take on the case as a way of challenging what he saw as an unconstitutional use of grand juries to coerce people to testify regarding their political opinions and relationships.

At the same time, he had a sense of the futility of such a project, feeling "there was no way we could win" (Sedler 1986). He thought, however, that the six would eventually testify and that in the meantime, the case would serve to draw public attention to the abusive use of the grand jury as an information-gathering arm of the FBI. He indeed advised the six to cooperate, feeling that while their principled resistance was admirable, it wasn't worth "damaging their lives" should the worst-case scenario—ending up in prison for contempt of court—occur. As this scenario unfolded, Sedler continued to advise them what the consequences of their decisions could be: he told them to "take it a step at a time" and to weigh their decisions carefully (Seymour 1987b). He did not want them to go to jail.

It soon became clear to Sedler that the principal motivation of the group in its decision to resist was not to protest grand jury abuse, though that later became the central issue, but rather to uphold the ethos of "sisterhood." Their lesbianism, he realized, was more than a sexual orientation and identity; it was a political expression of solidarity with other women, which required loyalty and commitment (Sedler 1986). Even the FBI seemed to sense their solidarity. As one of the Lexington agents told an interviewer, "You know how those lesbians are—they all stick together" (Gatz, February 19, 1975).

As the case evolved, Sedler came to feel that the FBI had a special animus against the lesbian community. "I think," he told a reporter for *Majority Report*, a feminist journal, "the FBI really believes in this huge lesbian underground responsible for hiding fugitives" (Lafferty 1975a). After all, shortly before he died, J. Edgar Hoover in 1970 sent out a directive warning the bureau that the "women's liberation movement" "should be viewed as part of the enemy, a challenge to American values" (Rosen 2000, 245–46). That the FBI was focused on the lesbian and gay community in its search for Saxe and Power is verified in its records. New York agents canvassed "gay areas of Manhattan's West Village" (FBI, January 25, 1975). And Cincinnati agents, following a list of ten gay bars it had obtained, checked out the "homosexual bars" in that city (FBI, February 4, 1975).

The FBI was facing criticism for its failure to find Patty Hearst and other women fugitives. Marla Seymour felt, in analyzing FBI motivations, that they were frustrated and mystified as to how these women fugitives were managing to elude them. "How did they do this? How did they hide? How did this lesbian community function?" (Seymour 1987b). Sedler also came to feel that there may have been a "titillation" factor at work with the FBI agents questioning the Lexington women: "Let's find out what these women do" (Sedler 1986).

That the FBI continued to have rather bizarre notions about lesbians is suggested in information provided to an agent by a New York City source, who told him that lesbians "are easily victimized. . . . Although they may attempt to come across very hard, they are 'pussycats' when action starts" and fall apart when "relationships with lovers" break up (FBI, February 8, 1975). While this information seems comical today, it may have guided Lexington officials to believe they could easily break the Lexington Six. They were soon to learn how wrong they were.

The same New York source also provided the agent with the startling observation that "most women's groups into 'health foods' . . . are revolutionary, feeling that health foods keep the body healthy for the revolution" (FBI, February 8, 1975). Such information would be laughable if the consequences of such false beliefs had not been so dire.

While the FBI was intensifying its Lexington operation, another radical woman fugitive, Jane Alpert, who had surrendered to the FBI in November 1974 after four years underground, was sentenced in New York on January 13, 1975, to twenty-seven months in prison. Alpert's trajectory somewhat paralleled that of Saxe and Power. Like them, she was an honors graduate of an elite eastern school, Swarthmore, who had become active in a militant wing of the antiwar movement. With her then-lover Sam Melville, she planted bombs at major banks in New York City in the late 1960s. (Melville was arrested in 1969 and sent to prison in Attica, New York, where he was killed in the Attica uprising in September 1971.) During her time underground as a fugitive, part of which was spent with Pat Swinton, who had been part of their bombing ring, Alpert, like Saxe and Power, discovered radical feminism and became critical of the sexism of the New Left men, including Melville.

When Alpert was a fugitive, Robin Morgan, a sister reporter at the radical journal *Rat*, wrote in May 1970 a "Letter to a Sister Underground," a prose poem expressing solidarity with Jane. It concluded, "In Sisterhood, in struggle, . . . but mostly because I think I love you" Morgan 1970b, xl) — a feeling of sisterhood felt by the Lexington Six women in their own struggle.

Alpert wrote up her critique of the male New Left in an article, "Mother Right," the first part of which was entitled "Dear Sisters in the Weather Underground." The article was published in the July–August 1973 issue of *off our backs* and a full-text version appeared in *Ms.* magazine in August with an introduction by Gloria Steinem, giving it a mainstream feminist imprimatur. In the article Alpert repudiated her male former colleagues in the New Left, naming names, including her former lover Melville, and giving specific details about their boorish sexist behavior. She concluded, speaking of Melville's and other radicals' deaths in Attica, "I will mourn the loss of 42 male supremacists no longer" (Alpert 1973).

Alpert's article proved controversial, and during the spring of 1975 as the Lexington Six case unfolded, explosive denunciations of Alpert appeared in the feminist press, along with equally impassioned expressions of support. The controversy raised questions about movement women like Alpert, Saxe, and Power, who had actively participated in New Left violence but had turned away from "all that," as Robin Morgan once put it (Morgan 1970a) and embraced feminism. The debate (discussed more fully below) came to feature Susan Saxe as the main Alpert antagonist, to the point where it is now referred to as the Saxe-Alpert controversy. It was a debate in which Jill Raymond was to take part.

On January 24, 1975, Alice Grusse, an executive in a silverware-manufacturing plant in Meriden, Connecticut, was approached at work by two FBI agents. They said they were seeking to locate her daughter Ellen regarding a bank robbery. Grusse was shocked. It was inconceivable that her daughter could have been involved in any such thing, so she told the agents to hold on while she called Ellen, who then lived in New Haven. Ellen, who had been part of the Hartford lesbian feminist community along with Saxe and Power, already knew about the FBI dragnet in Lexington (Harris 1976a, 50) and had resolved not to talk to its agents. However, she told her mother to give the agents her address, feeling that she would have to face them sooner or later and not wanting to further burden her mother. Shortly thereafter the same day, the agents arrived at the New Haven apartment Ellen shared with her lover, thirty-one-year-old Marie Theresa "Terri" Turgeon. After the mother's phone call, the two women had quickly contacted a lawyer who advised them to talk to the FBI only if they had an attorney present. They told this to the FBI agents at the door, who then threatened them with subpoenas, saying they could be indicted for harboring fugitives (Harris 1976a, 50). It appears that the Connecticut U.S. attorney, William Dow III, realized that the Connecticut federal court would not have jurisdiction over a Massachusetts bank robbery, so any indictment would have to be based on a charge of harboring fugitives within the court's jurisdictional range.

Three days after the FBI visit, on January 27, Turgeon received a subpoena to appear before a federal grand jury in New Haven the following day. The next morning Ellen Grusse received her subpoena, ordering her to appear three-and-a-half hours later before the same grand jury (Harris 1976a, 52). The two thus had little time to collect their wits and decide how to handle this shocking development. But somehow from the first they were determined to resist the FBI and grand jury investigation. It felt like a violation of the lesbian-feminist community in which they had found a haven, and feelings of loyalty to that community fueled their resistance. As with the Lexington Six, they felt a reflexive emotional revulsion against government intrusion into their personal lives and associations.

Ellen had in fact known Lena Paley and May Kelly well as part of the nascent women's liberation community in early 1970s Hartford. She first met them in 1972 at a forum on Marxist-feminism at the University of Connecticut at which Lena and May were participants. Ellen was then taking courses at the university toward a degree. Soon after, a friend (and soon-to-be lover) of Ellen's, Carol Romano, formed a consciousness-raising (CR) group that included Lena and May, which Ellen joined. Also in the group were Mary Anna Palmer and Terri Turgeon. Carol and her husband, Jim, were committed feminists, having taken part in an early feminist action, the 1969 protest of the Miss America pageant in Atlantic City. They ran a feminist bookstore/center in Hartford.

Lena and May dominated the CR group sessions with their intense, radical political perspective and their dazzling intellect. Mary Anna remembered "being totally intimidated by the people in this group" (Palmer, email to author, May 4, 2018). "It was in this CR group," Ellen recently recalled, "that I became politically conscious and active. . . . My friendship with May and Lena and certainly [Carol] deepened during the next year" (Grusse, email to author, February 23, 2018). After Lena and May left Hartford, Ellen and another member of the CR group visited them in Lexington. Sometime in early to mid-August 1974, May, as noted, returned to Hartford.

During this visit May revealed her true identity as Kathy Power to Ellen, who later acknowledged, "I was totally in shock and incredulous" at the news. Shortly thereafter, Ellen and Carol, to whom May had earlier disclosed her past, took a short trip into New York City during which it became clear to Ellen that Carol was turning against May. When Ellen began to suspect that Carol might be on the verge of informing on their friend, she excused herself from Carol on the spot, found a payphone, and called May to warn her: "I told her to leave immediately" (Grusse, email to author, February 23, 2018). Ellen never knew whether Carol actually informed on May. (It appears from FBI records that she didn't actually cooperate with them until early 1975.) But, not taking chances, May heeded Ellen's warning and left town.

Mary Anna Palmer was also shocked when she learned of Lena's and May's true identities. "I did not know who May and Lena were," she reported, "until after we learned about the FBI being in town. They did not tell me their real identities. When I learned who they were, I went down to the public library and looked up the Boston bank robbery and shooting. I was shocked. . . . I couldn't imagine May or Lena being involved in such an activity" (Palmer, email to author, May 4, 2018).

Both Ellen Grusse and Terri Turgeon had grown up in conservative Catholic families but found a new social and ideological home in the women's movement. "The women's community," Grusse came to realize in the course of succeeding events, "is also my family now" (Harris 1976a, 92). "Feminism," Turgeon felt, had given her "a new sense of . . . dignity as an individual" (Harris 1976a, 67). She and Ellen met in 1974 and had fallen in love that fall, shortly before the FBI intrusion into their lives.

Grusse's and Turgeon's lawyer, Michael Avery, attempted to have the January 28 subpoena quashed, but the judge, Jon O. Newman, a Nixon appointee, "contemptuously," Ellen thought, dismissed the motion and ordered the two women to appear before the grand jury that afternoon (Harris 1976a, 76). The women were terrified by this time but proceeded into the grand jury room and refused to answer the district attorney's questions on grounds of their Fifth Amendment rights.

The questions asked of Ellen Grusse were the following:

1. *Do you know or are you acquainted with SUSAN EDITH SAXE, who uses the alias of LENA PALEY, or KATHERINE ANN POWER, who uses the alias of MAY KELLY, and if so have you seen them in Connecticut and do you know where they resided or stayed when they were in Connecticut and when is the last time you spoke with either or both of these individuals?*

2. *Have you ever met or come into contact with or had conversation with either SUSAN EDITH SAXE . . . or KATHERINE ANN POWER . . . at 118 Babcock Street in Hartford; 7 Putnam Heights in Hartford during the years 1973 through the present date, and if so where, when and with whom did you have these discussions or conversations? (In re Ellen Grusse 1975, 1238)*

The questions asked of Terri Turgeon were similar but with added details:

4. *At some point in time you lived at 23 Marshall Street in Hartford and KATHERINE ANN POWER, also known as MAY KELLY, visited you there, most likely during the calendar year 1974. Indicate to the grand jury whether or not that is so and if so when she came there, who she was with, how long she stayed and where she was residing at the time?*

5. *During the course of their stay in Connecticut both KATHERINE ANN POWER . . . and SUSAN EDITH SAXE . . . made known to certain acquaintances the fact that they were fugitives and charged with certain crimes. Do you know the individuals to whom they gave that information?* (In re Ellen Grusse 1975, 1238)

The questions seem to be focused on getting information about Saxe's and Power's current or recent whereabouts, rather than evidence leading to a harboring indictment. Grusse's and Turgeon's attorneys, Michael Avery and David Rosen, concluded as much, that "the [grand jury] questions were based on nothing more than suspicion," which suggested the FBI knew little and was on a fishing expedition. Based on these and other questions, the attorneys concluded that "the grand jury was being improperly used as an investigative body" (Harris 1976a, 82). It was, according to FBI records, at about this time that Carol Romano and her husband began cooperating with the FBI, so the grand jury questions may have been prompted in part by the information they were providing. On the same day that Grusse and Turgeon refused to testify, a federal court in Hartford issued subpoenas for two other Hartford women, Diana Perkins and Mary Anna Palmer, who had also refused to cooperate with the FBI. Perkins eventually gave limited testimony, but Palmer's case was dropped.

Back in their apartment after the hearing Ellen and Terri experienced "real terror." "We had no idea what would happen to us. . . . The government seemed so vicious and relentless that we thought it could do anything," Terri recalled. Moreover, the ensuing publicity "was the worst imaginable invasion of our privacy." As she later recounted, "Being a celebrity was the last thing I wanted. I just wanted . . . to be left alone in peace in my own way" (Harris 1976a, 88, 89, 76).

The nightmare continued when on January 30 the FBI outed Terri to her mother and other family members who had not previously known that she was a lesbian. Agents further sought out Terri's sister at her workplace where, with other workers present, they asked pointed questions about Terri's personal life. Two uncles in Maine and a cousin in Baltimore were also contacted by the FBI, as well as a couple in North Carolina Terri and Ellen had once visited (Harris 1976a, 92).

Meanwhile, the FBI investigation in Lexington was expanding exponentially. Agents began a campaign of intensive surveillance: the recalcitrant noncompliers were tailed; phones were tapped; mail was opened; trash was rifled through; relatives, friends, and employers were contacted. And as "the whole thing mushroomed," one activist recalled, fear became rampant throughout the gay and lesbian community; everybody began wondering if they were on "some list" (Hackney 1989). The atmosphere was "a cross between bewilderment and paranoia," another community member recalled (Sutherland 1986). "It's a miracle we didn't fall apart with all the paranoia," another recollected (Kundert, phone interview with author, April 19, 2018).

After his repudiation of FBI agent Wayne McDonald, Carey Junkin found himself being tailed on campus ("four steps behind") by another agent (Junkin 1987). (You could generally identify agents by their short hair, shaven faces, and business suits.) Later, on February 4, 1975, as he was hitchhiking to Cincinnati, Carey was stopped by the police on three occasions and asked for identification. As he had phoned a friend in Cincinnati earlier that day to let him know he was coming, Carey realized his phone had been tapped and the police alerted (Transcript 1975, DE 30).

One time Marla Seymour was driving along with Gail Cohee and Debbie Hands in a car, and they noticed a Fayette County school car following them. Taking a closer look, they realized it was Special Agent McDonald (Seymour 1987a). Jill Raymond later recounted that it was "a very bizarre experience" to find oneself under such surveillance, "the feeling . . . that somebody out there who you can't see is focusing their attention on your life: on what you're doing, what you're saying, the mail you're getting" (Raymond 1989, 294). There was a real sense of "Big Brother is watching" (Kundert 1986).

Having by then obtained the phone records of the recalcitrants, the FBI proceeded to contact relatives and friends. In several cases the FBI agents outed daughters, sons, or siblings to parents or other family members, as they did with the families of Terri Turgeon and Ellen Grusse—a practice the bureau developed during the earlier Red and Lavender Scares. It is hard to figure what legitimate purpose the FBI had in providing these revelations. Had they used outing as a threat to the Lexington Six individuals themselves, it might be construed as coercing their testimony. But the agents don't seem to have done this. They may have thought that by informing family members and other acquaintances that their relative or friend was "sexually deviant," they could enjoin those contacts to coerce the recalcitrant to cooperate, but this seems a far-fetched strategy (and in any event, it didn't work). One is left with the conclusion that the FBI outed the Lexington Six to friends and family (and, through publicity, to the public at large), deliberately exploiting a socially stigmatized identity, as a means of intimidating and harassing the lesbian and gay community, which the bureau saw as a threat to American normality. This would be consistent with their by-then apparently ingrained COINTELPRO tactics.

In an affidavit later filed with the U.S. district court, Jill Raymond testified that since the fall of 1974, she had made phone calls to the following friends and family members: Susan Palanas and Peter Briggs in Albuquerque, New Mexico; Laurie Raymond in Seattle; Alan Russel in Detroit; Dierdre Foss in Springfield, Ohio; Dorothy Raymond in Cleveland; Larry Kamins in Washington, DC; and Bonnie Proctor in Ayden, North Carolina. "Subsequently, all of these persons were visited by [FBI] agents" (Transcript 1975, DE 29).

The following were visited in this order: Peter and Susan Briggs on January 28; Dierdre Lynn Foss, Jill's foster sister, on February 1; Laurie Raymond, Jill's sister, on February 3; Alan Russel on February 3; and Dorothy Raymond, Jill's eighty-year-old grandmother, on three occasions on February 8, 9, and 11, 1975.

The FBI was received with varying degrees of resistance from all these people, although none of them had been forewarned about the case and Jill's putative involvement. Susan Briggs, earlier Susan Palanas, was a former member of the Red Star Sisters who recently moved to New Mexico. In a brief conversation with FBI agents who came to her door in Albuquerque Susan told them she had met Lena or May, accompanied by Jill, at a women's meeting. The FBI agent asked her if Jill was "into terrorism." Susan replied no. He also asked odd questions such as whether Lena's "hair fashion was mannish" (suggesting that the FBI's notions about homosexuality hadn't evolved much since the time of J. Edgar Hoover's vacuous 1964 conversation with Lyndon Johnson). At the conclusion of the interview, the agent asked Susan "if it was true that [she] did not like them [the FBI agents]." Susan reported, "I answered that that was true" (Transcript 1975, DE 34).

Later the same day, January 29, the FBI agents returned to interview Peter Briggs, who was even less cooperative. He announced, "I did not want to answer their questions or supply them with information. . . . I told them if they want to know what Jill Raymond did, they should ask her." The agents asked him if he knew that "harboring felons was a crime. I answered that I knew that." At this point the agents began to defend themselves, assuring Peter that their motives were not political. Peter "expressed doubt about this" and asserted "that the FBI was political" and that it had engaged in "wire tapping . . . and general investigation of United States citizens who had committed no crime but were politically dissident"—a fact that was well known thanks to the revelations in the COINTELPRO files obtained from the Media, Pennsylvania, FBI office. One of the agents then threatened Briggs, saying they had information on him that could implicate him "more deeply in their criminal investigation." Briggs told them to go ahead and subpoena him "if they so desired" (Transcript 1975, DE 33). The agents left the premises, and Peter heard nothing further.

Dierdre Foss, Jill's foster sister, was at work on February 1 at the Odd Fellows Home in Springfield, Ohio, when an FBI agent named John Finnegan approached her and told her "an acquaintance" of hers in Lexington, Kentucky, "had been held been held in contempt of a grand jury and that she probably was already in jail" (Transcript 1975, DE 46–47, 519). This false information was news to Dierdre, who asked the agent to doublecheck his facts. He later called her and acknowledged that Jill had been subpoenaed but not yet held in contempt of court (getting ahead of the story, it seems). In the course of this forty-five-minute conversation, the agent intimidated Dierdre by boasting about the power of a grand jury. He said, "The two most important people in the world were Jesus Christ and the judge of the grand jury, and not necessarily in that order" (Transcript 1975, DE 46–47, 520). (The agent presumably meant the judge in a court wherein a grand jury is empaneled, because the grand jury per se does not have a judge.) Finally, Dierdre, who had contacted Jill to find out what was going on, reported back to the agent this significant detail: Jill told her she hadn't known who Saxe and Power were when they were in Lexington and didn't know where they were at the present time (FBI, February 1, 1975).

Alan Russel, a friend of Jill's in Detroit, was contacted by FBI agents two days after Dierdre, on February 3. They told Russel that Saxe and Power were dangerous fugitives and might "decide to get rid of Jill," so he should warn Jill and get her to cooperate with the FBI for her own safety (Transcript 1975, DE 37). They also said, "Did you know Jill is a lesbian?" Alan was indignant at this and called Jill as soon as the agents left (Raymond 1989, 295).

The same day as the Russel noninterview Jill's sister, Laurie Raymond, received a visit from the FBI in Seattle. Laurie refused from the get-go: "I said I didn't have anything to say to them." The agents persisted, however, producing the posters of Saxe and Power. Laurie recollected the ensuing exchange:

> FBI: *Do you realize these women are wanted for* murder?
> ME: *I have nothing to say.*
> FBI: *Do you mean you're unwilling to cooperate in catching a murderer?*
> ME: *Yes, that's right.*
> FBI: *Why?*
> ME: *Well, for one reason what with the biggest war criminal of all time still living freely at taxpayers' expense and immune to prosecution for his domestic crimes, I can't work up much excitement for one little murder. (Transcript 1975, DE 36)*

Laurie was alluding to the fact that President Richard Nixon had never been prosecuted for war crimes or for the domestic crimes associated with the 1970 Watergate break-in of the Democratic National Headquarters.

The FBI agents proceeded to threaten her: "If we find that these women have been here, we can get you for harboring a fugitive," stressing once again that "this isn't something political. This is just murder." Laurie replied, "Frankly, I feel more threatened by the government you're working for than by any murderers. . . . Why don't you leave?" (Transcript 1975, DE 36). The FBI report filed the same day of the interview noted that Laurie Raymond "displayed extremely uncooperative attitude and open hostility toward the FBI" (FBI, February 3, 1975).

On February 8, the FBI contacted Jill's grandmother in a nursing home where she resided. Agents told her Jill was "suspected of harboring or aiding fugitives." Dorothy Raymond, "very polite and hostess-like" (Raymond 1989, 295), told them, "I did not think Jill or her sisters . . . would want to take in such people" (Transcript 1975, DE 38). As Jill later recalled, "She backed me up" (Raymond 1989, 296).

The agents returned the next day and again on February 11, when Jill was visiting her grandmother. During these visits the agents told Dorothy that Jill was a "socialist, and wasn't that awful?" (Raymond 1989, 295), and moreover that she was a lesbian. The grandmother "scolded" the agents for their impertinence (Raymond 1987a). Dorothy Raymond later asserted to the U.S. District Court of Eastern Kentucky: "Jill . . . is a girl of intelligence and integrity. . . . I am confident she is innocent of the charges" (Transcript 1975, DE 38).

Other parents and relatives of the Lexington Six were less supportive when informed of their child's sexuality. Carey Junkin's father, a retired U.S. Army officer, was deeply upset and in the course of the ensuing court hearings had a heart attack. Members of Carey's father's Alabama family, who were in the Ku Klux Klan, offered to shoot Carey on sight when they learned he was gay (Junkin 1987). Marla Seymour's parents said that while they loved her, they couldn't support her and eventually cut her off entirely (Seymour 1987). Other parents were also deeply disturbed when they learned from the FBI or from news coverage that their daughter was a lesbian (Raymond 1987a).

Attorney Robert Sedler was shocked at the lack of parental support. It was the only case he had ever handled, he came to realize, in which the parents did not support their children. Their "hostile attitude" was palpable. One mother exclaimed to Sedler, "how *could* my daughter become a lesbian?" Sedler felt that not only did such hostility make it harder for several of the Lexington Six; it also likely affected the judge in the final hearings that no parents were in the courtroom to support their children, an unspoken comment that weighed against the six (Sedler 1986). Carey Junkin remarked how in those hearings the judge "treated us like bad children, not thoughtful adults. . . . We had been abandoned by our parents" (1987).

Up until the time they received subpoenas to appear before the federal grand jury, most of the members of the targeted lesbian feminist and gay communities didn't take the whole process entirely seriously. There was an element of unreality about it, in part because of the suddenness of the January appearance of the FBI, in part because they knew they were innocent of any crime and believed they would be vindicated. "None of us believed at any point in the process," Jill Raymond later recalled, "that it was going to go any further. Your logical faculties go into play, and you say 'It's not reasonable for them to pursue this. There's nothing here. We have no information here.' And we certainly didn't believe we were going to jail" (1989, 296). There was "a certain naivety" among the group, Sally Kundert reflected. "We thought, well, we're innocent, we don't know anything. . . . We didn't even know they could strip you of your rights" (1986).

Jill agreed in retrospect that there was a "dissonance" between the seriousness of their prospects and their somewhat oblivious, nonchalant attitude. We were "somewhat naive," she acknowledged, "about the political implications." The decision not to cooperate was based more on "our own relationships with one another and with Lena and May. . . . It was something we did from the gut—because we felt that way." So, while those who were resisting the FBI felt good about standing up for principle and proud of their stand, it "hadn't occurred to any of us that we were going to spend a year or even a week in jail. . . . We didn't believe we were going to have to sacrifice a lot" (Raymond 1987b).

Accordingly, the resistance of the Lexington Six was not a planned, thought-out political action but rather a series of ad-hoc decisions made seriatim. "We were flying by the seat of our pants," recalled Barbara Sutherland, a second-year law student who worked for the legal team. It all happened so fast that even the counsel staff representing the six barely had time to think out a legal basis for its positions. It was a matter of "you develop principles and reasons as you go along" (Sutherland 1986). Fortunately for them, the New York–based Center for Constitutional Rights came to their aid in providing already well-rehearsed legal arguments for use in subsequent hearings.

During much of the month of January—that is, before the subpoenas were issued—several of those targeted by the FBI gathered to consult, to theorize, to conduct research, and to worry about their friends Lena and May. After all, the revelations about their past meant that the two fugitives were in real jeopardy. Felony murder in Massachusetts, their Lexington friends learned, could carry the death penalty or at least life without parole. So they worried about what Lena's and May's fates could be if they were captured. "Here were these two people who'd befriended me, and I could imagine them both going down in a hail of bullets," Raymond later noted, recalling the SLA conflagration in Los Angeles in which several militants died thusly. "I wanted to do something. I wanted to be able, not to hide [Lena and May] from the law . . . but to stand up for them in some way, for the people I knew them to be then, not as crazies who thought shooting people and robbing banks was a good way to fund a movement" (Raymond, email to author, March 19, 2018). In addition, Jill recalled, she felt a sense of "loyalty to the antiwar movement"—the context in which Saxe and Power had committed their crime. It was a matter of "political identity, loyalty, personal connection." At the same time, she felt a certain "helplessness" that she couldn't do "something to take care of them [Lena and May]" (Raymond 1987a).

CHAPTER THREE

Grand Jury Resistance

As events continued to unfold for them in late January 1975, some of the Lexington Six felt its unreality intensify. It seemed "like a play that we were props in," Carey Junkin recalled. "You're just sort of washed along" (1987). Marla Seymour also had a sense of disbelief in what was happening. Nothing from her past had prepared her: "I [ended up] in jail, I never expected to be. I was in real danger, never expected to be. . . . I felt exposed and helpless, situations I'd avoided at all costs in my life before" (1987a). Yet, despite the foreboding signs, they continued to feel that in the end their own innocence would become apparent and save them. Even attorney Robert Sedler persisted in thinking, "they're not going to lock up a couple of girls—UK students"—and all white (Raymond 1987b).

By the end of January, however, things turned more ominous when subpoenas were issued for five of the Lexington Six, ordering them to appear February 3 before the grand jury of the U.S. District Court for Eastern Kentucky. (The term *subpoena* stems from the Latin *sub poena*, which means "under penalty"; in other words, one will suffer a penalty if one disobeys the order.) It remained unclear why these five—Gail Cohee, Carey Junkin, Debbie Hands, Jill Raymond, and Marla Seymour (and later Nancy Scott)—were targeted, except for the fact that they were lesbians and gay. Others who had refused to answer FBI questions were not subpoenaed (Kundert 1986). Many were called, it seemed, but few were chosen, and the chosen few were lesbian and gay.

In each case the subpoena—a formal order stamped with the seal of the court—was hand-delivered by a marshal of the court. In Jill Raymond's case, "I was coming home late one night after being out to dinner with a friend. It was after midnight and the U.S. marshals were just then walking away from the front door of my apartment. 'Here it is,' they said" (1989, 296). "YOU ARE HEREBY COMMANDED," Jill read, "to appear in the United States District Court of the Eastern District of Kentucky at Lexington, Kentucky . . . on the 3d day of February."

Once the subpoenas were issued, Sedler remained incredulous. "First he called the FBI and said, 'Look, this is a nothing case. Who are you kidding?'" But the FBI agent told him, "We're in this. We're serious" (Raymond 1989, 296).

Grand juries—or their antecedents—were first constituted during the reign of the English king Henry II, who under the Constitution of Clarendon in 1164 established a "jury of accusation." This was a large panel of individuals tasked with bringing a formal charge against a member of its community suspected of a crime. The jury panel then presented its determination to a court of "itinerant justices" appointed by the crown, who "ask[ed] the assembled jurors whether they suspected the defendant, and if the answer was affirmative, he was sent to the water." Being "sent to the water" meant a trial by ordeal, with the accused either having to put their bare arms in scalding water or being dunked in frigid water. If the defendant withstood and emerged unscathed from the ordeal, he or she was declared innocent (Berman 1983, 451, 57). Since the defendant generally failed these tests, the decision by the accusing jury was usually tantamount to conviction. In 1215, trial by ordeal was abolished by the Fourth Lateran Council, and the trial was gradually assumed by a petit jury, composed of a smaller number of persons than the grand jury (hence the name *petit*, which means "little"). This is roughly the system in the United States today: a grand jury brings an indictment or formal accusation; a petit jury (or sometimes a judge) decides innocence or guilt. (The United States is the only country in the world, other than Liberia, to retain the grand jury system.)

The Fifth Amendment to the U.S. Constitution specifies, "No person shall be held to answer for a capital, or otherwise infamous crime, unless on a presentment or indictment of a Grand Jury." Thus, the purpose of a grand jury historically has been to determine if an indictment is warranted, that is, whether there is "probable cause" of criminal activity on the part of the accused, which, if so determined, brings the accused to trial.

In practice, the grand jury system has often become a vehicle in political power struggles, with "the grand jury serv[ing] the interests of the government or the prejudices and passions of the local populace." In the antebellum South, for example, including in Kentucky, "one of the primary roles of the grand jury was to enforce the slavery laws" (Deutsch 1984, 1162, 1167). Under Reconstruction in the post–Civil War era, grand juries in southern states excluded Blacks and refused to bring indictments against members of the Ku Klux Klan, thus upholding the Jim Crow system of effective apartheid.

From the late nineteenth century to the present, prosecutors have consistently used the grand jury against (mostly) left-wing radical political movements. In the aftermath of the 1886 Haymarket Square massacre in Chicago, a grand jury indicted thirty-one anarchists and socialists, though there was no evidence that any of them had been involved in the bombing that precipitated the event. (Four were eventually executed.) In World War I, antiwar activists were routinely indicted by grand juries simply for publicly advocating dissident views (Deutsch 1984, 1171–73).

While the traditional role of the grand jury was to bring indictments, during the Cold War era in the United States it took on a new role, that of discovering rather than evaluating evidence (Deutsch 1984, 1178). This "investigative grand jury" became a powerful tool of the prosecution because of its *duces tecum* subpoena power—that is, the authority to command evidence—a power that was used in the Lexington Six case. (The incorrect record of the April 12, 1974, phone call, for example, was obtained under a *duces tecum* subpoena.) Because jurors knew little about the law and indeed often didn't even understand the function of a grand jury (as was the case with the Lexington and New Haven juries, as we shall see), they were easily manipulated by prosecuting attorneys and became in essence "a rubber stamp of approval for prosecutory requests." At the time of the Lexington Six case, for example, out of approximately 23,000 federal grand jury cases in 1976, 22,877 indictments were returned by the grand juries (Deutsch 1984, 1175 n.76). In other words, the juries followed the prosecutor's wishes in 99 percent of the cases.

So by the time of the Lexington Six case, grand juries had become commonly used by the government "as a tool against political activism" on the theory that "anybody who disagreed with the government was committing some kind of crime," Judy Peluso, a member of the New York Grand Jury Project, observed. "This country is very afraid of dissent," she added (Peluso 1987). During President Richard Nixon's administration, the use of grand juries against political dissidents reached its height; between 1970 and 1973, for example, over a thousand political activists were subpoenaed before more than one hundred grand juries in eighty-four cities (Deutsch 1984, 1179).

After attorney Robert Sedler realized that the FBI was serious—indeed, deeply invested—in the case of the Lexington Six, he filed a motion with the U.S. District Court of Eastern Kentucky to quash the subpoenas, that is, to have them dismissed. The motion to quash was filed on February 18; however, five of the Lexington Six had already been ordered to appear before the grand jury on February 3, a hearing that therefore proceeded forthwith.

Based on the way the FBI agents in Lexington seemed by late January to be focusing their questions on the composition and political orientation of the lesbian community, Sedler and others had come to the conclusion that the FBI had developed a theory there was a secret lesbian underground network, a lesbian cabal, stretching from New Haven to Lexington and points beyond, hiding elusive women fugitives like Susan Saxe and Kathy Power, as well perhaps as Patty Hearst, Pat Swinton, and maybe even members of the notorious Weather Underground such as Kathy Boudin and Cathy Wilkerson. That the FBI agents in Seattle seemed to suspect Jill Raymond's sister Laurie of harboring fugitives—and that the agents raised the issue in their interrogations of Jill's friends and family in Albuquerque, Cleveland, and Detroit—suggested how widespread the FBI considered this mythical lesbian underground to be. By the end of February, bureau agents had conducted investigations in nearly all the major cities in the Northeast, Midwest, and West Coast. The dragnet extended even to Honolulu (FBI, January 28 1975a) and the Canadian border (FBI, January 29, 1975).

At the same time that FBI agents were contacting Jill's relatives and friends throughout the country, an agent in Cincinnati, Mary Elizabeth Dunn, began interrogating members of the feminist community in that city. Dunn visited a gay bar where bartenders saw her walk out with a list of women "who want to make contacts," which was attached to the end of the bar (Anonymous 1975b). Dunn also contacted various women's groups, including the Cincinnati Rape Crisis Center, where "she started flashing her badge and had to be asked to stop intimidating people" (Von Hoffman 1975). Dunn asked Margie Robertson, president of the Cincinnati chapter of the National Organization for Women for a membership list with lesbian members highlighted. Robertson, who was nursing a sick child during the interview, heroically refused. "Not only can't you get a list," Robertson said, "but we don't keep track of who is a lesbian" (Raymond 1989, 294). As a consequence, the FBI wiretapped Robertson's phone, which she could tell by the buzzing sound and the clicking of a broken tape. When that happened, she told them (via the tapped phone), "Get it together, boys!" (Von Hoffman 1975).

With a growing awareness of the mammoth dragnet the FBI had cast, and angered thereby, five of the Lexington Six trooped to the federal court-house on February 3, determined to protect their community from what they saw as unwarranted and oppressive intrusion by patriarchal authorities. (Nancy Scott, the sixth member of the group, was subpoenaed later.) The courthouse is a massive limestone structure in downtown Lexington built in 1934 in classical revival style. Unlike the nearby county courthouse, it didn't have a statue of a Confederate general on horseback on its front lawn (the statue was removed in 2017), but its architecture nevertheless had an overpowering, foreboding feel. The grand jury room was on the fourth floor. The five "witnesses," as they were termed, assembled with their lawyer in the hall adjacent to an anteroom attached to the room where the grand jurors were seated. In the minutes before they were summoned into the jury room, the subpoenaed five huddled together with their lawyer to prepare a set written statement that each planned to read before the jurors.

Robert Sedler was not present that morning; instead, the five were represented by a young, recent (1974) graduate of the University of Louisville Law School, M. E. (Emmy) Hixson. In addition to the five, several supporters were also in the hall, many sitting on the floor, as there was only one chair in the narrow corridor. It was a noisy, "confused but tense" scene, a member of the legal team recalled (Sutherland 1987). No one on the counsel staff, including the lawyer, was allowed to accompany the witnesses into the grand jury room, and the witnesses, dressed in their usual everyday attire of blue jeans and sandals, went in, one by one, alone (Raymond 1987b).

Although the Lexington Six had certain things in common, they had varying degrees of political commitment and varying degrees of connection to Kathy Power and Susan Saxe. What they had in common was that they were all white, young (ranging in age from nineteen to twenty-three), either current or former UK students, liberal arts majors, educated in U.S. public high schools, middle-class, and struggling with a newly acquired lesbian or gay identity (as they were young, even those who had been out for a few years, such as Carey and Marla, were relatively new to the experience of being a member of a despised minority). They came from various parts of the United States, mainly the South or border states: Carey from Alabama, Nancy from Indiana, Jill from Ohio, Gail from Delaware, Marla from Ohio, and Debbie from Kentucky. All had been involved to one degree or another in the antiwar movement, generally leaned left politically, and all—including Carey—strongly identified with the rising women's liberation movement. Of the six, only Marla, Jill, and to a lesser extent Gail had known Lena and May well. Nancy and Debbie had met the two only a few times, and Carey, as noted, had merely said hello to them once or twice in the hall of his apartment building. And none, significantly, knew Lena and May as Saxe and Power.

Despite their commonalities, and although they all came to accept as the primary legal rationale of their case the issue of grand jury abuse and governmental overreach, each of the Lexington Six had differing motives for their initial resistance to the FBI and federal court authorities. For Jill Raymond it was primarily a matter of dogged loyalty to beloved friends, Lena and May, sister comrades in the fight against oppression. For Carey Junkin it was that he "just thought that what they were doing was wrong and abusive and somebody has to stand up to them" (Junkin 1987). For Carey, too, as perhaps for some of the others, it became an "acid test" to prove to himself that he had it in him to stand up for what he believed in. Marla Seymour's and Nancy Scott's resistance seemed to be fueled by a fierce indignation that their personal freedom and rights were being violated. "I am myself," Nancy Scott declared, "and refuse to be dictated by *anyone*" (Scott, letter [from jail] to author, April 30, 1975).

For Marla and Gail Cohee, as a committed couple, it was a matter of loyalty to one another and to the women's community in general. They vowed at the onset of the FBI siege in January that they would do everything together as they faced the onslaught. Both too, as well as Nancy Scott and Debbie Hands, were, like Ellen Grusse and Terri Turgeon, motivated by a passionate determination to protect the lesbian-feminist community they called home from violative intrusion by patriarchal authorities, "the Man." For Nancy Scott it was a matter of taking a stand against the authorities' "outright attack on feminism and lesbianism" and against this "iron-ruled patriarchal society" (letter to author, March 29, 1975). For the Lexington Six, political and personal passion had merged. The personal really had become political, and the political personal.

Jill Raymond recognized the link between personal resistance against privacy invasion and political resistance against unjust police-state authority: "Our personal lives were our personal lives. If you have the right to ask me what Lena Paley and I discussed on the night of October 3, 1974, when she and I went out to X bar and drank beer for three hours, if you have the right to quiz me about everything she said and I said, then I must surrender any privacy that would attach to that relationship" (1989, 298–99).

One other commonality the five shared that morning of February 3 when they faced the grand jury for the first time: they were petrified. "It was kind of terrifying," Carey recalled. "I didn't even know what a grand jury was" (Junkin 1987). "It was real scary," Marla agreed in recollection (Seymour 1987a).

Once the hearing began, each of the five was in turn called into the grand jury room alone to face twenty-one jurors lined up behind a long, L-shaped table at the corner of which the witness was seated. It was a small, windowless room, Jill Raymond recalled, and the feeling was "claustro-phobic" (1987b). Off to the right stood the U.S. district attorney, Eugene Siler Jr., who had issued the subpoenas and generally ran the grand jury proceedings, asking most of the questions. In the background was a court reporter who recorded the session.

The witnesses and their attorney were surprised to find two FBI agents and three federal agents from the Bureau of Alcohol, Tobacco, and Firearms sitting in the anteroom between the hall and the grand jury room. They were even more surprised to find FBI Special Agent Wayne McDonald acting as bailiff for the hearing, calling the witnesses into the grand jury chamber for their testimony—clearly an improper procedure, which the Lexington Six legal team highlighted in their appeal for reversal.

Marla Seymour was the first to be summoned by McDonald. "Marla, come on in," he said to her, somewhat snarkily, "and give your little speech" (Transcript 1975, DE 46–47, 358). McDonald had already addressed the grand jury that morning before the witnesses appeared, giving the jurors what was called "background information" about them and the case (Transcript 1975, DE 46–47, 475). As McDonald had apparently not been sworn in for this testimony, this too was improper. In a later hearing before district court judge Bernard T. Moynahan Jr., Sedler contended, "Mr. McDonald's unauthorized presence before the grand jury totally taints any indictments which this grand jury might return. . . . The only people who can give background information to the grand jury are sworn witnesses—but not an official of the government" (Gatz, March 8, 1975).

In the contempt hearing on March 8, laying out the case for an appeal, Sedler hypothesized that McDonald might have made the following statement to the grand jury in the February 3 hearing: "During the course of [its] investigation," the FBI had "uncovered evidence that led [the FBI] to believe that particular persons in Lexington knew that at the time they were here Lena Paley was Susan Saxe and May Kelly was Catherine [sic] Power." Moreover, again according to Sedler, McDonald allegedly said to the jurors: "We believe that certain persons in Lexington, in particular, the persons that have been subpoenaed before you today, know the present whereabouts of these persons, and we want you to help us, the FBI, get this information so that we can locate the fugitives" (Transcript 1975, DE 46–47, 486).

We cannot know for sure whether McDonald actually said these words, since grand jury records are secret and, in the case of this particular hearing, were destroyed in 1988 (Cindy Long, U.S. Attorney's Office, Eastern District of Kentucky, email to author, December 22, 2017). However, it seems likely that McDonald said something along these lines to the grand jury that morning. If Sedler's hypothesis is correct, Agent McDonald clearly saw the grand jury as an investigative tool of the FBI, as a means of coercing the noncooperative witnesses to provide officials with information about Saxe's and Power's whereabouts. That the grand jurors also saw themselves in such a role is evidenced by the answer given by the jury foreperson, Ralph Agee, of Richmond, Kentucky, to a question posed to him by Nancy Scott as to why she was being interrogated: "We want to find out where those two girls are and who they were with" (Transcript 1975, DE 46–47, 271). Thus, the grand jury in Lexington was clearly functioning as an investigative arm of the FBI, far afield from its originally prescribed historical function of bringing indictments. Saxe and Power had, of course, long since been indicted in both Pennsylvania and Massachusetts, so there could be no question of the Lexington grand jury collecting evidence to determine whether those two had committed a crime (which would have been a legitimate purpose for the grand jury). That determination had already been made. Nor apparently did the FBI think any of the Lexington Six had actually knowingly harbored fugitives—as was revealed in the final contempt hearing (see below). Nor were any of them suspected of any other crime.

In Sedler's second appeal, filed on June 5, 1975, before the Sixth Circuit Court of Appeals in Cincinnati (Appeal B 1975), he highlighted the supposition that in providing "background information" to the grand jury, McDonald had not raised the question of whether any of the Lexington Six harbored fugitives or been accessories after the fact, which are federal felonies. Indeed, those matters did not seem at the time of the contempt hearing to have been of central concern for the Lexington FBI agents or the U.S. attorney. They only became so ex post facto during the appeals process.

Escorted, then, by McDonald, each of the five witnesses proceeded one after the other into the grand jury chamber. Once Carey Junkin saw that the jurors were "average looking" folks who "looked like his parents' friends," he felt less intimidated (Junkin 1987). The jurors had been selected, as is typical in federal procedure, at random from a voter registration list. In this case, although under the 1957 Civil Rights Act, race and sex could not be used as criteria to select federal grand juries, there does not appear to have been more than one African American on the panel. Indeed, it had only been a matter of weeks since the U.S. Supreme Court had ruled in *Taylor v. Louisiana* on January 21, 1975, that exclusion of women from jury service violated the Fourteenth Amendment's due process and equal protection clauses and was therefore unconstitutional (Wortman 1985, 295). Women, however, had already been serving on Kentucky state juries since the 1920s. While the question of the grand jury being biased because of disproportionate racial and gender composition was not raised in the Lexington case, it was in the case of Ellen Grusse and Terri Turgeon in New Haven and other grand jury resistance cases (see below).

The procedure agreed on ahead of time by the Lexington Six and their legal advisors was one laid out in a manual entitled *Representation of Witnesses before Federal Grand Juries: A Manual for Attorneys*, published in 1974 by the National Lawyers Guild, a progressive association of lawyers that specialized *inter alia* in cases of grand jury abuse. This six-hundred-page loose-leaf binder covered all aspects of grand jury cases, including an outline of the stages of a typical grand jury case from the subpoena to the "show cause" and contempt hearing, as well as a lengthy checklist of legal objections to be made during its course, based on detailed descriptions of legal precedents. The attorneys for the Lexington Six—on this occasion, Emmy Hixson, a National Lawyers Guild member, undoubtedly followed the instructions laid out in the manual closely.

The first tactic specified in the manual is that a witness before a grand jury should only answer his or her name and address, and with each subsequent question ask to be excused to leave the room to consult with his or her attorney (National Lawyers Guild 1974, 3–25). This was necessary because lawyers are not allowed to accompany their clients into a grand jury room. It was also an obstructionist tactic because it delayed the proceedings considerably; each consultation in the Lexington case took from three to five minutes, according to the court reporter (Transcript 1975, DE 46–47, 282).

Once the witness was seated, U.S. Attorney Siler asked the questions, beginning with "State your name." This was the only question that any of the Lexington five answered directly. The following verbatim testimony of Gail Cohee (as recorded in the contempt hearing transcript) presents a typical exchange:

Q. *[from Siler]. State your name, please?*
A. *Gail Cohee.*

Q. *Now, Miss Cohee, I am going to show you here a picture entitled Catherine [sic] Ann Power. I want you to look at that and tell this grand jury if you have ever seen that girl before in your life?*
A. *May I consult with my attorney?*

THE FOREMAN: *Yes.*
(Reporter: The witness left the room, and returned).
Q. *All right, the question asked you was: Have you ever seen this girl in the picture entitled Catherine Ann Power before in your life?*
A. *Mr. Foreman, on advice of counsel, I respectfully refuse to answer that question, based on my rights under the First, Fourth, Fifth, Eighth, and Ninth Amendments to the United States Constitution, applicable sections of the United States Code, and on the additional ground that the subpoenas and the question constitute an abuse of the grand jury function and process by the U.S. Attorney. (Transcript 1975, DE 46–47, 274)*

Cohee was reading from a statement prepared ahead of time by Hixson in consultation with legal staffs at the National Lawyers Guild and the Center for Constitutional Rights, which had become involved in the case (see below). Each of the five witnesses answered all substantive questions with this identical statement.

Occasionally, however, the exchanges went off script, as the witnesses registered symbolic resistance to the proceedings. Cohee, for example, questioned the wording of the following question:

Q. *Now, Miss Cohee, let me ask you this question: Is it not a fact that during 1974 you lived with these two girls whom I have shown you in the picture identified as Catherine Ann Power and Susan Edith Saxe?*
A. *May I consult with my attorney?*
(Reporter: The witness left the room, and returned).

Q. *You are Gail Cohee, again?*
A. *Yes, I still am.*

Q. *And before you went to consult with your attorney you were asked: Is it not a fact that you lived with these two girls, Catherine Ann*

Power and Susan Edith Saxe shown in these pictures during 1974?
A. *I don't understand the question. Would you please explain to me what you mean by "lived with"?*

Q. *Lived with, in the same quarters.*
A. *May I consult with my attorney?*
(Reporter: The witness left the room, and returned).

Q. *Now, do you understand the questions asked, and, if you would, tell the grand jury your answer?*
A. *Mr. Foreperson, upon advice of counsel. . . . (Transcript 1975, DE 46–47, 277–78)*

Noteworthy in the above exchanges is a subtle battle being waged over terminology. Cohee uses the nonsexist term "Foreperson," not then common (though now accepted), instead of "Foreman." The court officials uses the term "Miss" instead of "Ms," which would have been preferred by the women witnesses. And throughout, young women such as Saxe and Power—then in their twenties—are referred to by Siler and the foreperson as "girls," a somewhat dismissive and derogatory term for adult women.

Also noteworthy is Cohee's noncooperative attitude, which was manifested by each of the witnesses in turn in their nontestimony. Marla Seymour's hostility to the proceeding is quite apparent in her interrogation, picked up here when she returns to the jury room after consulting her attorney:

Q. *Okay, you are Marla Seymour again, right?*
THE WITNESS: *Right.*

Q. *And what is your present living address?*
A. *I don't see why you need to ask that question since I received my subpoena.*

Q. *Okay. You refuse to answer?*
A. *I have been issued my subpoena at a certain address.*

Q. *All right. Do you have an attorney?*
A. *Yes, I do.*

Q. *And what is your attorney's name?*
A. *I need to consult with my attorney.*

MR. SILER: *All right, we will wait for you.*

(Reporter: She returned to the room later).

Q. *Okay, you are Marla Seymour again, right?*

A. *Yes, I am.*

Q. *Okay. Did you answer the question whether you had an attorney?*

A. *Yes.*

Q. *And what is the name of that attorney?*

A. *She said that she would be glad to tell you if you went out in the hall and asked her.*

Q. *Well, you have to tell us, because I don't have the authority to find out from an attorney.*

A. *Well, I will have to go consult. May I be excused, Mr. Foreman?*

THE FOREMAN: *Yes.*

MR. SILER: *We will just strike that. Sit back down. I have another question to ask you. Forget about that right now.*

THE WITNESS: *I have been excused by the Foreman*

THE FOREMAN: *We struck the question.*

MR. SILER: *Yes, we struck the question.*

Q. *Okay, I'm going to show you a picture here of Susan Edith Saxe. I want you to look at that and tell the grand jury whether you recognize that girl at all.*

A. *I have to consult with my attorney. May I be excused?*

MR. SILER: *All right.*

(Reporter: And she left the room, then she returned).

Q. *All right. Your name is Marla Seymour, right?*

A. *It still is.*

Siler proceeds to ask Marla again whether she recognizes Susan Saxe from the photo.

A. *I have seen that photograph in the papers a lot, yes.*

Q. *Do you recognize the person?*

A. *Just the picture.*

Q. *Just the picture. Have you ever seen this girl in the picture before?*

A. *I need to consult with my attorney. . . . (Transcript 1975, DE 46–47, 246–49)*

This tactic of delay and obstruction—what has been called a "tap-dance routine"—was one recommended by the National Lawyers Guild: "You refuse to answer any questions without consulting [your attorney]. You write down the first question asked (what is your name?), trot out to the hall, consult and return with your answer. . . . This strings out the proceedings and wastes everyone's time" (Homer 1975, 19). Apparently, it was felt that this tactic prevented a witness from inadvertently providing potentially incriminating answers and thus preserved her Fifth Amendment rights. It also may have been designed to prove—given the repetitiveness and vacuity of the questions—that the proceeding was pointless and absurd.

Although it was a legal tactic advised by their attorneys, this obstreperousness might not have served the Lexington Six well. After all, it likely irritated the grand jurors to have to endure endless delays and trivial obfuscations, which in the end may have prejudiced the jurors against the witnesses. After succeeding hearings, Sedler concluded as much, intuiting that the grand jury had come to feel "a great deal of hostility" toward the Lexington Six (1986). On the other hand, if it was not strictly a legal tactic, the witnesses' palpable hostility toward the proceedings may have simply expressed the anger and disrespect the Lexington Six had come to feel toward the FBI and the court for intruding into their lives, in effect destroying them. For it was clear by this time that there was no going back to their peaceful lives antebellum. As Marla Seymour reflected in retrospect several years later, "I was angry. . . . I still don't think it's a fair way to proceed. I have a real sense of personal outrage that that happened—that people can be railroaded in that legal fashion" (1987b).

Ten days after the first grand jury appearance by the Lexington group, up in New Haven on February 13, Ellen Grusse and Terri Turgeon faced federal district court judge Jon O. Newman, a Nixon appointee, on a motion filed by government attorney William Dow III that they be granted "use immunity" and forced thereby to testify. "Use immunity" was a concept developed by the Justice Department under President Nixon; it was included in the Organized Crime Control Act of 1970, which has been called "the most undemocratic and repressive piece of legislation" passed by the U.S. Congress "in a generation" (Harris 1976b, 96), not least because of the "use immunity" clause, which effectively enabled prosecutors to skirt the Fifth Amendment protection against self-incrimination. For under a grant of use immunity, "anyone who was compelled to testify could not be prosecuted directly on the basis of that testimony" (Harris 1976b, 94). (However, the witness could still be prosecuted if the evidence were gathered independently of the individual's own grand jury testimony.) Once granted use immunity, a witness is compelled to testify or be held in contempt of court and sent to jail for the life of the sitting grand jury, generally up to eighteen months. In 1972, the Supreme Court, under Nixon appointee Chief Justice Warren Burger, upheld the law in *Kastigar et al. v. United States* as constitutional, overturning decades of the Court's affirming "the doctrine of absolute immunity" guaranteed by the Fifth Amendment. "With [this] decision," legal journalist Richard Harris observed, "the long struggle to stop government from forcing its way into the innermost privacy of peoples' thoughts, associations, and consciences largely came to an end" (Harris 1976b, 98, 99). The government was thus free to ask just about any question of a witness, who had no recourse but to answer or go to jail.

This was the situation faced by Ellen Grusse and Terri Turgeon that February day in Connecticut. Their situation was compounded by the fact that Grusse's testimony could be used against Turgeon and Turgeon's against Grusse. Had they been legally married, this might not have been the case. Under the doctrine of "spousal immunity," spouses cannot be compelled to testify against one another. Of course, in 1975, the reality of—even the idea of—same-sex marriage lay far in the future. But it did seem unfair to Grusse and Turgeon and to the Lexington Six that a heterosexual married couple might be granted a privilege denied to a lesbian or gay couple.

Shortly before their court appearance on the use immunity motion, Ellen and Terri issued an eloquent statement explaining their reasons for refusing to testify or cooperate with the FBI. The statement was released by the recently formed Grand Jury Project of the New York Women's Union and published in the February 1975 issue of *off our backs*. In the statement the two women gave as the principal reason for their resistance a belief that same-sex couples deserved the same rights as heterosexual married couples: "We believe that the right to privacy and confidentiality in human relationships goes beyond those traditionally recognized confidences such as attorney/client, spouse-to-spouse, doctor to patient, etc. . . . Every person has the right to keep her affairs private without [interference] by government agents." But, they contended, the reality was that under current FBI and grand jury practices of harassing and gathering information on feminists and left-wing activists, "anyone can be subject to harassment and even jailed for not answering even the most personal and/or irrelevant questions about themselves or friends or acquaintances. This is a total invasion of privacy and should not be tolerated" (Grusse and Turgeon 1975).

Like the Lexington Six, Grusse and Turgeon felt their lesbian-feminist community—which they considered a kind of sanctuary, their home—was under siege. "Outside of these communities," they wrote, as lesbians "we are oppressed, degraded, and dehumanized both on personal and collective levels. The existence of such communities is a threat to the patriarchal power structures and it is in their interest to infiltrate these communities to create fear, mistrust and division" (Grusse and Turgeon 1975).

The women concluded their statement with a feminist critique, equating the FBI and judicial violation and invasion of their lives with the threat of violation every woman faced every day, "living with the fear of rape, brutalization by men, defining herself through her man, etc." Resistance was thus a matter of refusing to "play . . . the Man's games, which deny us our basic rights, dignity and responsibility and control over our lives." It was time, they asserted, to end this "chain of invasions" (Grusse and Turgeon 1975).

The Lexington Six, shortly after their own grand jury appearance, endorsed Grusse's and Turgeon's position in a statement of their own in which they emphasized the unfairness of the fact that as lesbians they were denied spousal immunity. "The legal system," they noted, "presently acknowledges certain 'sacred' relationships in which people retain legal privacy, including that of husband and wife. We agree with the Connecticut women that the kinds of personal relationships to which we claim the same right to privacy go beyond these traditional ones" (Cohee et al. 1975a, 1975b).

The Lexington Six essentially claimed that "spousal immunity"—the idea that certain relationships are sacred and protected from government or police intrusion or violation—should extend to lesbian and gay relationships, as well as to the bonds of solidarity they had formed with one another, with lovers, or indeed with Susan Saxe and Kathy Power. In other words, the Lexington Six in their statement argued for a kind of comrade or sisterhood immunity, acknowledging the intensity and committed nature of such bonds.

The idea that the immunity privilege should be extended to committed relationships beyond the heterosexual husband-wife dyad gathered force as grand jury resistance committees became organized. The theory emerged that the immunity privilege should be granted to all members of "intentional communities," such as communes and convents. David Rosen, one of Grusse's and Turgeon's attorneys, succinctly explained the idea in the closing arguments of their final contempt hearing on June 6, 1975: "No one," he said, "should have to choose between perishing and betraying a friend" (Harris 1976c, 89).

Their eloquence notwithstanding, Grusse and Turgeon were on February 13 granted use immunity by the New Haven district court judge, who ordered the two to appear the same day before the sitting federal grand jury and answer its questions. The women proceeded down the corridor of the courtroom to the grand jury chamber where the jurors awaited them. After the two conferred with their attorney, Michael Avery (who, like Sedler, thought the case was hopeless [Harris 1976c, 56]), Turgeon was summoned into the grand jury room by the U.S. attorney, William Dow III.

After swearing her in, Dow reminded Turgeon that under the grant of use immunity she no longer had the right to remain silent and that if she lied, she would be subject to perjury charges. From the first seemingly innocuous question—whether she had previously appeared before this grand jury—Turgeon followed a procedure similar to that used by the Lexington group. She wrote down the question, asked to be excused to consult with her attorney, and returned to the jury room to read essentially the same prescripted statement as that used in the Lexington case, invoking several Bill of Rights amendments but with the additional claim that the government had conducted "illegal electronic and personal surveillance" which contributed to making the entire proceeding "an abuse of the grand-jury process" (Harris 1976c, 56), thus raising two of the issues that would form the basis for an appeal.

In further questioning Dow asked Turgeon if she knew Saxe and Power and "when [she] last saw" either of them: "Where that was, when that was, who they were with, and where they were residing at the time?" These questions suggest the primary interest remained that of capturing the two fugitives. Turgeon followed the same procedure, consulting and refusing to answer. Dow then asked her whether Saxe and Power had visited Turgeon at her residence at 23 Marshall Street in Hartford during 1974. Same response. Dow also claimed that during their stay in Connecticut, Saxe and Power had revealed "to certain acquaintances that they were fugitives and charged with certain crimes. Do you know the individuals to whom they gave that information?" Same refusal. Had Turgeon answered this question she might have implicated her lover in the crime of being an accessory after the fact, since Ellen Grusse had known of Kathy Power's identity and had acted on her behalf in warning her that Carol Romano might be about to inform on her. Finally, Dow asked Turgeon if she had received any communication from either Power or Saxe in the preceding three months (*In re Ellen Grusse* 1975, 1236). Once again Turgeon "respectfully refused to answer on the ground that it and these proceedings violate my rights under the Constitution" (Harris 1976c, 56).

Turgeon was then dismissed and Ellen Grusse called into the jury room. The New Haven grand jury consisted of twenty individuals—twelve men and eight women—all white. Grusse's and Turgeon's attorneys made a charge of racial and gender discrimination in the selection of the jurors in the contempt hearing before Judge Newman on February 19. In the claim of gender discrimination the witnesses pointed out that "of 155 persons selected or rejected for the venire, about 60% were female," but "only 28% were selected for service, compared to 45% of the men." The judge ruled, however, that these statistics did not prove discrimination because there could be other reasons why women might decline to serve, such as "a need to care for young children at home," thus explaining the gender discrepancy (*In re Ellen Grusse* 1975, 1236).

Once seated in the grand jury room, Grusse was asked essentially the same questions as those posed to her partner Terri Turgeon: "Have you ever met or come into contact with or had conversation with either SUSAN EDITH SAXE, with the alias of LENA PALEY, or KATHERINE ANN POWER, with the alias of MAY KELLY, at 118 Babcock Street in Hartford;

7 Putnam Heights in Hartford during the years 1973 through the present date, and if so where, when and with whom did you have these discussions or conversations?" (*In re Ellen Grusse* 1975, 1238). Grusse refused to answer, invoking the same litany of rights as Turgeon had. She added, however, a personal appeal to the jurors: "My decision not to speak [to the FBI] is based on the moral belief that the investigation . . . will violate my basic constitutional and human rights. . . . You, the jurors are being used as tools of the FBI to further their investigation. This is not a legitimate use of the grand jury" (Harris 1976c, 58).

Ignoring her statement, Dow asked Grusse if she planned to refuse to answer all of the questions. But he was interrupted by the foreperson of the grand jury, seemingly in response to Grusse's plea. "Could I ask one question?" the foreperson requested of Dow, who was apparently surprised but agreed. "Do you understand," the foreperson asked Grusse, "that the purpose of this grand jury is to investigate a crime that was committed in Boston in 1970?" Realizing that the foreperson was basically acknowledging an illegitimate purpose for the grand jury, Dow immediately interrupted him and awkwardly attempted to cover for his statement. "Let me amplify . . . if I could, Mr. Foreman, to indicate that the scope of the inquiry goes beyond the crime itself . . . in Boston, but [includes] activities . . . in Connecticut . . . such as possible assistance to those [Boston] suspects. . . . Is that your understanding?" (Harris 1976c, 58). The foreperson agreed, showing once again how grand jurors often fail to understand that the purpose of a grand jury is to indict, based on evidence presented to it by law enforcement officials and others, not to act as an agency of law enforcement by gathering evidentiary information.

Dow's hasty coverup was an attempt to shift the issue away from the pursuit of Saxe and Power, who had long since been indicted by other federal grand juries and whose crime had been committed in another state. Dow clearly wished to deflect the question of whether the New Haven grand jury even had jurisdiction over that case. Instead, he turned to the crime of harboring fugitives, where the Connecticut court would have jurisdiction, thus casting Grusse and Turgeon as potential subjects of a criminal indictment. That indictment was never issued, however, because apparently there was no evidence that either of them had knowingly harbored Saxe or Power.

It is true that Ellen Grusse tipped Kathy Power off in the phone call, noted previously, in which she warned that Carol Romano might be about to turn Power in, and that this could conceivably have made her liable to charges of being an accessory after the fact, in that she took actions to impede the apprehension of a fugitive. However, her action was based on a hunch and no law official was involved, so it seems the government would have had a weak case. Nevertheless, it was used by the U.S. attorney as a justification for the grand jury interrogation: "The Government informed the witnesses with the concurrence of the grand jury foreman, that the grand jury was investigating possible violations in the District of Connecticut of statutes punishing accessories after the fact, 18 U.S.C. §3, and those who harbor fugitives, 18 U.S.C. §1071" (*In re Ellen Grusse* 1975, 1238). That there was similarly a lack of harboring or accessories-after-the-fact evidence in the Kentucky case is probably why that matter was never raised there—that is, until the appeals filings wherein the U.S. attorney raised the harboring issue as an attempt to legitimize the case against Jill Raymond.

Having thus refused to answer grand jury questions despite the grant of use immunity, Grusse and Turgeon were officially ordered to do so in a hearing before Judge Newman the following day, February 14, Valentine's Day. Newman ruled that despite the witnesses' claims that their privacy was being invaded, he saw no evidence "of unnecessarily personalized inquiry" or of "intimate personal details . . . being probed for no apparent legitimate purpose" (Harris 1976c, 62). Newman ordered the women back to the grand jury room to answer the questions or be held in contempt of court and jailed. They returned to the grand jury room that same afternoon at 2 p.m.—their third appearance—and refused to answer the same set of questions, whereupon Dow filed a motion that the two be held in contempt. The contempt hearing was held on February 18.

The legal team filed a forty-two-page brief in which they claimed that Grusse's and Turgeon's refusal to cooperate with the FBI was justified in part because the grand jury questions were based on information obtained illegally by FBI through electronic surveillance—wiretapping of the women's phones. Michael Avery, the attorney, also attempted to subpoena the FBI agent in charge of the search for Saxe and Power in Connecticut in order to prove that the FBI already knew the answers to all the questions being asked of Grusse and Turgeon (which would seem to be evidenced by the specificity of the questions as to street addresses and time spans) and that therefore there was no purpose to the grand jury inquiry other than harassment—or to procure information that would lead to Saxe's and Power's capture (Harris 1976c, 63), both of which are illegitimate purposes. Avery also wanted to call Dow to swear under oath whether he planned to give the FBI whatever information he gleaned from Grusse's and Turgeon's grand jury testimony. Since grand jury testimony is supposed to be secret, this would be illegal and would reveal that the improper purpose of the New Haven grand jury was to gather information for the FBI. Judge Newman denied both of Avery's requests, and since the government attorney filed an "affidavit of denial," which asserted that "there has been no electronic surveillance" of those involved in the case, the judge held Grusse and Turgeon in contempt of court and ordered them to the custody of a U.S. marshal, pending appeal, during which time they were released on a $10,000 bail bond (*In re Ellen Grusse* 1975, 1238).

At this time the National Lawyers Guild became involved. A guild lawyer, Kristin Booth Glen, prepared a forty-seven-page appeals brief, which highlighted the issue of illegal wiretapping by the FBI and the improper use of the grand jury. U.S. Attorney Dow filed a twenty-seven-page response brief, which evidently was persuasive, as the U.S. Court of Appeals for the Second Circuit under Chief Judge William Timbers, a Nixon appointee, in *United States of America v. Ellen Grusse and Marie Theresa Turgeon*, turned down the appeal, citing as its authority the Organized Crime Control Act of 1970. Terri Turgeon later commented, "We are two innocent women, and yet we have the whole United States government against us" (Harris 1976c, 95). One judge, James Oakes, dissented, claiming the government's denial of wiretapping was insufficient. A further appeal to the U.S. Supreme Court justice Thurgood Marshall was denied on March 5, 1975 (Harris 1976c, 71–72).

All this legal maneuvering seemed Kafkaesque to Grusse and Turgeon. "Incredible helplessness" summed up how they felt, Turgeon reported. "When the values we hold dear are translated into legal language they lose all meaning" (Harris 1976c, 64). The motivations that had fueled their original resistance—loyalty to and love for one another and beloved friends—had now become a legal case primarily focused on grand jury abuse and other objectionable government activities. Of course, the legal case was rooted in the women's ardent desire for privacy and for protection of their lesbian community from patriarchal intrusion and destruction. But that position would have been incomprehensible in American law; it had to be translated into concepts serviceable in the legal domain.

In mid-January 1975, a New York attorney, Rhonda Copelon, was called out of a meeting in Manhattan for an emergency phone call. It was Robert Sedler in Kentucky asking for help in the emerging case of the Lexington Six. Copelon was a lawyer with the Center for Constitutional Rights, an organization that specialized in social justice cases. Founded in 1966, it had defended numerous antiwar and civil rights dissidents, and with the rise of the political manipulation of grand juries under President Richard Nixon, had developed strategies for litigating these kinds of protest cases. In 1974, its attorneys had, for example, defended grand jury resisters in the case of the "Gainesville Eight," members of the Vietnam Veterans against the War, two of whom were jailed for refusing to cooperate with a federal grand jury.

The Center for Constitutional Rights was also involved in another Kentucky case at the time, that of Alan and Margaret McSurely, political activists in Appalachia prosecuted under a Kentucky Sedition Act, later ruled unconstitutional (a 1967 case in which Sedler filed an *amicus curiae* brief); the McSurelys were also held in contempt of Congress in 1970, a decision reversed on appeal. (They subsequently sued Senate officials for damages, a suit that was decided in their favor in 1982). Sedler had also worked with the center in another case argued by center lawyers Morton Stavis and Doris Peterson concerning a Kentucky attorney held in contempt, a decision that was reversed by the U.S. Supreme Court in 1974 (*Taylor v. Hayes*).

Sitting next to Rhonda Copelon in New York when she was called out of the meeting to take the urgent phone call from Sedler was Janet Gallagher, a friend and colleague who had been a political activist in the antiwar movement and was familiar with earlier cases of government persecution of dissidents. When she and Copelon learned about the Lexington case, they therefore already appreciated its significance as a renewed example of the FBI's abuse of the grand jury process. While the FBI had been relatively quiescent in the years immediately following the Watergate and COINTELPRO revelations, the Lexington situation seemed to indicate that its old practices were reviving.

Gallagher was a member of the New York Women's Union, a feminist organization, and in that capacity was involved in planning a socialist-feminist conference to be held that summer of 1975 in Yellow Springs, Ohio, the planning committee of which was located in Lexington. On that committee were Jill Raymond and other members of the Red Star Sisters. On February 7, 1975, Janet flew down to Lexington to meet with them. After meeting her at the Bluegrass Airport, they took her to Off Hand Manor, an old Victorian mansion on Nicholasville Road where several of them lived.

"I think you should know this house is surrounded," Jill semi-jokingly told Janet as they drove up to the house. In fact, the FBI had been sur-veilling the place for days. By then five of the Lexington Six had been subpoenaed and had just appeared (on February 3) before the grand jury and refused to cooperate. Janet brought with her materials about grand jury resistance and strategies prepared by the Center for Constitutional Rights, whose attorneys subsequently worked with Sedler in preparing for the showdown between the Lexington Six and the federal court. He was soon joined by Judith Peterson, an attorney recommended by the center, who served as co-counsel in the case. Likely included in the materials provided by Gallagher were a forty-three-page pamphlet put out by the National Lawyers Guild in 1972, "By the Government, For the Government, Against the People: A Booklet for Grand Jury Witnesses," and a twenty-five-cent leaflet on grand jury resistance also prepared by the guild in 1972 entitled "Non-Collaboration."

The position of the Center for Constitutional Rights was indeed that of "non-collaboration": "it was crucial," Gallagher felt, "that *nobody* talk to the FBI, that safety for everyone was non-collaboration." The center had developed this stance in reaction against what it saw as mistakes made by activists during the McCarthy period when government agencies, such as the House Un-American Activities Committee, "picked" people "off one by one" (Gallagher 1987). Had activists held together in solidarity and refused to cooperate, presenting a solid wall of resistance, the government would have been much less successful in destroying peoples' lives, it was felt.

The introduction of the New York radical lawyers into the case reinforced the position of the Lexington Six, who were already inclined to resist of their own accord and for their own reasons. At the same time, the militancy and absoluteness of the New York contingent seemed somewhat alienating to the Lexington activists, who were used to a more laidback, genial, southern style. Janet Gallagher sensed during her February visit that her hosts saw her as alien: "We were strangers from New York City" (1987).

When Gallagher returned to New York after her Lexington visit, she, Rhonda Copelon, and several other activists decided to establish the New York Grand Jury Project to "build . . . support for the Kentucky people" and to spread the word about FBI harassment and grand jury abuse so as "to prepare women's communities" about them (Gallagher 1987). The founding members of the project were, in addition to Gallagher, Judy Peluso and Julie Schwarzberg. From the onset it was a feminist operation, staffed largely by feminist women and in conjunction with feminist attorneys.

Alarmed by the evident revival of the political grand jury in Lexington and New Haven, activist attorneys determined that a national strategy was needed to contest it. On April 13, 1975, the Massachusetts chapter of the National Lawyers Guild held an organizational meeting in Boston. Attending were representatives for various grand jury resisters, including Fred Soloway of the newly formed Coalition to End Grand Jury Abuse, who spoke about the Lexington Six and the case of Jay Weiner in Pennsylvania (subpoenaed in connection with the Patty Hearst hunt). Michael Avery, Ellen Grusse's and Terri Turgeon's attorney, reported about their case; Karen Jo Keenan, about a San Francisco case concerning a radio station disc jockey, Doron Weinberg, who had been subpoenaed for audiotapes of poetry readings by women in the Weather Underground; and Fred Cohen, an attorney for Pat Swinton. Janet Gallagher represented the New York Grand Jury Project at the meeting.

The consensus at the Boston conference was that starting with the Lexington Six case, a new wave of FBI harassment and grand jury abuse had begun, and with it—initiated by the stand of the Lexington and New Haven resisters—a new wave of resistance was emerging. The attendees reaffirmed the position of "non-collaboration" developed in the early 1970s but noted that "the issue around Grand Juries has really died down over the past few years and is just now reviving. Therefore—we've got a lot of work to do on educating folks" (Blum 1975, 4).

The conferees further proposed that the New York Grand Jury Project put together informational material and serve as a locus for "centralization of information." Karen Jo Keenan, likely voicing a general opinion, said she "felt good that there was a Guild network" already in place around which national organizing could proceed (Blum 1975, 4, 5).

The establishment of the New York Grand Jury Project as the organizational locus of the national grand jury resistance movement was formalized in August 1975 at a meeting in Philadelphia where representatives of several recently formed grand jury defense committees gathered to strategize about how to coordinate the various localized resistance efforts. Attending that meeting were members of the Susan Saxe Defense Committee, the Lexington Grand Jury Defense Committee, and the New Haven Grand Jury Defense Committee, as well as other committees from Boston, New York, and Washington, DC. With the assumption of the New York Grand Jury Project as the central organizational and communication center for the scattered committees, organizers established a network linking the disparate committees, enabling the formation of a nationwide resistance community.

In detailing the origins of the Grand Jury Project in its inaugural newsletter, *Quash: A Grand Jury Newsletter*, in October 1975, the project collective noted how the resistance of the Lexington Six had served as a catalyst: "The New York Women's Grand Jury Project was begun in mid-February to help publicize and resist the FBI/grand jury invasion of the women's and lesbian communities in Lexington, Kentucky, and New Haven, Connecticut . . . to alert the women's community in New York to the problem and to share legal/political information about resistance to FBI/grand jury witch hunts" (Anonymous 1975f).

The collective reiterated the theory developed at the April Boston conference that "as part of the effort to impose a post-Vietnam 'normality,'" a "second wave" of grand jury abuse had begun, the "first wave" having abated in the wake of the Nixon administration scandals (Anonymous 1975f). In a later issue of *Quash*, its editors again highlighted the critical importance of the resistance of the Lexington Six: "The Lexington case drew national attention to the government's renewed used of grand juries for intelligence gathering and harassment . . . and *spurred grand jury resistance efforts around the country*" (Anonymous 1976d; emphasis added).

Appreciation of the significance of the Lexington and New Haven resistance cases lay far in the future, however. At the time — in mid-February 1975 — it was a matter of confused preparation and desperate scrambling to get legal strategies lined up, supporters organized, and defense groups formed. In early February, a Lexington Grand Jury Defense Committee was organized to provide support for the Lexington Six and to disseminate information about FBI harassment and grand jury abuse through press releases and flyers. At one point the committee issued "I Am Kathy Power" buttons for sympathizers to wear, proclaiming their solidarity with the resistance movement against the FBI (Goldman 1998, 27). The button derived from the FBI's original assumption that Sally Kundert was Kathy Power when they surrounded her house on January 12. It also recalled the Danish resistance movement during World War II when non-Jewish Danes began wearing yellow Stars of David armbands after Nazi occupation officials ordered all Jews to wear the identifying stars. The point was both to confound the Nazi officials and to show solidarity with the Jews. The Lexington "I Am Kathy Power" buttons were likewise to show resistance to the FBI as well as solidarity with the Lexington Six and other political dissidents.

The original core of the Lexington defense committee was a group of activists who lived as a collective in Off Hand Manor, which served for a time as the committee's headquarters. Living in the collective were Mary Dunn and Sharon Myrick, a lesbian couple; Lucia Gattone and David Walls, a heterosexual couple; Sue Ann Salmon; and Barbara Sutherland — all of whom became members of the defense committee or active in its discussions. A second-year law student, Sutherland worked on the legal team of the Lexington Six doing research. Also on the defense committee

Figure 1. "I Am Kathy Power" Button Worn by Supporters of the Lexington Six.
Photograph by the author

were Margaret Shanks, Dierdre Foss, Terri Willingham, Jack Beckford, Diane Dorris, Nancy Collins, Dick Burr, and Carolyn Burr. There were no official leaders of the group—decisions were by consensus—but Mark Paster and Sally Kundert served as co-treasurers because somebody had to sign checks. All of these individuals had been involved in radical political movements for some time, and some either considered themselves socialists or were sympathetic to socialist positions. Some of the women had been members, for example, of the Red Star Sisters.

Although some on the committee were inclined toward a socialist analysis, their publications related to the Lexington Six betrayed little of that perspective, hewing largely to a liberal civil liberties position. Despite the presence of at least two lesbians in committee discussions, it tended to underplay the lesbian-gay aspect of the case. This was largely a tactical decision, apparently born of a fear that a too heavy emphasis on gay-lesbian issues would alienate otherwise sympathetic supporters—a further sign of how stigmatized homosexuality was in 1970s Kentucky.

Meanwhile, the New York Grand Jury Project proceeded to get organized; it established an office in Brooklyn, set up a speakers' bureau, and began publishing leaflets and posters enjoining women not to cooperate with the FBI. The project even eventually published a twenty-four-page comic book, "Just a Few Easy Questions," and put out "We Won't Talk" t-shirts. And in conjunction with the National Lawyers Guild, Grand Jury Project members worked to educate lawyers about the issue. Eventually, the project cooperated with filmmaker Mary Lampson in producing a docudrama based largely on Jill Raymond entitled "Until She Speaks." It was shown as a feature on the *American Playhouse* television series in 1981 with Ellen Grusse and Terri Turgeon in cameo appearances.

Thanks to these efforts the alert about potential FBI harassment spread rapidly to communities at risk across the country, and grand jury resistance committees formed in various cities. As the word spread, supporters for the resisters readily stepped forth. Some 150 supporters of Grusse and Turgeon, for example, were in the courtroom for their February 19 hearing.

As early as February 2, a letter to the editor of the *Real Paper*, a Boston alternative weekly, warned people in radical communities against cooperating with the FBI or even with newspaper reporters, pointing out as evidence John Wood's January 12 *Boston Globe* article about Saxe and Power in Kentucky, in which "friends [of Saxe and Power] exposed a wealth of information about how fugitives live, survive, and stay free." Wood, the writers claimed, "is now trying to get the FBI to follow up on his research" (Whitehorn and Ryan 1975). (Whether this allegation is correct is uncertain, but the FBI clearly jumped on the case immediately after the January 12 appearance of the Wood article.)

The writers of the *Real Paper* letter also pointed to Jane Alpert's alleged cooperation with the FBI following her November 1974 arrest—an issue that was soon to erupt in heated pro and con Alpert exchanges in feminist journals. Alpert's detailed testimony about life underground, the writers contended, likely helped "fill in gaps in the government's knowledge of how fugitives from American injustice live." The letter concludes, "PEOPLE SHOULD NOT TALK to the FBI or other government investigators. We have the right and the duty to remain silent" (Whitehorn and Ryan 1975). That a copy of this letter ended up in the FBI file of William Gilday, one of the Brighton bank robbers, suggests how aware the FBI was of this growing resistance movement.

To further publicize FBI tactics, the various grand jury resistance groups put out comical, attention-grabbing posters. One, "Who's That Knocking at My Door?" created by the Boston Grand Jury Project, depicted a cartoon picture of two male FBI agents with characteristic fedoras, rolled-up raincoat collars, and mustaches captioned "We're Feminists." An article entitled "Prosecutor: 'Are You Trying to Show Contempt for This Court?' Mae West: 'I'm Doing My Best to Hide It'" by Julia Homer in *Second Wave*, a feminist journal, was accompanied by a cartoon of an FBI agent as the wolf in the Little Red Riding Hood fairytale: "Hell-o! We're from the FBI and we'd like to ask a few questions. May we come in?" In the second panel, a woman replies, "Not by the hair on my chinny-chin-chin!!" Prominent on the wall behind her is a poster: "Sisterhood is Powerful!" (Homer 1975).

A few months earlier, on Women's Equality Day, August 26, 1974, the anniversary of the ratification of the Women's Suffrage Amendment, the Washington, DC, branch of the National Organization for Women put out a flyer that was a mock "Wanted by the FBI" poster. Issued by a "Feminist Bureau of Investigation," it listed "Ten Most Wanted Men for Offenses against Women." On the poster were photos of various political figures including the secretaries of labor and the treasury (FBI, September 9, 1974).

As the FBI intensified its activity in lesbian communities in the spring of 1975, *Majority Report*, a feminist journal, published an article entitled "I Was a Lesbian for the FBI," accompanied on the journal's front page by a shadow-picture sketch of a Nancy Drew–type sleuth holding a magnifying glass over evidence (Anonymous 1975c). The article, retitled "I Was a Feminist for the FBI" in the following issue, by Tina Fox, recounted the story of a woman who had worked as an informer for the FBI on feminist groups in Buffalo, New York, going so far as to attend "Sisters of Sappho dances" (Fox 1975). *Majority Report* also published a "Civics Lesson" about grand juries written by Cathy (Kathy) Boudin, who was then in the Weather Underground, and Brian Glick. The article, originally published in 1968, gives a somewhat dated primer on the "use . . . and abuse" of grand juries (Boudin and Glick 1975).

By May lesbian-feminist groups around the country had been fully alerted to the FBI menace. The National Coalition of Gay Activists issued a "SPECIAL ALERT" flyer with a headline warning of "a major FBI campaign against the feminist and gay movements" that "has emerged in Connecticut and Kentucky." Jean O'Leary of Lesbian Feminist Liberation announced a meeting of lesbian activists from New Haven, Philadelphia, New York, Washington, and Boston to coordinate resistance to the FBI and grand jury "collaboration," which was seen as having the "potential for destruction within the lesbian and feminist communities" (Cordova and Doczi 1975).

Meanwhile, an opposite position to that encouraging FBI/grand jury resistance was circulated by Carol Romano, the woman who cooperated with the FBI in Hartford. She and her ex-husband, Jim, wrote a leaflet and booklet defending her position, claiming that the policy of non-collaboration was part of a "plot by the 'male left' to destroy feminism." The leaflet, entitled "A Warning to Women's Liberation," supported this thesis and claimed that Saxe and Power were "agents of the 'new left.'" The booklet, "Diary I," which was circulated mainly on the West Coast, expanded on this conspiracy theory. Grusse and Turgeon wrote an exposé of these publications in an "Open Letter" published in Quash in 1977 (Grusse and Turgeon 1977).

Ironically, a member of the Gay Caucus of the National Lawyers Guild picked up on the Romano flyer's implication that the left had been, if not hostile, at least negligent regarding feminist, lesbian, and gay issues. Citing the flyer in part, Renee C. Hanover on April 10, 1975, addressed a letter to a guild colleague urging the association to take the ongoing harassment of the "lesbian community" seriously, referring to the FBI siege in Lexington and New Haven as a "Lesbian Witch Hunt." "Lesbians throughout the country," Hanover noted, "are being terrorized." Hanover reported that the Romano flyer charged that "lawyers of the movement who advised women to refuse to answer questions . . . 'demonstrated their sole interest to be that of the male-dominated left.'" Acknowledging that "the fear" registered in the flyer— "that the interest of the straight, male-dominated left will prevail, is real," Hanover asserted, "Gay interests have never been taken seriously by the left." She urged, therefore, that the guild support the lesbian-gay communities in the current crisis (Hanover 1975). It seems, however, that, given the legal assistance already being rendered in the Lexington and New Haven cases, the National Lawyers Guild, as well as the Center for Constitutional Rights, was already doing so, though in terms of their own concerns about Bill of Rights infringements, rather than as a lesbian or feminist cause against patriarchal oppression.

CHAPTER FOUR

Contempt of Court and Jail

On February 18, 1975, attorney Robert Sedler filed a motion with the U.S. District Court of Eastern Kentucky to quash—that is, to dismiss—the subpoenas of the Lexington Six issued for their February 3 appearance and for a further appearance on February 18. The basis for the motion was a theory Sedler had developed (following guidelines developed by the National Lawyers Guild) that the "dominant purpose for the issuance of said subpoenas is to coerce and to trick the witnesses into committing perjury." Such a purpose, Sedler argued, "constitutes a gross abuse of the grand jury process" (Transcript 1975, DE 3, 1).

Sedler based his claim on the testimony of an Alfalfa restaurant employee, Laura Schuster, who "on or about February 6" learned from another employee, Mary Martin, that Letty Ritter, described by Sedler as an "informant" for the FBI, told Mary that the FBI had told her that if the subpoenaed Lexington Six lied to the grand jury, the FBI "would know, because they . . . had 'letters'" (Transcript 1975, DE 4). This claim that the FBI had letters addressed to or from the Lexington Six is thirdhand information and therefore not as strong as a firsthand report; it nevertheless raised the question of whether the FBI was intercepting the witnesses' and their supporters' mail, which was likely the case, despite FBI denials.

To support this claim, Judith Peterson, a National Lawyers Guild attorney from Tampa, Florida, who had joined Sedler in the case, filed subpoenas for Letty Ritter, Mark Oram, and John McCauley, agent-in-charge of the Lexington office of the FBI. McCauley was also ordered under a *duces tecum* subpoena to produce and bring to the hearing any letters the FBI might have that were to or from the Lexington Six (Transcript 1975, DE 7–9). Their hearing was held on February 20.

Peterson had joined the case on the recommendation of the Center for Constitutional Rights. She had worked as a counsel in the "Gainesville Eight" case and thus had some experience with grand jury resistance issues. Peterson came to Lexington armed, as she put it, with "all the ammunition," likely referring to the legal instructions laid out in the 1974 National Lawyers Guild manual. With this preparation Peterson conceived the case of the Lexington Six within its prescripted scenario and so instructed Sedler. Her job, as she saw it, was simply to make the by-then standard arguments. As she acknowledged, "what I was doing in court was not terribly original." Similarly, the six witnesses were given scripts to follow in the grand jury hearing: "They could read every single word. Everything [was] written for them" (Peterson 1987).

Peterson also adhered to the Center for Constitutional Rights' conception of the purpose of trials and legal hearings as tools of political education. One of the guiding principles of the center was to use a case as "a teaching and organizing tool" or "an organizing catalyst." Such a designated case was termed "an impact case" or "prophetic litigation." "Even unsuccessful cases," it was held, could "focus and catalyze movements for social change." As Nancy Stearns, the center attorney who tapped Judith Peterson for the job, put it, the center saw cases as "an organizing device." This sometimes meant regarding "the courtroom as theater" (Ruben 2011, 29, 31, 30, 32, 112, 172).

Judith Peterson approached the Lexington case with these ideas in mind. It was to be "an impact case," a catalyst for social change. She considered it a matter of "going through the processes in order to make a point." And that point was to publicize the importance of non-collaboration. "My approach," Peterson said, was that "not testifying before the grand jury was the ultimate point and everything was structured around that." In this she and Robert Sedler had significant disagreement: "He did not agree with the idea of not testifying," whereas "my position was people shouldn't testify."

The two "agreed to disagree," however, in order to best serve the interests of their clients (Peterson 1987).

Sedler was not sympathetic to the idea of using the Lexington Six as poster children for grand jury resistance. Like others in the Lexington community, he was disinclined to see them in abstract theoretical terms as a symbol of resistance but as individuals who could be greatly harmed by the jail experience. This conflict of views between those—mostly local—who saw the six as separate and, in many cases, cherished individuals versus those—mostly coastal politicos—who put the larger cause first escalated as the case began to draw national attention.

As a young woman attorney—then something of a rarity—Peterson had to deal with sexist attitudes in her Lexington court appearance. The judge objected, for example, to her wearing pantsuits in court instead of a dress or skirt. Peterson also felt she had to cede most of the oral argumentation to Sedler on the theory that, as a man, his words would have more weight with a traditional judge. It was irksome, she reflected, "having to let the male member of the defense team make arguments simply because they might be listened to with more credibility—particularly when they were my arguments" (Peterson 1987).

In her testimony on February 20, regarding the question of whether the FBI had intercepted the mail of the Lexington Six, Letty Ritter confirmed that one of the FBI agents, John Gill, had told her "that they had all the answers to all the questions that would be asked, and that the girls, or the people subpoenaed so much as said that they didn't know something when they did, then they would be given—they would be charged with perjury and given five (5) years for this" (Transcript 1975, DE 46–47, 391). Presumably, the FBI had "all the answers" because of knowledge gleaned from the letter cache the Lexington Six legal team assumed it to have.

In his testimony, however, John McCauley denied that the FBI had any of the subpoenaed letters: "There are no such documents or letters" (Transcript 1975, DE 46–47, 411). But in a teletype from the Louisville FBI bureau dated the same day, it is noted that U.S. Attorney Eugene Siler "has stated he will vigorously oppose the production of any and all such letters or documents which are in the possession of the FBI" (FBI, February 20, 1975), suggesting the FBI did in fact have such illegally intercepted letters.

Sedler attempted to ask John Gill, the relevant agent, in his testimony under oath whether he had told Letty Ritter about a potential perjury charge because of letters the FBI had allegedly obtained, but Siler objected to the question and Sedler dropped it (Transcript 1975, DE 46–47, 427–29). In his argument defending his motion to quash, Sedler stressed as well the issue of grand jury abuse, noting that the FBI was using the grand jury to aid in its investigations because of its own failure to capture various fugitives: "They don't have a very good record of finding people these days. They can't find Patty Hearst and they can't find Saxe and Power and they're so frustrated they're willing to abuse the law" (Mitchell 1975a).

Meanwhile, on the same day that the motion to quash was filed, February 18, U.S. Attorney Siler filed a motion granting use immunity for the Lexington Six. As noted in the case of Ellen Grusse and Terri Turgeon, once granted use immunity, witnesses subpoenaed before a grand jury are compelled to testify. If they refuse to do so, they can be held in civil contempt by the court and sent to prison for the duration of the grand jury term.

The hearing on both motions—to quash and to grant use immunity— was held in the main courtroom of the U.S. District Court before Judge Bernard T. Moynahan Jr. on February 21, 1975. Sedler had encountered Judge Moynahan in earlier cases—most notably in a 1967 judicial hearing concerning the indictments of Alan and Margaret McSurely, Carl and Anne Braden, and others under a Kentucky sedition law. Sedler had joined William Kunstler, a Center for Constitutional Rights attorney, in successfully arguing that the law was unconstitutional. Judge Moynahan voted with the two-to-one majority to void the law (Fosl 2002, 308, 388 n.42).

But this was the first time the Lexington Six had actually seen the judge, and for some like Jill Raymond it was the first time they had even been in a courtroom. It was an awesome and intimidating experience. "It felt like church," Jill recalled, with Judge Moynahan sitting up there "like God" (Raymond 1987b). It was a "large, cold room," Marla Seymour remembered, filled, it seemed, with a "lot of big men"—FBI agents, marshals, bailiffs, and so on. "We felt dwarfed." The judge, big, burly, and balding, reminded Marla of her Irish grandfather. He spoke slowly, with a southern drawl, and his demeanor was "stern and distant" (Seymour 1987b). Moynahan, although very conservative, was actually a Democrat, appointed to the bench by President John F. Kennedy shortly before his assassination in 1963. A graduate of the University of Kentucky Law School, Moynahan was a World War II combat veteran, having served as an officer in the Army Air Corps and as a prisoner of war of the Germans, a point he raised in his final contempt judgement.

Sedler and Peterson proceeded to present their arguments in defense of the motion to quash, and Siler, whom the FBI was finding "very cooperative" (FBI, January 23, 1975a), presented his in support of the motion to grant use immunity. By this time the case was beginning to attract national attention. An article covering this hearing appeared in the February 23 issue of the *New York Times*: "FBI Misuse of Grand Jury Alleged by Lawyers in Fugitive Case" (Anonymous 1975a).

Despite their newfound and not entirely welcome notoriety, the Lexington Six sat mutely through the proceedings, feeling strangely distanced from it all, as the lawyers went through complex legal arguments that they barely understood. "We were pretty far removed from the legal work and how it was being done," Jill recalled (Raymond 1987b). They sat almost in an awed stupor at what was happening to them, with the bizarre feeling of watching helplessly as their destiny unfolded in the hands of a group of mostly men formally engaging in legal niceties while their lives were at stake.

Marla Seymour had the impression that Moynahan had already made up his mind about the case based on his assumptions "about what kind of people we were" (1987b). She sensed a camaraderie between Moynahan and Siler and a certain hostility on the part of the judge toward Sedler and especially toward co-counsel Judith Peterson, whom he treated at times like a brash upstart needing correction but at most times simply ignored or dismissed. "He treated her like a bad little girl," Barbara Sutherland thought (1987). When Peterson was first introduced to the court at the beginning of the February 18 hearing, Moynahan instructed her to remember that she had an equal responsibility to the court as to her clients, and "that one shall not be lost sight of in pursuing the other" (Transcript 1975, DE 46–47, 7). Presumably, Moynahan anticipated overzealous representation of the Lexington Six on Peterson's part. It was during the same hearing that Moynahan apparently called Peterson to the bench and told her not to wear pantsuits in his court (Sutherland 1986). In a later hearing during a cross examination of Meredith Moore, the judge snapped at Peterson in the following exchange:

> MISS PETERSON: *Excuse me, Your Honor, I believe that her earlier testimony was—*
> THE COURT: *Well, the objection is sustained. This is a cross examination, Ma'am. Take your seat. All right—is overruled—take your seat. Don't interrupt when a question is being propounded. Wait until it is propounded, and don't make a speech about it.* (Transcript 1975, DE 46–47, 505–06)

Peterson had not in fact interrupted, and the judge appeared flustered— changing his ruling in mid-sentence from sustained to overruled. It seems Peterson rattled him. Seymour thought Moynahan had trouble dealing with such a strong, unsmiling woman (1987b).

The whole atmosphere in the court was one of open animosity, Barbara Sutherland reflected: "real hostility, distrust and appearance of unfairness." "We [supporters of the Lexington Six] hated the judge and were suspicious of him," feeling that, as Marla Seymour noted, he had "already made up his mind about it," that "it was all a sham." Sensing the spectators' disrespect for the proceedings, the judge repeatedly admonished them "to be quiet and respectful" (Sutherland 1987). The sense of confrontational hostility was enhanced by the fact that the U.S. attorney inadvertently referred to the Lexington Six as "defendants" several times during the proceedings and at one point to Judith Peterson as "defense counsel" (Transcript 1975, DE 46–47, 128). The Lexington Six were not defendants, had not been accused of a crime, and were not under indictment, though it may have felt that way. But Eugene Siler, with prosecutorial zeal, seemed to have forgotten this.

Apparently also, as with Peterson's pantsuit, the judge felt the attire of the Lexington Six—blue jeans, T-shirts, plaid country shirts, bandanas, and so forth, the normal wear of UK students at the time—was likewise disrespectful. Indeed, on the day of the final contempt hearing, March 7, Carey Junkin showed up in a T-shirt that read "Stop FBI Harassment." Judge Moynahan ordered him to remove it. In a conference with Sedler and Peterson, Moynahan said he wanted Junkin "to take it off. He can't put on a show like that in this courtroom" (Bailey 1975a). Carey left the courtroom and returned with a jacket loosely covering it, but the judge objected again to that arrangement. Carey then pulled the shirt off, in the full courtroom, turned it inside out, and put it back on with the message hidden.

The hostile confrontationalism probably didn't help the case of the Lexington Six. In any event, a few days after the February 18 hearing, the judge rendered his perhaps foregone decision: all six were granted use immunity on February 24 and the motion to quash the subpoenas was denied on February 25. When he heard about the use immunity decision, Carey Junkin felt himself "shaking to the point of throwing up" (1987). The Lexington Six now knew they were really in for it.

Once the news that the U.S. Supreme Court had turned down their appeal of the contempt decision reached New Haven on March 5, Ellen Grusse and Terri Turgeon were sent to prison. Back in the federal building late that afternoon, the two women were searched for weapons, hand-cuffed, and chained together before being led off to a police van. Their lawyer Michael Avery later protested that this demeaning protocol was "just another official attempt to humiliate and degrade people who stand up to the system." While federal officials undoubtedly follow this procedure with every prisoner, it seemed unnecessary at best with Grusse and Turgeon, who voluntarily turned themselves in after the Supreme Court denial. Fully armed police lined the hall and the parking lot as the two were led away. "They had come to view us as hardened, dangerous criminals," Grusse observed. "And we were merely two women who had vowed not to discuss their personal lives with anyone." As they were leaving the building, they happened to pass U.S. Attorney Dow, who was watching. Grusse lifted her manacled hand to wave at him, calling, "Thanks a lot, Willie." Dow gave a Pontius Pilate reply: "I didn't do it. It's not my fault" (Harris 1976c, 74).

Grusse and Turgeon were sent to the Connecticut Correctional Institution at Niantic, a women's prison about fifty miles east of New Haven. They were both terrified at what they imagined prison would be like. "All I knew about prison life," Terri reflected, "was those old movies and stories about Attica—bars and cells and sadistic guards and vicious criminals. There was nothing, absolutely nothing, in my past experience to prepare me for what lay ahead, and I was paralyzed by fear." Ellen was also afraid of how other inmates—likely "Black and poor"—would view two white, educated, privileged women. "I was frightened most of all by what they might do to us when they found out that we were lesbians" (Harris 1976c, 75).

Happily for them their fears were soon dispelled. Niantic was a relatively benign institution. The other inmates—mostly Black prostitutes or in for drug-related charges—were friendly, welcoming, and surprisingly supportive. There were no bars, and the "cells" were private rooms in cottages. While no prison experience can be considered cushy, this was about as good as it got. Nevertheless, psychologically it was devastating for the two because of the feeling of being totally under others' control and the sense of complete and helpless dependency it induced. It seemed to Terri that the whole purpose of the court system and prison—agents of society at large—was "to destroy every shred of individuality in anyone who stands up to it" (Harris 1976c, 76).

Fortunately for Grusse and Turgeon, the term of the grand jury they had defied expired on April 1, and as their confinement was limited to that term, the two were released from prison that day. They had been in prison over three and a half weeks. But just as the marshal released them, he served them with another subpoena, to appear before a newly empaneled federal grand jury on May 6. Their ordeal continued.

The Lexington Six were heartened by the defiant stand taken by their comrades in New Haven, whose resolve helped strengthen their own. For the day after Ellen and Terri were jailed, the Lexington Six faced their own Golgotha. Subpoenaed to appear on March 6 before the federal grand jury in Lexington, the six gathered once again in the federal building still firm in their determination not to comply with the government's orders. But because they had been granted use immunity, they could no longer use the Fifth Amendment defense and therefore knew that the consequences of their refusal to testify meant that their fate would likely be the same as Ellen's and Terri's: contempt and jail time. The Lexington Six came to the courtroom on March 6 prepared for the latter with small suitcases filled with the sorts of things one might pack for a weekend trip—toothbrush, toothpaste, hairbrush, a few books, and clothes. Preparations had been made for care of their pets, plants, cars, and apartments, which friends and members of the newly formed Lexington Grand Jury Defense Committee helped out with.

The first order of business that Thursday morning was for the six again to appear before the grand jury in their second encounter. They and their attorneys had decided on a new tactic: they would attempt to bypass the U.S. attorney and appeal directly to the jurors in hopes of eliciting some sympathy and appreciation for the stand they were taking. As Carey Junkin explained, "We wanted [the jurors] to see that 'they' were a 'we'" (1987). The witnesses hoped to get across to the jurors that they were innocent of any crime, that their refusal to testify was a matter of principle—the right of every American to have their private lives free from government control and interference. They figured that since some of the jurors were likely from eastern Kentucky where FBI and government tax officials—the "Revenuers"—had long been hated because of their persecution of "moonshiners," illegal liquor distillers, their position might strike a chord with at least those jurors.

The Lexington Six also wanted to try to educate the grand jurors on the proper historical function of a grand jury and how it was being used improperly by the FBI. This was a somewhat quixotic and perhaps counterproductive tactic, because it was highly unlikely that adults were going to hearken to college kids' lectures about grand jury function and history over the official position of establishment authorities.

Carey Junkin led the procession into the grand jury room that Thursday morning. In his appearance, after the initial tap dance, Carey spoke to the jurors directly. Surprisingly, the U.S. attorney didn't cut him off but let him proceed for several minutes as he catalogued his complaints about the investigation and the injustice of the procedures:

> Mr. Foreman, Ladies and Gentlemen of the grand jury, as a resident of Lexington and a student at the University of Kentucky, I would like, for the record, to state that I have been harassed and intimidated by agents of the FBI and the United States Attorney. When I was first contacted by Agent Wayne McDonald, on the telephone, I was asked if I knew two women named Lena Paley and May Kelley. As I

*am not in the habit of giving out information on who I know or don't
know . . . to total strangers on the phone, I refused to answer. . . . Upon
refusing, I was informed that if I did not agree to talk to them I would
be subpoenaed and forced to tell all I knew about these two women,
and anything else the grand jury might wish to ask me.*

Carey amplified by appealing directly to the jurors sitting before him:

*Ladies and Gentlemen of the grand jury, if you would be called by
a total stranger, who said he is an FBI agent, but offered no proof
of his position, and was asked about family, friends and political
persuasion, how would you react? Would you be willing to answer
questions about things you consider private? I leave it up to you. Does
the United States prosecutor have the right to ask me these and other
questions for the FBI, or is he using the powers of the grand jury and
using you to help him in the invasion of my privacy? (Transcript 1975,
DE 46–47, 235–36)*

Carey concluded his oration with an eloquent plea that could well have
been addressed to the heavens, reflecting as it did his own existential plight:

*When I appeared before the grand jury the first time I was asked
questions about my personal life and about people I was supposed to
have known. Never at any time was I told why I was being questioned
either by the FBI or the grand jury.*

*Could someone on the grand jury please tell me why I am here
and what you want to know about my personal life?*

Apparently, the U.S. attorney or someone else in the room made a gesture to
silence Carey because he then protested, "I'm not through." He continued,

*What was the purpose of bringing me here? The standard purpose of
the grand jury is to indict people for specific crimes.*

*Of what crime am I accused? Of what am I to be indicted? I really
want to know the answer to these questions. . . . I would like an answer,
please, from someone? (Transcript 1975, DE 46–47, 235–36)*

Siler and the foreperson of the grand jury ignored Carey Junkin's plea as if it hadn't been uttered and proceeded to ask him if he had lived on South Broadway in 1974, but Carey protested, "Is nobody going to answer my question?" Siler replied, "I take it that nobody wants to answer your question. You see, the grand jury is not here to be interrogated" (Transcript 1975, DE 46–47, 236–37).

Having made his unsuccessful plea to the grand jury, Carey then agreed to partially answer a few trivial questions—another last-ditch attempt on the part of the legal team, apparently in hopes that partial cooperation would soften the growing hostility and intransigence of the government attorney and jurors. So in answer to the question of what type of car he owned in 1974, Carey said he bought an Opel in October or November. When asked if he had ever "lived with" Susan Saxe at 367 South Broadway, Carey answered somewhat casuistically, "Without waving my objection to the subpoena and the asking of the question constituting an abuse of the grand jury process, my answer to this question is that I do not recognize the person in this picture as anyone I have lived with" (Transcript 1975, DE 46–47, 238, 240). Technically, this was true. Carey hadn't lived in the same apartment or shared a bed with Susan Saxe, but he had lived in the same building and knew her enough to recognize her picture. When asked in a follow-up question whether he had ever *seen* Saxe, Carey took the Fifth.

As with Carey Junkin's rhetorical appeal to the heavens, the testimony of Debbie Hands had the feel at times of absurd theater, perhaps a play by Samuel Beckett or Herman Melville's story about another famous recalcitrant, "Bartleby, the Scrivener." The session began with some tactical sparring back and forth between Hands and the U.S. attorney in which she questioned why Siler was running the proceeding, which, she implied, was an improper protocol: "Can I ask why the prosecutor is asking the questions? . . . Do you know that the grand jury was not designed for the prosecutor to even be in the grand jury room? I want to know why other people [the jurors] aren't asking questions. This is set up for communication . . . between myself and you [addressing the jurors], and the prosecutor has nothing to do with it except advise" (Transcript 1975, DE 46–47, 254–55).

Hands made a further, even more scorching point, implying that Siler's motives in pursuing the case of the Lexington Six were to further his career. "Have you people," she asked the jurors, "read in the paper where Siler wants to be the Federal Judge and that catching famous people . . . will . . ." (Transcript 1975, DE 46–47, 246–47). Here, Siler interrupted. (Siler was indeed promoted to a federal judgeship six months later by President Gerald Ford.)

Like Carey, Debbie received no answer to her questions. She returned the favor by refusing to answer the questions posed henceforth by the U.S. attorney, remaining for most of the rest of the session sitting before the jury in stony silence:

MR. SILER: . . . *My question was . . . have you ever seen the girl [showing a photo of Kathy Power] before?*
(Reporter: No response from the witness).
Q. Are you refusing to answer?
(Reporter: No response from the witness). . . .
Q. Are you refusing to answer the question which was put to you?
(Reporter: No response from the witness).
Q. . . . Have you ever in your life known a person by the name of Susan Edith Saxe or Catherine Ann Power?
(Reporter's Note: No response from the witness).
Q. Are you refusing to answer?
(Reporter: No response from the witness).
Q. All right, listen closely to this question. Have you ever in your life known a person by the name of May Kelley or Lena Paley?
(Reporter: No response from the witness). . . .
Q. My question is, if you will kindly listen . . . did you not meet these girls shown in the picture during the summer of 1974? Do you refuse to answer that?
(Reporter: No response from the witness).
Q. Approximately what date was it when you first met the two girls . . . ?
(Reporter: No response by the witness).
Q. Are you refusing to answer?
(Reporter: No response by the witness). (Transcript 1975, DE 46–47, 255–57)

This charade went on for several minutes—a charade because Siler knew the answers to all the questions. As Hands's pointed comment about Siler's political ambitions shows, the Lexington Six were coming to feel they were being used as props in a political show trial to further the U.S. attorney's career.

The political atmosphere in 1975 Kentucky was ripe for such theatrics. The traditional "town-gown" division between universities and surrounding towns had been exacerbated by antiwar demonstrations on the Lexington campus, so the regional populace was not prone to sympathize with shaggy, unkempt, disruptive college kids who were thus fair game for prosecutorial zeal. The "law-and-order" mantra of the Nixon years continued to hold sway; stern prosecutors and judges were in favor, which enabled them to ride the tide to successful careers. (Siler eventually replaced Moynahan on the Eastern Kentucky District Court and ended up as a judge on the Sixth Circuit Appeals Court in Cincinnati.)

Marla Seymour was also called before the grand jury around midday on March 6. The atmosphere in the courthouse had by then grown increasingly chaotic. There were sixty or so supporters lining the hall where the six and their attorneys conferred, and the government officials seemed that Thursday to be eager to rush the proceedings along, perhaps fearing that, if prolonged, the hearings would go into the weekend—which, as it turned out, they did. In her appearance before the grand jury, Marla complained about the frenzied atmosphere, with the U.S. attorney "in a merry-go-round of yelling in the hallway for a specific witness while our attorney is trying to advise those witnesses." It seemed, she said, that Siler was just "running us through here for his own purposes" and not allowing witnesses to have their full say (Transcript 1975, DE 46–47, 249).

The situation became even more intense when Siler suddenly filed motions that the witnesses—Carey Junkin, Debbie Hands, and Marla Seymour—be held in contempt. The motion for Junkin was issued at 1:30 p.m., for Hands at 2 p.m., and for Seymour at 2:30 p.m.; all three were ordered to appear in the main courtroom at 3 p.m. for a hearing on the contempt motion. This left the legal team with just a few minutes to prepare. Robert Sedler was in fact back at the university teaching a regularly scheduled class, so it was up to Judith Peterson to conduct the plea. She did so by immediately questioning the abruptness of the decision to file a motion for contempt, claiming that the Lexington Six were entitled to five days' notice. But Judge Moynahan rejected this contention out of hand, saying, "You're not entitled to five days in this case" (Mitchell 1975b). Shortly after the hearing began, Sedler rushed back to the courtroom to resume his role as co-counsel. Meanwhile, interrogation of the remaining three members of the Lexington Six—Jill Raymond, Nancy Scott, and Gail Cohee—continued up in a grand jury room on the fourth floor.

In her second appearance before the grand jury, Jill Raymond took the occasion to address the jurors directly, trying to make the case that the FBI was operating improperly and illegally:

> MR. FOREMAN, *when agents of the FBI came to my door they mentioned that I might be called before the grand jury. It seems to me a little bit strange for law enforcement officials to be threatening people, who have a right to refuse to talk with them, with prosecution. . . . What I have read in the newspapers recently about the FBI led me to conclude that it is an agency which has overthrown the powers initially delegated to it. It appears that this institution is beyond the control of the legislative officials of this country, these supposedly duly elected representatives of the people. (Transcript 1975, DE 46–47, 281)*

In all probability the jurors heard this as an academic discourse at odds with their own understanding of the FBI, likely themselves unaware of the COINTELPRO revelations about illegal FBI activity, and that Jill's attempt to inform fell therefore on deaf ears. As Jill herself commented years later, we hoped to "connect with the grand jurors" by addressing them directly. But "it was like two cultures really not understanding each other" (Raymond 1989, 297, 292).

Siler interrupted Raymond at this point in her speech. "I hate to break in," he said, "but I think you can answer the questions yes or no." The question had been whether she had lived "in the same building with the two girls," Saxe and Power. The answer to that question was in fact "no," as Jill had never lived in the same building as Saxe and Power, but she took the Fifth, after asking once again to address the jurors: "It just seems to me that you all wanted me to make statements to you, so I have a statement to make." But Siler cut her off and dismissed her, ordering her "excused until in the morning [March 7] at 9:30. I intend to file contempt proceedings against . . . you" (Transcript 1975, DE 46–47, 281, 280, 282).

Nancy Scott made her first appearance before the grand jury that same March 6 day. She also attempted to give the jurors a primer on the history of grand juries:

> Mr. Foreperson, I have a statement that I would like to make first: In the days of early England, like in the 1700's, like a real strange system of criminal justice was in effect, like the poor were arrested and jailed irregularly (sic) and a lot of this was just because they were poor and they didn't have any rights . . . like if you were an enemy of the King you could be arrested for anything at anytime, the Star Chamber was used for inquisition and often for torture, imprisonment most often followed and death was a frequent result. The people were so irate that panels of citizens were called . . . known as grand juries, and they were formed to determine if anybody. . . . (Transcript 1975, DE 46–47, 264–65).

U.S. Attorney Siler cut Scott off at this significant point, where she was about to inform the jurors that the purpose of a grand jury is to indict, her overall point being that grand juries were instigated to halt egregious injustices, especially to the poor and "enemies of the King" but that today, perversely, they were being used as Star Chambers were in earlier times. "We appreciate your discourse here," Siler interrupted sarcastically, "but the grand jury has got to get on." Scott objected, "But you all want me to talk, and this is something I want to say" (Transcript 1975, DE 46–47, 265).

The inquest proceeded into the ritual of the witness exiting the room to consult with her attorney and returning to read the prepared script, refusing to answer based on various Bill of Rights amendments, the U.S. Code, and allegations of grand jury abuse. Like Carey Junkin and Gail Cohee, Nancy quibbled with the attorney over the meaning of the term "lived with" and finally answered "no" to the question of whether she had resided with Saxe and Power (Transcript 1975, DE 46–47, 270).

At this point the foreperson, Ralph Agee, asked Scott if she would answer the questions if he personally asked them instead of Siler. After consulting with her lawyer in the hall outside the grand jury room, Nancy returned to ask, "Mr. Foreman, can you explain to me why the questions are being asked?" This may have been an entrapment question; if so, it's a trap Agee fell right into when he gave the answer noted previously—"we want to find out where those two girls are" (Transcript 1975, DE 46–47, 271)—thus revealing his own misunderstanding of the purpose of a grand jury.

Scott then asked the foreperson what questions he had for her. He in turn asked Siler to "give [him] the list" of questions prepared by the U.S. attorney, revealing how the proceedings were governed and determined *not* by questions the grand jury had but by questions channeled to the jury room through the U.S. prosecuting attorney from the FBI. The first question on the list—not surprisingly—was whether Nancy had ever known Susan Saxe, to which Nancy, after another attorney consult, pled the Fifth, making the usual prepared statement.

At this point Siler erupted and chastised the witness:

> MR. SILER: *Let me tell you something, young lady. You are trifling with the grand jury. You led this foreman to believe that if he asked you these questions . . . that you might answer. . . . You just dragged your feet, went out in the hallway, and these people [the jurors] need to get home to their families, and you are fiddling with them. I have warned you about that, I think it is inexcusable for a person with your background and education to be involved in activities of this sort. (Transcript 1975, DE 46–47, 272)*

Siler's exasperation seems in part an expression of annoyance at the delays and obfuscations, but he also sounds personally peeved that Nancy appeared to be betraying her class. Nancy was in fact the most ostensibly middle-class and conventional-looking of the Lexington Six, having been in her prefeminist days a "sweetheart of Sigma Chi," as one acquaintance put it (Hackney 1989), and indeed "a Greek festival queen" a year previously (Seymour 1987b).

The various efforts by the Lexington Six to instruct the grand jurors as to their proper role were likely resented by the jurors, seen as condescending attempts by members of the educated class to challenge their authority. By the end of the hearings, attorney Robert Sedler discerned "great hostility on the part of the grand jury" (Sedler 1986). Testimony by Ralph Agee during the contempt hearing verifies Sedler's conclusion. Under cross-examination Agee revealed his animosity: "I hope they get the maximum," he reportedly said in an earlier hearing, as reported by Sedler, who asked Agee what he meant by the statement. Agee replied, "Well, the best I can understand this situation is these defendants have been granted immunity, and if they don't answer the questions that we ask them, or the U.S. Attorney asks them, then they are in violation of the law . . . and if they are in violation of the law, then they are upholding a criminal, and, we, as a jury thought they should be given a maximum sentence, which would probably be jail, or a fine, until they cooperate" (Transcript 1975, DE 46–47, 323–24).

Of course, the fact that the six weren't answering the questions didn't mean they were "upholding a criminal." But Sedler didn't zero in on this logical flaw in Agee's reasoning; rather, he seized on Agee's incorrect reference to the witnesses as "defendants." "You said they were defendants. Had the United States Attorney advised you that criminal charges were pending against these people?" Agee quickly covered himself: "I wish to strike the word 'defendant.' I used that on my own. Witness, I should say" (Transcript 1975, DE 46–47, 325).

But Sedler pursued the point: "But that's how you felt, that they were defendants?" Agee replied, "With the cooperation we have been getting, yes." Sedler continued, "In other words, you were very upset, personally, that they didn't answer your questions?" (Transcript 1975, DE 46–47, 325). Siler objected to this, and Judge Moynahan sustained the objection, which ended the discussion. The point had been made, however, that Agee and the other jurors were out to get the Lexington Six.

Clearly the situation had assumed mythic proportions. It was no longer a matter of ordinary citizens claiming Fifth Amendment and other constitutional rights, nor was it even a matter of capturing Susan Saxe and Kathy Power, who by then were long gone and whose trail was cold. Indeed, as Sedler later commented, neither the U.S. attorney nor Judge Moynahan really believed any of the six knew where Saxe and Power were or even had known who they were during their time in Lexington (Sedler 1986). No, the issue had become a question of defending the natural order against obstreperous upstarts who held that order in contempt. Not only had the Lexington Six shown their contempt by their resistant, obstructive behavior in the grand jury hearings but their very demeanor—their clothes, for example—were seen as a defiant comment on social norms. As Jill Raymond later commented, "The problem was that none of us cared about being respectable" (Kirkharn 1976). Underlying this cultural confrontation was the most shocking aspect of their defiance, the incontrovertible but never overtly stated reality that these unrepentant rebels were lesbians and gay, sexual deviants. It seemed they needed to be taught a lesson, chastised, and brought back to their proper conforming place in the natural order.

On March 7 and 8, the final hearings were held in the main courtroom, which was packed with supporters of the Lexington Six (I, the author, was present for the March 6 and 8 hearings). The grand jurors were also in attendance, along with the Lexington Six, seated at the front before the judge, as well as attorneys Robert Sedler, Judith Peterson, and Emmy Hixson; the U.S. attorneys; marshals; bailiffs; and the FBI agents who had initiated the whole process, Wayne McDonald, John Gill, and John McCauley. Much of the March 7 hearing was taken up with the court reporter's reading of the transcripts of the grand jury hearings aloud in the courtroom (which is why we have a record of those hearings).

But the legal team for the Lexington Six mounted one last major offensive, an attempt to prevent a contempt order by casting the whole process as corrupted by the FBI's illegal use of electronic surveillance—wiretapping of peoples' phones. Several affidavits were introduced in support of a motion asking for the government to conduct an internal search for and to reveal any evidence it had that such surveillance occurred. For, the motion read, "an accurate determination whether there has been unlawful surveillance that has tainted these proceedings cannot possibly be made without a full search of the records of every agency that conducts electronic surveillance" (Transcript 1975, DE 25, 12–13).

Affidavits claiming that their phones had been wiretapped were filed by several people connected to the case, including Rhonda Copelon, the attorney for the Center for Constitutional Rights in New York. She asserted that "extreme static, buzzing and . . . squeaks and squeals," which occurred during her telephone conversations with people in grand jury resistance cases, were evidence of wiretapping. On several occasions during phone conversations with University of Kentucky law student Dick Burr, who was assisting the Lexington Six legal team, Copelon's phone had gone dead for thirty seconds and then resumed (Transcript 1975, DE 26, 1–2).

Doris Peterson, another staff attorney for the Center for Constitutional Rights, reported similar problems (Transcript 1975, DE 27, 1–2). Judith Peterson stated that while she was staying at the Off Hand Manor collective, the phone was likely tapped. She based her claim on a suspicious incident that occurred on February 19. When she had a law clerk place a telephone call to "the local FBI office, there was no answer," so the clerk hung up. But when Peterson then tried to place another call on the same phone, "the phone was dead" (Transcript 1975, DE 28, 2–3). While such anecdotal evidence of wiretapping is hardly conclusive proof, it does suggest that the FBI was interfering with the phone service at Off Hand Manor. Robert Sedler also filed an affidavit claiming that since taking on the Lexington Six case, "I have experienced an inordinate amount of telephone interference" on both home and office phones (Transcript 1975, DE 31, 2).

Jill Raymond and Carey Junkin similarly submitted affidavits alleging wiretapping of their phones (Transcript 1975, DE 29, 30). Jill asked how several of her friends and relatives were contacted by the FBI so soon after she had phoned them, indicating at the very least the FBI had her phone records. And Carey recounted the February 4 trip to Cincinnati in which the police stopped him three times, all shortly after he had phoned a friend there to say he was coming.

All of this effort to establish a claim of illegal wiretapping by the FBI was for naught, however, as U.S. Attorney Eugene Siler immediately filed a denial affidavit, claiming that no wiretapping had occurred. He had apparently conducted the requested search of FBI files in a matter of hours. "My office has inquired," Siler swore under oath, "of the appropriate federal authorities to determine whether there has been any electronic surveillance or interception of the wire or oral communications" of the Lexington Six "or their attorneys. . . . Based on the results of such inquiries I hereby state that there has been no electronic surveillance or interception of wire or oral communications of those individuals" (Transcript 1975, DE 32, 1). Since several of those who filed affidavits claiming wiretapping—namely Rhonda Copelon and Doris Peterson—were not named in Siler's denial, the affidavit left open the question of whether their New York phones were tapped.

Beyond this, it is doubtful, moreover, that Siler's claim that no wiretapping occurred is correct. As we know from the COINTELPRO documents, illegal wiretapping was longstanding standard operating procedure in the FBI and, given the evidence presented in the affidavits, it seems unquestionable that wiretapping occurred. Whether, therefore, FBI agents lied to Siler or whether Siler was himself lying is unclear.

Knowing that Siler's sworn denial would suffice to convince Judge Moynahan and thus moot the accusation, Sedler attempted in the contempt hearing to get the FBI agents themselves to admit under oath that wiretapping and other illegal activities were among their procedures. He did this by delving into the details of FBI operations. But Siler objected to this line of questioning, and the judge sustained his objection: "I don't think," Moynahan told Sedler, "you are entitled to get into the workings of the Office of the Federal Bureau of Investigation . . . in that kind of detail" (Transcript 1975, DE 46–47, 399–400). Moynahan's reasoning was that it would diminish the FBI's effectiveness if such details were known publicly.

Sedler persisted, however, asking Senior Agent John McCauley of the Lexington FBI office whether he had actually conducted the search for letters allegedly seized by the FBI, as asserted in the subpoena filed in connection with the motion to quash the subpoenas on February 18:

> [Sedler]: Did you, in response to that subpoena, direct agents to make a search for those documents?
>
> MR. SILER: Objection.
>
> THE COURT: The objection is sustained.
>
> Q. Did you make any effort to obtain the documents outlined in the subpoena? . . .
>
> A. No, Sir, I did not.
>
> Q. Why not?
>
> A. Because there are no such documents or letters. (Transcript 1975, DE 46–47, 410–11)

McCauley's somewhat circular answer implies one of two things: either he did conduct some sort of search; otherwise how would he have known that there were no letters? Or, his certainty that there were no letters precluded the possibility of there being such letters. No evidence necessary.

Sedler continued his interrogation:

Q. How do you, as Speical [sic] Agent in Charge go about determining whether electronic surveillance has been engaged in by FBI agents, or by others?
MR. SILER: *Object, Your Honor. (Transcript 1975, DE 46–47, 416)*

Judge Moynahan then called Sedler, Peterson, and Siler to the bench to hear their reasoning in private. Sedler told him,

Your Honor . . . we are trying to get into the question of how Mr. Siler . . . how the existence of an electronic surveillance is determined. Mr. Siler filed an affidavit saying he had made a check since yesterday afternoon to determine that none of the agencies had engaged in electronic surveillance of myself, of Miss Peterson, or any of our clients. Now, what I am trying to do now is simply find out how the FBI goes about determining whether or not anybody is engaged in electronic surveillance. (Transcript 1975, DE 46–47, 416–17)

Judith Peterson amplified the implication made in Sedler's statement that you couldn't conduct a thorough records search in a matter of hours; instead, she suggested, "it would take two weeks to come up with that kind of information—not two hours" (Transcript 1975, DE 46–47, 418). Siler made a technical objection about proper legal procedure; Sedler agreed with his point and withdrew the complaint, apparently feeling he now had enough on the record to use in an appeal.

By then it was late in the day so the March 7 hearing was recessed at 5 p.m., with the session to resume at 9:30 a.m. the following day, Saturday, March 8, ironically International Women's Day but a day of reckoning for the Lexington Six.

In that Saturday morning session, after Sedler concluded his interrogation of the relevant FBI agents, most of which was blocked by judge-sustained objections by Siler, the proceedings wound up with Sedler attempting to "show cause"—the purpose of a contempt hearing—why the Lexington Six were refusing to obey the court's order under the grant of use immunity to answer the questions posed by the grand jury (actually, as we have seen, by the U.S. attorney).

Figure 2 (left). Jill Raymond in the Lexington courthouse for the contempt hearing, March 7–8, 1975. Photograph by Mark Cantor Paster. Used by permission

Figure 3 (right). Marla Seymour in the Lexington courthouse for the contempt hearing, March 7–8, 1975. Photograph by Mark Cantor Paster. Used by permission

Once the wiretapping claim had been dismissed by the court—Judge Moynahan said the claim was "preposterous" (Bailey 1975b)—the Lexington Six were ordered back before the grand jury for one final appearance. After they refused once again to answer the questions, each was questioned directly by the judge to verify that she or he was in fact refusing to testify. Each confirmed the refusal.

Judge Moynahan then held each of them in contempt of court:

IT IS NOW THEREFORE ORDERED AND ADJUDGED that the witnesses, James Carey Junkin, Marla Seymour, Jill Raymond, Gail Cohee, [Nancy Scott], and Deborah (Debbie) Hands . . . are hereby adjudged in civil contempt of this Court, and it is FURTHER ORDERED AND ADJUDGED that said witnesses . . . be committed to the custody of the United States Marshal for the Eastern District of Kentucky until such time as they shall have purged themselves of said contempt by complying with the order of this Court directing them to answer certain questions propounded to them by the aforesaid grand jury . . . provided that such period of confinement shall not exceed the term of the aforesaid grand jury . . . and in no event shall such period of confinement exceed eighteen (18) months. . . . Bernard T. Moynahan Jr, Judge. (Appeal A 1975a, 8a–9a)

A collective gasp rippled through the courtroom as people realized what this meant: Gail, Carey, Debbie, Jill, Nancy, and Marla were going to jail. Robert Sedler jumped to his feet to announce that the Lexington Six had a formal statement to make to the court, which he proceeded to read. "We," the Lexington Six, he began,

believe that we have just cause for the refusal to answer the questions propounded to us by the grand jury. We state to the Court that none of us know the present whereabouts of the persons known to us as Lena Paley and May Kelley.

We further state to the Court that we have no knowledge or reason to believe that Lena Paley or May Kelley were persons other than the persons they claimed to be, or that they were fugitives from justice.

Because we believe that we have just cause for the refusal to answer the questions propounded to us by the Grand Jury, we must respectfully decline to answer these questions and must appeal the decision of the Court directing us to do so. (Transcript 1975, DE 46–47, 613)

In the end, thus, the Lexington Six declared forthrightly to the court that they knew nothing about the whereabouts of Susan Saxe and Kathy Power nor did they have any "reason to believe" that Lena Paley and May Kelly were in fact Saxe and Power or that they had been fugitives from the law. Of course, by this time, simply by reading the papers the Lexington Six had "reason to believe" who Paley and Kelly really were, but they did not have nor had they ever had direct, firsthand knowledge of the women's true identities.

Some may ask at this point, why then didn't the Lexington Six just say this to the grand jury and spare themselves much suffering and grief? The reason lies in their belief that the real purpose of the FBI and the FBI-controlled grand jury was not just to capture "those girls," as Foreperson Agee, put it, but to delve into their personal lives and in so doing to stigmatize and demean them and their community. That the FBI did so ostensibly to elicit information about what it imagined to be a vast network harboring dissident radical women only intensified their resolve to resist. The Lexington Six, like the Connecticut women, felt the FBI and grand jury intrusion as an attack on their private lives, their friends and comrades, and their community—which had become, as Ellen Grusse put it, their "family," their cultural home (Harris 1976a, 67).

In this the Lexington Six resistance bears a resemblance to the 1969 Stonewall Inn uprising in New York City. There too the motivation of habitués to fight back against police harassment lay in the feeling that a gay "home" place was under siege. In the case of Stonewall, the home was a largely male gay bar, whereas for the Lexington and Connecticut women it was a lesbian feminist community. And while the campy riotous scene of the Stonewall protest, led largely by drag queens, couldn't have differed more from the austere orderliness of the Lexington and New Haven district courts, nevertheless the feelings that motivated the resistance in each case were not far removed. One Stonewall participant described that event as "swishy queen[s] . . . make up dripping and gowns askew, fighting for their *home*" (Segal 2019, 123; emphasis added). Likewise with resisters in Kentucky and Connecticut in 1975: their private "world of love and ritual" (to use Carroll Smith-Rosenberg's celebrated phrase, coined the same year) was being assaulted by the overpowering, patriarchal "strong arm of the law." As a matter of political loyalty to a beloved community, they couldn't stand by and let that happen.

Robert Sedler concluded the Lexington Six contempt hearing by asking the court to have the grand jury members polled on the question of whether they still wanted the six to testify, having now heard the witnesses' avowal that they had no pertinent information in the search for Saxe and Power. Judge Moynahan agreed to this somewhat unusual request, and so the jurors left the courtroom to hold a vote on the question. Were the jury to decide against further questioning, that presumably would have abrogated the contempt decree and the six would have been freed of the matter once and for all. Sedler was gambling that the witnesses' direct appeals to the jurors had had the desired effect of persuading them that the Lexington Six had no knowledge of or involvement in the Saxe-Power case.

The courtroom was filled with a tense and dreadful silence during the jury's six-minute absence. Carey Junkin had the feeling that some of the women on the grand jury were sympathetic to the Lexington Six: "We represented an alternative to their locked-in life-style of being married and rejoicing at the new Kenmore washer" (1987). So, he imagined, frustrated with their repressed suburban lives, these women might identify with the rebelliousness of the resisting young women of the Lexington Six. Apparently, at least some members of the grand jury—possibly the women—voted against pursuing matters with the Lexington Six, perhaps believing the official statement of denial read in the courtroom by Sedler. He himself later said he believed the grand jury had not been unanimous on the question of whether to continue prosecuting the case (Seymour 1987b). Nonetheless, given the rapidity of the jury's decision-making process, there can't have been too much of a debate. In any event, Agee returned with the jury's decision in the affirmative: they wanted the case to go on. The contempt order held.

The next and final issue was Sedler's request that the six be released on bail until the appeal—which he was filing forthwith—was decided. In a "colloquy" at the bench among the judge, Sedler, and Siler on the question of bail, Siler argued against granting bail on the implausible grounds that this plea was but another delaying tactic, which would just give Susan Saxe and Kathy Power "more and more time . . . to change their identity and take off or hide out further with other people in this vicinity" (Transcript 1975, DE 46–47, 632). Siler once again betrayed the fact that he saw the grand jury's purpose as aiding in the pursuit of Saxe and Power—an improper conception of the grand jury.

But for the court the case was no longer a matter of catching two fugitive women—indeed, as noted, Sedler had come to believe that Moynahan didn't really think that any of the six knew where Saxe and Power were (Sedler 1986). No, it was now a matter for the judge of defending the natural order against defiant blasphemers: the case had become a microcosm of the broader 1960s confrontation between the establishment and rebellious youth. It was an unbridgeable divide. And this despite the fact that the judicial authorities—the judge, the U.S. attorney, and probably most of the grand jurors—and the Lexington Six were of the same race and class.

"We knew we were completely innocent," one supporter observed, and we "had parents that Siler and Moynahan would have liked," and yet because of our politically dissident positions, to them we were "the wrong people" (Sutherland 1987), demonized as the enemy. Judge Moynahan's response to the bail plea revealed that for him, Sedler noted, it had become a matter of defending a "whole system and way of life" (Sedler 1986).

"I have never," Moynahan exclaimed, in explaining his final judgment, "seen a case where a group of witnesses have shown greater contempt for the power of a Federal grand jury." Moynahan proceeded to cite instances of the Lexington Six offering flippant replies to questions and lecturing the grand jury about its history and function. "I have never," Moynahan continued, "seen a more flagrant abuse, callous disregard and total lack of responsibility, and contempt for the powers of a federal court" (Transcript 1975, DE 46–47, 633).

Moynahan concluded by alluding to his fifteen months as a prisoner of war in Nazi Germany. Having experienced prison time "as an unwilling visitor in Hitler's Third Reich," after his plane was shot down over Germany during World War II, Moynahan said he appreciated what prison was like. "It's a very sobering experience," and "I'm sorry that these young people have to be confined." But given their "callous attitude" and "total and irresponsible disregard of the power of the grand jury," their behavior "cannot be tolerated. . . . For that reason, the motion for a stay and the motion for bail are overruled, and these witnesses are remanded to the custody of the Marshal" (Transcript 1975, DE 46–47, 633–34).

One of the ironies of this case is how each side justified and rationalized its position by analogizing itself to World War II resistance against Nazism. Moynahan clearly prided himself on having been a fighter against the totalitarian tyranny of Hitler's Germany. But the Lexington Six and activists in the antiwar movement in general equated the American administrations of Lyndon Johnson and Richard Nixon with Nazi Germany, a fascist regime carrying out an unjust war, suppressing civil rights and liberties, and persecuting dissidents. That Nixon's name on antiwar posters and flyers was often spelled with a swastika for an X and America with a K (Amerika) was symptomatic. The shadow of Nazi Germany and the Holocaust hung heavily over the political movements of the 1960s and 1970s. A generation that had come of age in the immediate postwar era and well apprised of Nazi atrocities was determined not to be "good Germans," enabling and collaborating with evil. So another unspoken motive driving the Lexington Six—unspoken because it was so well understood—was the determination not to be "good Germans" but to resist what they saw as Gestapo-like tactics of the FBI and the grand jury. As a grand jury resister in Seattle commented, "I feel like I'm in Germany in 1935" (Celarier 1976).

After the final order came down to send the six to jail, Robert Sedler made one last plea for bail. Since, he argued, he believed "that we may prevail on appeal," and "if we have prevailed, then these persons will have suffered irreparable injury," could the court at least grant bail for a few days to see whether the appeals court of the Sixth Circuit would grant a stay?

In response Moynahan read from a U.S. Supreme Court decision, *U.S. v. Bisceglia*, which had been issued only a few weeks previously on February 19, 1975. In this decision the Supreme Court upheld an earlier decision, *Blair v. United States of America* (1919), which granted very broad powers to the grand jury. The *Blair* decision had been issued during an earlier era—the World War I "Red Scare" period—in which civil liberties were drastically curtailed in the United States, and the decision reflected that era's mood. The Supreme Court's decision in *Bisceglia* upheld a lower-court decision made in fact by Moynahan himself but overturned by the Sixth Circuit Court of Appeals, thus vindicating Moynahan over the appeals court, which may have strengthened Moynahan's confidence that he would win the appeal in the case of the Lexington Six.

In the colloquy with Sedler over the bail decision, Moynahan quoted from the *Blair* decision, as recently modified by the Supreme Court in *Bisceglia*: "A witness is not entitled to set limits to the investigation that the grand jury may conduct. It is a grand inquest, a body with powers of investigation and inquisition, the scope of whose inquiries is not to be limited narrowly by questions of propriety or forecasts of the probable result . . . or by doubts whether any particular individual will be found properly subject to an accusation of crime." Moynahan then terminated the discussion: "There's no point in belaboring it any further. . . . Let the witnesses be forthwith remanded to the custody of the Marshal" (Transcript 1975, DE 46–47, 635, 636).

The Lexington Six were now prisoners of the state. With the decision announced, the six held hands as the marshal led them out of the courtroom. They could feel murmurs of support from the audience. "That meant a lot," Marla Seymour later recalled (1987b). "We felt very strong," Jill Raymond recounted, "not quaking" as they were led away (1987b). In an adjacent anteroom, a holding cell, the six were put in handcuffs and chained together at the waist, receiving the same punitive and demeaning treatment as Ellen Grusse and Terri Turgeon.

"It had never occurred to us that they would put us in chains," Marla exclaimed. When Marla saw her lover Gail Cohee in chains, she felt tears of helpless rage well up. The chains were composed of large heavy links attached to the handcuffs and wrapped around their waists. "It was very, very offensive" (Seymour 1987b). Jill, Gail, and Debbie were chained together; Marla was chained to Nancy Scott, with Carey chained separately.

While they were waiting in the holding cell to be driven off to their respective jails, several supporters managed to line up near the exit door. When the six began to leave the building, Sally Kundert ran up and hugged Marla. Both were crying (Seymour 1987b). "It was extremely emotional," Sally reported, to see them led off in chains (Kundert 1986). Beholding Jill in shackles was "like seeing your sister dragged away. It really hurt," another supporter, Sue Ann Salmon, recalled. "I felt empathy. . . . I felt like it was me being in jail" (Salmon 1987). It was "terrible" and "shocking" to see one's friends chained and demeaned in this way, Barbara Sutherland recalled. As a final gesture of defiance and solidarity, Jill attempted to raise her manacled hand in a power fist to her supporters (Sutherland 1987).

Although in the courtroom myself, albeit near the rear, I wasn't sure as the hearing ended what was happening to the Lexington Six. The crowd in the courtroom soon dispersed, and I was about to leave, wishing that there were something I could do and like the others feeling angry and helpless. It occurred to me that the authorities would have to ferry the prisoners to the jails somehow and that they might be leaving through the rear of the building. So I went around to the back parking lot, and there I saw Jill sitting in the back seat of a squad car. Strangely, there didn't seem to be any police or wardens around, so I went up to the car and gave her a few words of encouragement and support through the half-open window. She grinned and tried to raise her hand to grip mine but her wrists were shackled. I couldn't see anyone else in the car—it was a darkened window—but Gail, Carey, and Debbie must have been there too. A guard soon came up and told me to back off. Then another official showed up, got in the car, and they drove off. At the time my main feeling was anger at the appalling injustice and inexcusable cruelty transpiring before me. This was America!

CHAPTER FIVE

Jail Time

The police car carrying four of the condemned and chained Lexington Six left the federal courthouse that Saturday afternoon, March 8, 1975, headed south to two separate jails: Jill Raymond and Gail Cohee to the Bell County Jail in Pineville, Kentucky, in Appalachia near the Tennessee border, and Debbie Hands and Carey Junkin to the Madison County Jail in Richmond, about an hour south of Lexington. Marla Seymour and Nancy Scott, chained together in another car, were sent to the Franklin County Jail in Frankfort, the state capitol. That the six were sent separately to dispersed county jails and not to a federal prison—despite theirs being a federal case—suggested a punitive and vindictive intent on the part of the judiciary, for county jails—especially in Kentucky—are much more primitive and gruesome than the more modern federal facilities. Also, the fact that the officials separated the six—especially lovers Marla and Gail, who were devastated by this unexpected development—suggests a further, deliberate attempt to make the prisoners suffer emotionally as well as physically. And with Carey and Debbie placed in separate sections of the Richmond jail, Debbie ended up in an intolerable situation of solitary confinement. Presumably, the purpose of placing the six resisters in such grueling conditions was to force them to cooperate and testify. If so, the rationale is not far removed from that of the trial-by-ordeal the grand jury was designed centuries ago to replace, and which the Fifth Amendment's prohibition of forced self-testimony and the Eighth Amendment's ban on "cruel and unusual punishments" were designed to prevent.

At the time of their contempt hearing and incarceration, the Lexington Six issued a lengthy statement explaining their position. Printed up as a flyer and distributed by the Lexington Grand Jury Defense Committee, it was less a civil liberties manifesto than a forthrightly lesbian feminist and gay theoretical take on the situation. "We are five women and one man," the statement begins, whose overall political philosophy coheres in the belief that we need to "turn society around so that it will stop draining people's humanness away for profit, and molding them to perform roles created by a violent masculine culture" (Cohee et al. 1975a).

The Lexington Six damned the "entire procedure" that had led to their contempt and incarceration, which revealed "the extent of the grip that male institutions and masculine value-systems have on the lives of all of us," reflecting the "patriarchal premise that the most effective way to relate to people is through the use of power." In particular, "Women who separate themselves from men, sexually and psychologically, pose a totally unique kind of affront to the masculine power, and we are likely to suffer the vengeance of the police and the courts in an especially severe way. Though everyone suffers the consequences of patriarchy, the women's movement is one of its prime targets now, for it challenges the validity—the virility, if you will—of all of its structures and definitions" (Cohee et al. 1975a).

Carey Junkin added a concurrence of his own:

The male witness among us . . . would like to [add] . . . the following remarks: By our lifestyle, we, as gay people have effectively frightened the patriarchy to the point where the government feels it must repress us and put us away where we can no longer pose a threat to its definitions of how a person should live his/her life. Gay people are one of the most vulnerable minorities in this country today. . . . Therefore, we as gay people . . . seek changes in the country which we live in to hopefully make it a less oppressive environment in which to live our lives as we damn well please. (Cohee et al. 1975a)

A few days after the Lexington Six were carted off to Kentucky county jails, Pat Swinton was apprehended on March 12, 1975, in Brattleboro,

Vermont, at a food coop where she worked. Since her arrest came just two months after Jane Alpert's sentencing on January 13, some on the left believed that Alpert's alleged cooperation with the FBI had led to it. Along with Alpert, Swinton had been a member of Sam Melville's anti-war bombing gang in New York City during the late 1960s, and after her indictment in 1969, had gone underground to avoid arrest. During her first year underground (1970–71), Swinton traveled with Alpert but the two split up and went separate ways thereafter. While a fugitive, Swinton lived in Brattleboro in a pacifist community, the Total Loss Farm, under the name Shoshana. Like many other women antiwar fugitives of the day, she awakened to feminism in the early 1970s. Before Alpert turned herself in in November 1974, Alpert visited Shoshana in Vermont and warned her she could be in jeopardy and should move on, but Swinton didn't heed Alpert's advice. After her arrest, Swinton was held in jail a few weeks but released in mid-April on a $200,000 bail bond until her trial in the fall of 1975.

At first Swinton herself did not share in the theory that Alpert had betrayed her. In an interview entitled "Pat Swinton: Jane Taught Me Feminism," Shoshana said "in a direct unhesitant manner that she does not believe Jane Alpert was responsible for her arrest or that 'Jane would knowingly collaborate with the authorities.'" Indeed, Shoshana attributed her own feminist awakening to Jane Alpert and Robin Morgan. "Jane . . . was always talking to me about feminism and you know I was dragged around to some meetings." On the other hand, Shoshana implied in the interview that Alpert might have inadvertently given the FBI pertinent information: "It's a mistake for anyone to think they can talk to the FBI and not have it used. . . . There's no such thing as a little cooperation with the FBI" (Shinell 1975).

Within a few months, however, Shoshana had changed her tune. In an interview that summer, she said Alpert "decided to be as cooperative as she could, in terms of giving a lot of details about where she'd been and what she'd been doing. And that was enough to lead to me. And it did, indeed, lead to me" (Shoshana 1975).

But despite Swinton's initial support, Alpert's repudiation of the male New Left in her 1973 "Mother Right" article had left her persona non grata in leftist circles, and through "smear and innuendo," as feminist activist Susan Brownmiller put it, Alpert was stigmatized as an informer. Brownmiller recalled, "I watched in horror as the virus spread into feminist circles" (1999, 229). In fact, Alpert refused to testify at Swinton's trial against her former comrade or others underground, and as a consequence was held in contempt of court with four more months added to her prison term, so that she ended up serving two years (Asbury 1975). Pat Swinton was eventually acquitted of all charges on September 26, 1975.

The so-called Alpert Controversy was triggered by the letter Jane Alpert sent to her "sisters" underground (and included in her "Mother Right" article). Even before Pat Swinton was arrested, a petition, issued largely by those "sisters" connected to the Weathermen, was circulated that claimed Alpert's alleged "cooperation" with the FBI constituted a "betrayal" of the movement. (The U.S. attorney in Alpert's case, Paul Curran, had praised Alpert for "fully cooperating" [Shinell 1975]). The petition, published on March 8, 1975, urged that Alpert be expelled from the movement and blacklisted: "Anyone who reveals such information ['about people in struggle'] acts in the same manner as an agent of the State." For "if we don't speak out against those who betray the confidence of friends and comrades, we dishonor those women who refuse to 'cooperate' and we endanger our entire movement" (Clark et al. 1975). Such a statement, issued the same day the Lexington Six were sent to jail, raised the stakes considerably on the question of FBI/grand jury cooperation and weighed heavily on the Kentucky resisters as they continued to struggle with the issue. The petition was signed by approximately ninety radical women, some identified as members of the New York Women's Union and the Prairie Fire Distributing Committee—the latter an operation of the Weather Underground. The lead signatory was Judy Clark, a Weather woman later convicted and imprisoned for her role in the Nyack, New York, Brinks robbery in 1981.

A second petition damning Alpert was issued by Ti-Grace Atkinson, Florynce Kennedy, Susan Sherman, and Joan Hamilton. Entitled "The Crisis in Feminism," it condemned "betrayal" in somewhat abstract terms, implying that Alpert was guilty of such and treated leniently by the courts because of her white-race privilege. Instead, the four urged feminists to remain allied with men in the left. "We do not 'support' or 'not support' the brothers of Attica. We *are* Attica" (Kennedy et al. 1975).

A third petition was published in the same March 8 issue of *Majority Report*. Entitled "Vindication of the Rights of Feminists," an echo of Mary Wollstonecraft's feminist treatise of 1792, it was a defense of Jane Alpert signed by most of the leading figures of second-wave feminism, among them Susan Brownmiller, Judy Chicago, Kate Millett, Robin Morgan, and Gloria Steinem, and including several prominent lesbians—Sidney Abbott, Rita Mae Brown, Jill Johnston, Audre Lorde, Phyllis Lyons, and Adrienne Rich—altogether sixty-eight women. Also couched in abstraction, it deplored the purge mentality exhibited in the two condemnatory petitions and the "slur on the character of a sister" who has exhibited "great integrity and strong feminist commitment." The signers further noted that the "female defenders" of the "male-dominated left" had yet to adequately address and respond to the critique of the New Left Alpert issued in her "Mother Right" article. The petition concluded, "We have an organic commitment to all oppressed peoples—but we affirm our own priorities as *women*" (Abbott et al. 1975).

The "Women of the Weather Underground" added a further contribution to the Alpert controversy a few weeks later, published (ironically) in the same issue of *Majority Report* as the Pat Swinton interview that more or less exonerated Alpert. This missive, "Did Jane Talk? The View from Women Underground," was delivered to the feminist journal in a clandestine manner, as most of its authors were underground fugitives wanted by the FBI. An anonymous phone call in early April to the editors of the journal informed them that a document "on the subject of Jane Alpert and 'collaboration'" had been secretly deposited in a litter basket in Manhattan's Greenwich Village near the Grove Street office of the journal. The editors retrieved the envelope from the litter basket and published the letter a few days later. The missive is dated April 10, 1975; it appeared in the April 19 issue of the journal (Women of the Weather Underground 1975).

The letter opened with a rather broad definition of "collaboration" and proceeded to indict Jane Alpert under the terms of this definition. Collaboration means "agreement to cooperate with the state to reveal any information" about the movement. Like Pat Swinton, the Weather Underground women warned that one cannot cooperate just a little with the FBI. Any information one revealed could endanger fugitives. Alpert's letter to her underground sisters was thus, according to the authors, a form of collaboration: "Her letter was a betrayal which endangered us, made our lives harder, and made it more difficult to maintain a secure underground" (Women of the Weather Underground 1975). The letter further suggested that Alpert had given officials information leading to Swinton's arrest and that Alpert received a relatively light sentence as a result. This allegation was picked up in a prison newsletter, *The Midnight Special*, published by the National Lawyers Guild. It named the prison in which Alpert was being held, "in order to point out to the sisters inside that there is a traitor in their midst" (Lafferty 1975a). Alpert supporters saw this targeting of Alpert's prison location as endangering her life.

Finally, the Weather Women suggested in their letter that Alpert's alleged collaboration encouraged the FBI to pursue the cases in Lexington and New Haven more vigorously: "A wave of FBI visits, Grand Juries," and arrests followed in the wake of her testimony. "By her collaboration," they concluded, "Alpert made herself an enemy of the people" (Women of the Weather Underground 1975).

The letter ended by calling for widespread resistance to FBI and grand jury investigations, lauding those like the Lexington Six who had resisted, and urging solidarity with those who, unlike Alpert, had refused to collaborate: "How could we embrace our heroines like Lolita Lebrun [*sic*], Ethel Rosenberg, the women currently imprisoned in New Haven and Lexington, Assata Shakur, Sarah Braveheart [*sic*] Bull, and not expose Alpert's treachery?" (Women of the Weather Underground 1975). All of these "heroines" refused to cooperate with the authorities in various investigations, for which they paid a heavy price: Ethel Rosenberg with her life for refusing to give testimony against her husband, Julius, in an atomic spy case. She was condemned to the electric chair and executed on June 19, 1953. Lolita Lebrón, a Puerto Rican nationalist, spent over twenty-five years in prison for her refusal to cooperate (as well as for leading an armed attack on the U.S. House of Representatives in 1954). Assata Shakur was a member of the Black Liberation Army then in prison awaiting trial, while Sarah Bad Heart Bull was an imprisoned activist in the American Indian Movement who had been beaten, arrested, and sent to prison for five months for taking part in a demonstration in Scotts Bluff, Nebraska, in early

1973, protesting a lenient charge brought against the murderer—a white man—of her son, an Oglala Indian. That the Lexington Six were being elevated into this pantheon of resisters raised their profile considerably, but, ironically, such national exposure put additional pressure on them by upping the condemnatory stakes should they decide to testify. Such pressure soon came to feel oppressive.

In their letter the Weather Women explicitly applauded the resistance of the Lexington Six: "In New Haven, Conn. And Lexington, Ky. six women remain in jail in fierce defiance of the grand jury investigating Susan Saxe and Kathy Power; many more people have been mobilized to support them" (Women of the Weather Underground 1975). The letter concluded by citing an exhortation by Terri Turgeon and Ellen Grusse to resist the government's attacks on movement communities.

The term *collaboration* used in these documents served to raise the cases of the Lexington Six and New Haven women to a historic level. Collaboration in the minds of postwar Americans meant collaboration with the Nazis, as seen during the Nazi occupation of Europe in World War II, a shameful betrayal of friends and comrades to the forces of evil. The Lexington Six now found themselves being held to this standard: to cooperate with the FBI had become equated with collaborating with the Gestapo. Indeed, a letter to the editor of *Majority Report* written by a lesbian refugee from Nazi Germany, published in the same issue as the Weather Women's statement, emphasized the equation: "I came out of Nazi Germany, to escape Hitler. I hoped to find freedom in the U.S. Today my telephone is tapped, I am followed by the police and so are friends who come to visit me. I think this is . . . in part because of my lesbian and feminist activities," as well as antiracist actions (Lee 1975). The letter writer joined in condemning Alpert's alleged collaboration with the Nazi-like authorities.

Similarly analogizing the FBI to Nazi police, Devie Wiseman, an op-ed contributor to the University of Kentucky student newspaper, the *Kentucky Kernel*, wrote on March 16, 1975, in reaction to the incarceration of the Lexington Six:

I am writing in rage and bewilderment to protest the treatment accorded to six young people by the so-called criminal justice system of this country. These six people have done nothing more than stand up for their principles and constitutional rights, yet they face jail terms of up to 18 months and more. Is this a fair exercise of the judicial process—or does it smack, just a tad, of Hitlerian "social democracy," communo-fascist purges, any society in which blanket oppression of "undesirable" elements is a ho-hum, day-to-day occurrence? . . . Please let us do something about government infringements of personal liberty and constitutional freedom before the FBI decides to change its acronym to "S.S"!! (Wiseman 1975)

The S. S. was the *Schutztaffel*, the national police force in Nazi Germany.

Almost immediately on finding herself locked in solitary confinement on the third floor of the Madison County Jail, Debbie Hands realized she couldn't tolerate it. She had to get out. So she agreed to "purge" herself of contempt (the legal phrase) by testifying before the grand jury in order to gain her release. However, her request to be released was delayed, and she ended up spending nearly a week in jail in a panicky state. Finally, on March 14, she was released on personal recognizance and ordered to appear before the grand jury again on March 20. In the meantime, she stayed with Sally Kundert, a member of the Lexington Six defense committee. Sally recalled Debbie being "very brave" in her resistance thus far but that "she couldn't stand it" in jail. "She was claustrophobic" (Kundert 1986).

When the other five Lexington resisters learned of Debbie's decision, they were immediately moved by "raw instinct," as Jill Raymond later recalled, to issue a joint statement of support and solidarity, the purpose of which was to declare "she is still one of us" (Raymond, email to author, February 13, 2018). Issued on March 19, the statement from "five imprisoned witnesses" had a fresh tone of indignant anger and pain that reflected their own anguished condition of incarceration. "We know from our experiences of the last two weeks, in the jails of Bell, Franklin, and Madison Counties, that this is truly a brutal 'cruel and unusual' method of coercing innocent[s] into complicity . . . designed to devastate peoples lives . . . to break their humanity." The statement concluded by "reemphasiz[ing] our support for Ms Hands' decision. We are pleased that one of our sisters is again free to organize and help educate people about the abuses of the grand jury system" (Seymour et al. 1975). Jill later noted, "We felt we needed to support Debbie as a person, and not turn on her for not being politically correct" (Raymond 1987b).

The following day, Debbie Hands, clad in her customary jeans and denim jacket, went back to the grand jury whose questions she had defiantly resisted answering previously. During her three-hour interrogation, portions of which were obtained by the feminist journal *off our backs* and published therein, Hands was asked a number of seemingly off-the-wall questions by U.S. Attorney Eugene Siler, such as whether Lena Paley and May Kelly had bicycles and where they bought their groceries, what kinds of cars Marla Seymour and Jill Raymond drove, what Debbie had discussed in conversations with Lena and May, and the titles of the books and articles she read in discussion with them. Hands refused to answer the latter question on grounds that it violated her First Amendment rights, and Siler dropped the issue (Ward 1975a). The one pertinent question they asked was, "Did they talk about a bank robbery, killing a policeman, robbing a national guard armory?" Answer: "No." The grand jury next went into some detail about a trip Debbie had taken to Ohio and California in August 1974, wanting to know who she traveled with, who they visited, and why they went. Answer: "Wanted to see things" (Hands 1975). Had she met anyone by the name of Tanya (the guerrilla nom de guerre of Patty Hearst)? Answer: Negative.

Following Siler's questions, the grand jurors themselves seemed eager to question Debbie about her reasons for refusing to testify, apparently mystified because she obviously knew nothing about Susan Saxe's and Kathy Power's past or their present whereabouts. She told them she was "shocked" when she found out that the two had been accused of being "bank robbers and killers," an image so opposite to the women she had known, "two very sensitive, kind and really good people. . . . I was very fond of them," she said (Ward 1975a).

Finally, a juror asked the witness straight out why she hadn't answered these questions before, since evidently she had nothing of substance to say. Hands explained that her stand was based on principle, that she felt her rights had been violated in the process and the grand jury used improperly. Her testimony should also have cleared the other five resisters, because it was evident from her answers that none of them had any pertinent information.

Meanwhile, the remaining five of the Lexington Six were settling into their new jail abodes. When nineteen-year-old Carey Junkin arrived at the Madison County Jail late in the afternoon of March 8, having never even seen a jail before, he was surprised to find himself greeted by applause from the other prisoners who knew his story and appreciated the fact that he hadn't ratted on his friends. But his reception by the jailor was quite the opposite: "Goddam queer," he told Carey, "this is my fucking jail and you better behave" (Junkin 1987). In the course of his month-long stay, Carey was beaten and put in solitary confinement several times. "I felt trapped, caged, and dehumanized," Carey reported (Junkin 1975). On several occasions he and other inmates were sprayed with teargas by a guard. Beforehand, many, including Sedler, had been afraid that Carey—as a young, out gay man—might be subject to rape in jail, but these fears proved groundless. Carey found that, although most of the other inmates were largely illiterate and very racist, "homosexuality was no big deal" (Junkin 1987).

For Carey, the worst aspect of the conditions in jail was the food—largely fatback, greasy pork, cornbread, beans, potatoes—the same meal three times a day. To protest, Carey organized a food strike, demanding a more balanced diet with more greens and salads; for this he was put in solitary confinement. The jailors' attitude was that since "we were just animals, we were lucky to be fed at all" (Junkin 1987). The foam mattresses also left much to be desired—ripped and infested with bed bugs. "The Madison County jail can only be described as a place sterile of all feelings toward other humans," Carey concluded. "There was a concerted effort to break my will and humanity" (Junkin 1975).

When Jill and Gail left Debbie and Carey off at the Madison County Jail that Saturday afternoon, they got a glimpse of the place. "Pretty creepy," Jill thought (Raymond 1987b), not realizing that she was to end up spending nine months of her life there. The two, still shackled and handcuffed, were then driven off east toward their final destination, the Bell County Jail in Pineville, a "real Appalachian dungeon," as one supporter recalled (Salmon 1987). It was "a real shock!" Jill said when they first saw the six-by-eight-foot cubicle that was to be their home for the next several weeks: "a little dinky nineteenth-century cell about as big as my bathroom" lined with peeling concrete walls. "We hadn't counted on that," she admitted (Raymond 1987b). The arrangement in this so-called women's block was of two adjacent cells with two sets of bunkbeds in each cell and a toilet stall in the wall between them. A massive iron door was the only entrance. The door had one barred window about a foot square, too high for the women to reach. They had to move a bed to the door in order to look out. I, along with Anne Rhodenbaugh, visited Jill and Gail in the Pineville Jail shortly after they were imprisoned on April 27. I recall them having to stand on the bed and sort of hang over the window in order to talk to us. Despite the grim conditions, they seemed in buoyant spirits, and we spent much of the visit laughing and joking. I had taken them some homemade chocolate chip cookies, but given the poor food probably should have brought something healthier. Still, despite our attempts to redeem the situation with humor, it was an irredeemably grim, inhumane place. At least, the two had each other for companionship and spent hours in lively conversation, but Gail was wracked by her enforced separation from her lover, Marla, which made her situation all the more intolerable.

At the time many of the Lexington Six supporters worried about the dangers the women faced in jail. The Jo Anne Little case was in progress, reminding everyone how vulnerable imprisoned women are to sexual attacks by jailors. Little was a twenty-year-old African American woman who while serving time in a North Carolina jail had been sexually assaulted by her white jailor, Clarence Allgood. In defending herself on August 27, 1974, Little killed Allgood and escaped. A month later she was indicted for murder. Her trial began on April 14, 1975, and was in full swing while Jill, Gail, Marla, Nancy, and Carey were in jail. Little was eventually acquitted in July 1975 on grounds of justifiable self-defense. (On the Jo Anne Little case, see Angela Davis 1975.)

Although never sexually assaulted, Jill and Gail did have problems with jailors leering at them, so that when they undressed, one would have to hold up a sheet to screen the other. They also had problems with crazy inmates, one woman in particular in an adjacent cell who went on a rampage, banging and kicking on the walls incessantly. While not physically dangerous to them, the episodes were deeply unsettling (Raymond 1987b).

As it turned out, this woman, named Laurie, was an alcoholic in for public drunkenness. At first Jill and Gail failed to realize her addiction, and when she screamed at the warden that she was sick and needed to go to the hospital, the two believed her and paid her bail. But when she returned drunk the next day in worse shape, they realized her condition. But her agitation was so disturbing that they bailed her out again, this time to get rid of her (Raymond 1976a, 9–10).

When Barbara Sutherland, a member of the legal team, saw the "terrible, terrible" conditions in that "dungeon-like" jail, she was appalled. It was far worse than anything she could have imagined, and she began to wonder whether the sacrifice these young people were making was really worth it, considering the long-term effects it could have on their lives. She began having dreams about kittens being killed. "That was my feeling about the Bell County jail": two young innocents in real danger, "at the mercy of whoever was in charge." She came to regret having been involved in encouraging the six not to testify: "Those jails were so awful. They were just awful" (Sutherland 1987).

While they and their supporters worried about the safety of the Lexington Six in jail, some jailors perceived the women, as lesbians, being a threat to other inmates. In the Pineville jail, Jill and Gail found themselves locked off at night in a separate cell from the other women inmates. As this was not a customary practice, one of the inmates—a regular—asked the jailor why they were doing this. He said it was to protect the straight inmates from the two lesbians. In the Franklin County Jail, jailors would warn incoming prisoners to be on their guard lest the lesbians attack them. Happily for Jill, Gail, and the others, their sister cellmates were largely unimpressed by these warnings and generally proved friendly and supportive (Daly and Zakem 1975).

The first thing Marla Seymour and Nancy Scott did when they arrived in their cell in the Franklin County Jail was ask for a mop and disinfectant. They then spent their first day cleaning. As part of the federal building in Frankfort, the Franklin County Jail was less decrepit than Madison County and less dungeon-like than Bell County; however, it had other negative aspects. The cell Marla and Nancy shared was about fifteen feet by fifteen feet and lined with six bunks. With one side entirely open, if barred, it had the feel of a lion's cage in a zoo where you could see everything the animal was doing (Sutherland 1987). There was virtually no privacy. In addition, there was a closed-circuit surveillance camera focused on the cell with a monitor in the trustee's office, so he could watch their every move, including in the shower. "We always felt in danger," Marla recalled, and "real vulnerable" (Seymour 1987b).

On one occasion a jail break occurred and they were afraid the escapee might try to take them hostage because the cell was so prominent and the keys readily available. Every jailor had one. In addition, they received a lot of baiting from the jailors—all of them men—about being lesbian.

A few days after her incarceration, Marla summed up her feelings: devastation at being separated from her lover but feeling a strange sense of defiant victory in their show of resistance. "They've done the worst they could do by separating Gail from me," she wrote, "[but] even at that very dear personal cost—*man* has suffered a defeat and woman, a victory. I've never been more proud to be female; and I've never been more proud of womanlove—displayed in us and our friends" (letter to author, March 13, 1975).

Like Marla, Nancy Scott was separated from her lesbian lover, who remained on the outside and not involved in the case. Nancy had until a year previously considered herself bisexual but had since become a committed lesbian, and indeed a lesbian separatist, refusing to have anything to do with men (letter to author, March 29, 1975). She and Marla decided to uphold a separatist position in jail, prohibiting male visitors and dealing only with women reporters.

Marla's and Nancy's relationship was complicated by the fact that they had had a brief affair earlier, which ended badly, and thus had to work through "some bad feelings" as they found themselves face to face in confinement. But they managed to "reestablish a friendship of sorts" given their shared plight (Seymour 1987b). Marla said the relationship between them became like a bad-roommate situation with completely different sleep schedules and the like. However, they ended up playing canasta together amicably and otherwise managed to make their peace.

When Debbie Hands testified and was released, she faced a bombardment of criticism from radical groups around the country and indeed from some members of the Lexington Six's own defense committee, perhaps eager to be seen as correctly militant in the eyes of the radicals on the East and West Coasts. There was always the fear, as Pam Goldman noted, of being written off as "politically unsophisticated yokels" by radicals in New York or on the West Coast (Goldman 1998, 31).

The issue came to a head in the Lexington Grand Jury Defense Committee over a statement issued by a Trotskyite group called the Seattle Radical Women, which strongly condemned any cooperative testimony before the grand jury and any support for such cooperation, urging the remaining Lexington Five to continue their refusals. The Seattle women thus repudiated the March 19 statement the remaining Lexington Five had issued in support of Hands. Most of the members of the Lexington defense committee were angered by the Seattle women's letter and phone calls, considering that these women knew little and understood less about the local situation. Their condescending, intrusive militancy was not welcome; it reflected, one defense committee member thought, an "insulting" assumption that Kentucky people were "out of it" politically and needed to be educated by the enlightened Seattle women in radical political correctness (Salmon 1987).

Two members of the Lexington defense committee, however, sided with the Seattle Radical Women and wrote a letter, dated April 14, 1975, to the Seattle group criticizing the Lexington committee's support of Hands and disapproving of the position that "it is all right to resist no further than one feels personally able." The letter-writers also found fault with the committee for not having a consistent radical political analysis. In general, as Pam Goldman noted, "The letter seemed to position its authors as more radical than the other defense committee members" (Goldman 1998, 31). In addition, on the occasion of Debbie's release, committee member Mark Paster recalled, the two "hardliners" brutally confronted her in a session he found "real ugly" and "real unfair" (Paster 1987). The hardliners' letter was not well received by the castigated defense committee members, and its authors soon left the committee. Hands, who had borne the brunt of the opprobrium, herself criticized these members of the committee, feeling that they cared more about political principle than about the lives of the resisters (Goldman 1998, 31).

The whole question of collaboration or non-collaboration was given thoughtful consideration by Anne Braden in a letter written to the Lexington defense committee and later reprinted in *Quash*, the newsletter of the Grand Jury Project. Braden was a "movement heavy," to use the lingo of the day, having, along with her husband, Carl Braden, been jailed for civil rights activities in the 1950s. (Carl also served a year in prison in 1958 under a contempt order for refusing to cooperate with a congressional committee, the House Un-American Activities Committee.) Carl and Anne were well known in Kentucky for having defied housing segregation laws in 1954 by fronting for an African American couple's purchase of a home in a white neighborhood in Shively, a Louisville suburb. (After the sale the house was bedecked with Ku Klux Klan flaming crosses on the lawn and dynamited.)

Anne was very supportive of the Lexington Six resisters and wrote them each letters soon after their incarceration in which she expressed "my love, my admiration, and my hand in friendship and support. . . . It takes great courage to take the stand you all took. Anyone who takes such a stand is fighting a battle for all . . . who do not want to live in a police state" (Braden, letter to Jill Raymond, March 11, 1975).

She offered them encouragement, based on her own experience of political resistance and civil disobedience: "I hope you are not discouraged. I know how it is when one is in jail—sometimes it is hard not to feel that too few people outside care. But knowing you are right can be your strength. Also, I know from experience that it often takes time for support to build. . . . But in time it will; I feel sure of that" (Braden, letter to Jill Raymond, March 11, 1975).

Braden's letter-essay, published in *Quash* as "The 50s and Now," was written evidently in response to the noncondemnatory position the Lexington Grand Jury Defense Committee had adopted regarding those of the Lexington Six who ended up cooperating. She stressed the importance of resistance or non-collaboration but also warned against "rejecting or casting out or condemning forever the people who do not measure up to the standards we have set" (Braden 1975).

Those standards, forged in her case during the McCarthy era, she summed up as: "One thing you don't do, under any circumstances [is] to cooperate with the enemy." During the 1950s, she recalled, "All of us in that period went through . . . watching friends, people we trusted, collapse or compromise. And each time it happened we were diminished somewhat as human beings—and each time it did not happen, we were strengthened" (Braden 1975).

For positive models of resistance, she harked back to "our spiritual ancestors," such as the resisters in Nazi Germany or the Soviet Empire. In short, "What I really think boils down to this: . . . people involved in any movement against the power structure need to have a firm position on resistance. Not just to grand juries—but to every form of tyranny by the rulers. . . . We do not believe it is right *ever* to cooperate with the enemy." She ended her statement by taking the long view, a historical perspective: "The struggles of us who live today . . . are part of a whole long chain of strength in human history. To me this is a source of strength—and gives the whole thing meaning" (Braden 1975).

Pressure continued to mount, however, after Debbie Hands's testimony from other outside groups, such as the National Lawyers Guild and the Center for Constitutional Rights, as well as the Seattle Radical Women and the New York feminists who had castigated Jane Alpert. The remaining members of the Lexington Six defense committee decided, in resistance to outside pressure, to support all of the Lexington Six as "individuals with feelings and needs" (Sutherland 1986). They were not abstract symbols who could be sacrificed for political principle or expediency. They were individual people whom committee members knew and loved as family. As Jill Raymond recalled, "it mattered personally" to them "that I was in jail and things happen to us there" (1987b).

In the case of Debbie, committee members such as Sally Kundert knew personally of the agony she had undergone in jail and about her personal history. It did not seem right to judge and condemn a person according to abstract principles when one knew the exonerating circumstances of their unique situation. In this, perhaps unwittingly, the defense commit-tee members who supported Debbie, as well as the remaining Lexington Five, were reasoning in a manner similar to that of the women in Susan Glaspell's celebrated story "A Jury of Her Peers" (1917). In that work, two women silently shield a neighbor who had murdered her husband as they realize the exonerating circumstances that led to her act. The reasoning of the two women has been cited by theorist Carol Gilligan and others as an example of women's personalized "ethic of care," as opposed to a masculine ethic based on abstract principle (see Gilligan 1982). The perspective of the resisters' local supporters, who knew their personal stories, was thus quite different from that of many East and West Coast politicos, who had no personal involvement with the Lexington Six and saw them only in terms of abstract, ironclad political correctness.

The resisters themselves sitting in their jail cells also began receiving mountains of letters from outside groups urging them to continue their resistance. One particularly insistent harasser (as they came to see her) was New York radical feminist Ti-Grace Atkinson, one of the signatories of the March 8 statement against Jane Alpert. Nancy Scott, for example, received a letter from Atkinson in which she "plead[ed] with me . . . to stay in here until the very end. . . . She says that I'm now a 'symbol' and must continue to be that." Nancy commented, "I would replace the word symbol with martyr," but she rejected such martyrdom "as part of the old male left ideology." She nevertheless feared that "if I can't hold out, I'll be written off . . . like Jane Alpert was." Finally, she realized she had to "resolve within myself to stand up for myself—not only to the 'Man,' but also to other 'feminists.' I am myself and refuse to be dictated by *anyone*—no matter *who* they may be" (letter to author, April 30, 1975)—showing thus the spirited resolve that animated her resistance in the first place. Marla Seymour too recalled how the group received insistent phone calls and letters from Atkinson and other outside pressure groups but they "didn't affect one way or another. If I did something it was because something moved me," not in reaction to pressure from others (1987b). Carey Junkin also resented the pressure he was receiving from peripheral groups "who didn't understand what facing jail was like" nor the conditions in the Kentucky county jails. When they called, he said, he "blew up at them," angered at their condescension, how "they treated me like a child" (1987).

Since she lived in Seattle, Jill Raymond's sister Laurie attempted to explain the position of the Lexington Six in supporting Debbie Hands to a meeting of the Seattle Radical Women. About a hundred members of the group were in attendance when Laurie tried to clarify the Lexington

Six's "decision to support the subpoenaed witnesses if/when they decided to testify." But she was "shouted down" by the crowd, "booed and drowned out whenever I tried to contest their argument." Laurie was shocked at this hostile reception; she hadn't realized "how hard line they were about the absolute necessity of resistance to the point of martyrdom" (email to author, March 22, 2018).

The sad result of the harsh injunctions the Lexington Six resisters were receiving from outside groups was that they were coming to feel attacked from both sides: from the FBI and the judiciary on the one hand and from ostensible allies on the other. Jill Raymond addressed the issue in a statement published in *off our backs*, reflecting the painful effect this "friendly fire" was having on the Lexington Six. "We cannot," she warned, "become even more frightening to each other than the state is" (Raymond 1975a).

Late one Thursday afternoon, on March 27, 1975, Val Woolf (aka Aileen A. Hellman and Lena Paley) was walking down a Philadelphia street holding hands with her new lover, Byrna Aronson. They were headed to dinner at a nearby Chinese restaurant. Suddenly, a police car stopped across the street and the patrolman, Joseph Reid, approached them. "Excuse me," he said. "Would you tell me your name?" "Val Woolf" was the reply. "That's funny," he said, "you look a lot like someone I just had a briefing on, someone named Saxbe [*sic*]" (Wood 1975b). He then told them they would have to be taken in for questioning. In the squad car Byrna noticed that her companion looked uneasy and her hands were trembling. She made an effort to reassure her, but Val tried to open the car door and jump out. After this failed attempt at escape, the two were handcuffed.

Byrna, an out lesbian, had gone through this before and thought it was just routine police harassment of lesbians and gays. She had been arrested herself several years previously for kissing her lover in a gay bar. "You are under arrest," she was told. "What for? Sodomy" (Cooper 1975). But during the ride to the police station in the squad car, Byrna learned the truth: Val Woolf was Susan Saxe. The realization came as a shock. Byrna knew who Saxe was and how she had been a fugitive for over four years. Now, sitting next to her in the car, the woman "I loved and knew as Val," turned out to be the "most wanted" Susan Saxe.

In response to a memo issued by the new FBI director, Clarence Kelley, on March 11, 1975, the FBI had intensified the search for Saxe and Power, still on the FBI's "Ten Most Wanted" fugitive list. New posters of the two were issued on March 11 with relatively recent photos of Saxe and Power, including one of Saxe taken by a bank surveillance camera in Torrington, Connecticut, while cashing an unemployment check under the name Aileen Hellman in 1973. Kelley's memo warned that the two "should be considered extremely dangerous" (FBI, March 11, 1975).

On March 25, two days before Saxe's arrest, the FBI "detained" an unidentified woman in Philadelphia who "had been observed walking with SUSAN EDITH SAXE." This person "denied knowing true identity of SAXE or SAXE's present residence. [She] also denied knowing KATHERINE ANN POWER." The heavily redacted FBI memo, obtained through a FOIA request, further mentions some "letters, furnished to FBI laboratory for handwriting and latent print comparison" (FBI, May 13, 1975). The letters, which were from Saxe to Kathy Power about the 1970 bank robbery in Massachusetts, were possibly the letters thought to have been turned over to the FBI by Jim, Carol Romano's ex-husband, the Hartford informer. The letters were evidently identified in the FBI lab as being in Saxe's handwriting (Horan 1975). Once in custody, however, Saxe refused to give them a handwriting sample. When threatened with contempt, she replied, "What's [the judge] going to do put me in jail?" (FBI, May 13, 1975).

So the FBI in Philadelphia had for several days been on high alert for Susan Saxe, based in part on the information given them by this unknown woman. In addition, there must have been an even earlier informant or tipster who advised the FBI that this woman had been seen with Saxe. Reid, the policeman who accosted Saxe and Aronson and arrested them, claimed he had studied the newly issued "Wanted by the FBI" poster a couple of hours before he saw them on the Philadelphia street. The FBI claimed that Reid's encounter with the two was but a "lucky break" (Wood 1975b), but this was clearly not the case. They had actually been on to Saxe's presence in the area for at least several days. Many suspected that Reid had targeted the area around Aronson's office at the American Civil Liberties Union where she worked. It seemed likely that the ACLU phones were tapped by the FBI because Susan had called Byrna to suggest the dinner date just a few hours before the arrest. And, since the new bank surveillance photo on the poster was extremely fuzzy, it seemed unlikely a patrolman would have recognized Saxe and identified her from that picture alone.

In any event, Susan Saxe was now in custody, held on a $350,000 bail bond with an arraignment hearing set for April 7. The FBI director immediately issued an all-points teletype bulletin:

SUSAN EDITH SAXE . . . TOP TEN FUGITIVE, APPREHENDED BY PHILADELPHIA POLICE OFFICE. . . . DISCONTINUE EFFORTS TO LOCATE. ALL OUT EFFORTS SHOULD CONTINUE TO LOCATE TOP TEN FUGITIVE KATHERINE ANN POWER. (FBI, March 27, 1975)

The next day, the FBI issued another teletype memo marked "URGENT" with more details: "SUBJECT, AT TIME OF ARREST WAS USING NAME AILEEN A. HELLMAN, 320 CENTRAL AVENUE, NO., 4E, WHITE PLAINS, N.Y." She had in her possession a New York driver's license, a White Plains YMCA receipt, and a public library card: "CURRENT DESCRIPTION, 5'4", 144 LBS., RED HAIR, HAZEL EYES (WITH DOT OUTSIDE LEFT PUPIL)" (FBI, March 28, 1975).

Shortly after Susan's formal arrest, Byrna Aronson was released and appeared on the courthouse steps to read a statement to the press that Susan had hastily scribbled on a yellow legal pad. Wearing her signature studded leather bulldog collar, Byrna read this message:

First, a greeting to all my sisters. Courage, especially to all of my sisters underground in America. Stay free. Stay strong. I intend to fight on in every way as a lesbian, a feminist and an amazon.

Four years ago I was charged with a series of crimes against property, against the state, against the man.

They called me a "dangerous" woman. Dangerous to whom? To my people? To the sisters I love? No, only to the vicious patriarchal authority that kills, despoils and rapes in every corner of the world.

The love that I share with my sisters, my people, is a far more powerful weapon than any the police state can bring to bear against us. It reaches through all their walls, all their lives, and, yes, that love is "dangerous" to them

Keep growing, keep strong. I am a free woman and I can keep
strong. Pass the word: I am unafraid. (Wood and Anglin 1975)

The first and fourth paragraphs of the statement were circulated as a
message from Saxe to her "sisters" and published as an all-caps bulletin
in feminist journals, signed "Susan Saxe, City of Brotherly Love" (Saxe
1975a), an ironic take, of course, on the traditional epithet for Philadelphia.
Posters of Saxe with quotations from the statement were eventually widely
circulated (see Hobson 2016, 60).

After Susan Saxe was arrested, the FBI harassment of the lesbian-feminist
community in Philadelphia continued. The word *harassment* is given advis-
edly, because it is the term the FBI itself used for the Philadelphia operation. In a conversation with Byrna Aronson on April 2 at the Philadelphia
police headquarters, the FBI chief investigator, Don Egleston, told her
that the "lesbian feminist community" could "anticipate further FBI
and Philadelphia police harassment." Egleston immediately realized his
Freudian slip and corrected himself: "No, I shouldn't say that. I mean
further *intensive investigation* of your community" (Anonymous 1975e).

Egleston was true to his inadvertent word. Shortly thereafter, Aronson,
Jane Cooper, and Pam Murray were arrested by the police after an evening
of leafleting gay/lesbian bars about FBI harassment and grand jury abuse.
(Cooper said there were more FBI agents than lesbians in the bars.) The
police thought Murray was Kathy Power, whom she evidently considerably resembled. (Murray herself said that recent photos of Power looked
more like her than her own IDs.) The three were released about 3:30 a.m.
after the FBI realized they had the wrong woman (Flower 1975a). But
the FBI continued their siege of the community, going so far as to rent
an apartment just below Aronson's. Members of the local NOW chapter
were startled to find four patrol cars and a paddy wagon parked outside
a meeting (Anonymous 1975d). The FBI and the police seemed to think
that Kathy Power was still in Philadelphia — an improbable assumption.
Philadelphia was probably the last place on earth Power was likely to be
hanging out. Kathy Power was long gone.

Back in Kentucky, Jill Raymond and Gail Cohee were idly watching
Walter Cronkite on the CBS newscast that evening in late March on the one,

local channel their set received in their Pineville jail cell when they were shocked to see photos of the woman they had known as Lena Paley flash on the screen. Susan Saxe had been arrested in Philadelphia. To see "her being carted off in handcuffs" was very painful, Jill recalled (Raymond 1987b).

Watching the news show that evening with Jill and Gail were two other inmates who happened to be in the Bell County Jail—both poor, white, Appalachia women—one in for car theft, the other for public drunkenness. The latter, Laurie, the one they eventually bailed out, expressed admiration for Saxe, especially after hearing her "lesbian-feminist-amazon" statement. Laurie, reflecting perhaps the Appalachian clan loyalty code, said, "she thought people shouldn't ever talk to police about their friends"—thus tacitly supporting the Lexington Six's refusal to do so (Raymond 1976a, 9).

Over in the Franklin County Jail where Marla and Nancy were held, when the news came of the Saxe arrest, the jailors began taunting them. But Nancy responded defiantly: "We're feeling stronger than ever, coupled with feelings of rage and fear. We'll manage though" (letter to author, March 29, 1975). Marla felt deeply saddened on a personal level as she considered Saxe's fate: "I felt bad. I felt real bad that she had been captured. I knew her personally and she was in for a rough go. I was scared for her" (Seymour 1987b). But after reading Susan's defiant statement, she felt reassured.

Carey Junkin had a different reaction to the Saxe arrest. "After Susan was arrested," he reflected, "there didn't seem to be a point" in remaining in lockup any longer. "I'd been in jail for a month [actually three weeks]. I knew I had no information that could hurt anybody." So he decided to testify. He felt guilty about doing so but felt it was "silly to be a martyr for no reason. It made no sense to stay" (Junkin 1987). Another factor in Carey's decision was that on March 27, the same day as Saxe was arrested, the Sixth Circuit Court of Appeals, which handled Kentucky's federal district cases, turned down the Lexington Six's plea for bail. So their incarceration was destined to last another several weeks at best or even months until the appeal decision was made—their last hope for reprieve.

Unlike the Lexington Six women, who had received solid support from the Lexington and national feminist communities, Carey had gotten little support from the gay men's community, and he felt psychologically as well as physically isolated. The only real support he received came from his

Lexington Six sisters, who, despite the separatist inclinations of some of them, eventually embraced him as a brother. "When they realized I was in it for the long run," he later recalled, "the women accepted me. I was part of the family." In the end, Carey felt he had learned a lot from the women, who educated him about feminism in the course of the grand jury process, as well as about issues of class, race, and homophobia. "It made me a much more whole person," he reflected (Junkin 1987).

But he received no support from his family and little from the gay men's community, including his partner of the time, who cooperated with the FBI. "Most of my support," Carey ruefully acknowledged, "came from inside myself" (Junkin 1987). Lexington gay men's community was in fact traumatized and terrorized by the FBI dragnet that spread through it in the early months of 1975. Not only was sodomy a crime but being outed to one's employer could mean a lost job; to one's family, shame and expulsion; and to the press, beatings and harassment. Hence "low profile was a matter of survival for a lot of gay men." It was not, one gay activist sardonically recalled, "a fashionable thing to be gay at that time" (Hackney 1989).

Most gay men were reluctant to openly support Carey or the Lexington Six for fear of being themselves revealed as gay. The community was not politically organized—that came later with the AIDS epidemic that decimated the gay community nationwide in succeeding decades. The only local community institution at the time was an apolitical gay bar, the Montparnasse. Without a sense of communal solidarity, it was generally every man for himself; the instinct was to avoid trouble and focus on self-protection. Being openly gay was already a risky political statement in Lexington, Kentucky, in the 1970s. "To say 'I'm gay. I'm not ashamed of it. I'm going to live anyway'" was "a pretty big step" at the time, Peter Taylor, a gay activist, observed. Many felt that that in itself was a sufficient political act. It was also the case that Carey, seen as a flamboyant, ostentatious self-promoter by some, was not particularly popular in the gay community, another factor in their lack of support (Taylor 1987).

Taylor, speaking perhaps for the community at large, felt the resistance of the Lexington Six was pointless, and that they were being conned by left-wing lawyers and outside pressure groups "pursuing their own agenda." He felt "they were being made fools of. . . . I felt sorry for them." Taylor, who knew Jill, felt "really sorry for her. I felt she was a victim. I failed to see how spending X months in jail did [her] any good" (Taylor 1987).

Carey thus after the Saxe arrest notified his attorney that he was ready to purge himself of contempt by testifying before the grand jury. "The boredom, loneliness and repression just got to me," he explained, "and I was afraid of the serious damage that was being done to me physically and mentally" (Junkin 1975). A motion to purge was filed on March 28, and Carey was released on recognizance, ordered to appear on March 31 before the grand jury. The questions he received that day were different from the ones he had fielded in earlier sessions. Now they seemed to be focused on Patty Hearst, the Symbionese Liberation Army (SLA), and the Weather Underground—about which Carey knew nothing. That two members of the SLA were lesbian lovers—Camilla Hall and Mizmoon (Patricia Soltysik)—likely fueled the FBI theory that there was an underground network of violent radical lesbians. Indeed, in their search for Patty Hearst and other SLA members, the FBI had carried out a dragnet in San Francisco in 1974 that prefigured the one carried out several months later in Lexington—and may have provided a model for the tactics used therein. It featured "several raids of lesbian feminist households and community spaces" and "plainclothes [agents] in the bars and everywhere lesbians went" (Hobson 2016, 55).

The Lexington grand jurors also asked Carey Junkin about his "sexual activity," a question by then superfluous as he had long been openly gay. Carey refused to answer some of the questions and attempted to "make the feds look foolish" for having spent "all that money and effort for nothing," for he in truth had nothing pertinent to say (Junkin 1987). On April 1, 1975, Junkin was officially held by the judge to be "no longer in contempt by virtue of the fact that he has purged himself of contempt for which he was adjudged on March 8, 1975 and is released from custody of the United States Marshal" (Transcript 1975, Docket List, 2). The same day, U.S. Attorney Eugene Siler informed the FBI that Junkin "did not provide any information which would be of lead value" (FBI, April 1, 1975), corroborating Carey's assertion, and clearly indicating, once again, that the U.S. attorney was using the grand jury to elicit "leads" for the FBI in its quest for already-indicted fugitives—an improper use of the grand jury, as contended by Robert Sedler in the appeals litigation.

Also on April 1, up in Connecticut Ellen Grusse and Terri Turgeon were released from the Niantic prison, as the New Haven grand jury term expired. However, the moment they stepped outside the prison, the same marshal who had released them served them with a new subpoena to appear on May 6 before the newly empaneled grand jury.

A week later, on April 7, Susan Saxe was arraigned in Philadelphia. When Susan saw the fifty or so supporters gathered in the courtroom, she smiled and gave them a power fist. In entering a not-guilty plea, "She held her head high and spoke clearly. 'Isn't she strong and self-confident?' someone said. 'She's so charismatic,' another said" (Flower 1975b). Elaine Lafferty, a reporter for *Majority Report*, recorded how moved she was by Susan's show of strength that day: "While at this time I cannot say that as a lesbian feminist movement person I fully support the actions of Susan Saxe, while sitting in that courtroom hearing her vs. the United States government, I felt much solidarity with her" (Lafferty 1975b). Outside the courthouse supporters sang the old radical song "Give Me Bread and Roses" and another song written for the occasion about resisting the FBI with sisterly solidarity (Flower 1975b), adapted from the union anthem "Solidarity Forever."

CHAPTER SIX

Collaboration versus Resistance

At the same time as Susan Saxe was being arraigned in Philadelphia, a hearing was being held in Monterey, California, in another case that raised the issue of women turning to violence. Inez Garcia was an illiterate Cuban–Puerto Rican who was raped in March 1974 by two men, Luiz Castillo and Miguel Jiminez. The latter, who weighed three hundred pounds, held her down while the other carried out the rape. About a half hour later, one of them called Garcia and tauntingly told her they were coming back to do much worse. Inez grabbed a rifle and, as she later reported, "I loaded it and went out into the street looking for those two creeps. I'd have walked all night to find them. I said I was going to kill them and I did" (Fosburgh 1975).

Garcia was arrested on March 19, 1974. Her trial began in September. At one point during the several weeks' long trial, an unrepentant Inez burst out, "I killed the son-of-a-bitch because I was raped and I'd kill him again" (Bernikow 2008). When the judge ordered her to return to her seat, she screamed at the bailiffs, "Pigs! Take your hands off me!" (Brownmiller 1999, 281). Later, under cross-examination, Inez reiterated, "I'm not sorry I did it. . . . The only thing I'm sorry about is that I missed Luis the rapist" (Jordan 2000, 202). (She had killed Jiminez but missed Castillo.)

Garcia was convicted of second-degree murder on October 4 and given a sentence on October 21 of from five years to life in prison. Feminists rallied to her defense, especially after a jury member reportedly said, "A rapist is just trying to give her a good time" (Bernikow 2008). On February 7, 1975, a demonstration of more than three hundred of her supporters took place at San Francisco City Hall in which thirty-two women and six men were arrested. The protesters also presented a petition signed by 1,500 people to Governor Jerry Brown demanding Garcia's release. Many of her supporters were lesbians and gays (one of the signs at the demonstration was "Faggots against Rape"), protesting culturally sanctioned brutality against women and gay men. Garcia later thanked the lesbian and gay community by marching in the San Francisco gay pride parade in June 1976 (she was out on bail with a second trial pending) (Hobson 2016, 74).

Garcia's conviction was overturned by the California Court of Appeals on technical grounds on December 29, 1975. A second trial in which feminist attorney Susan Jordan, an associate at the Center for Constitutional Rights, forged a self-defense plea ended in acquittal on March 5, 1977. Inez's case solidified the foundation for the "battered women's defense," which was used to exonerate women like Jo Anne Little who killed their attackers and rapists in self-defense. While Inez's actions bordered on revenge, the fact that Miguel had threatened her and had a knife when she confronted him sufficed to justify a self-defense plea. A parallel case at the time involved Yvonne Wanrow, a Native American woman who killed a man who had molested her son and raped the daughter of a friend. Wanrow's conviction of second-degree murder was overturned by the Washington Supreme Court in 1977, further establishing the legitimacy of the self-defense pleas for battered or threatened women.

By the mid-1970s, feminists were coming to view all these women—Jo Anne Little, Inez Garcia, Yvonne Wanrow, Jane Alpert, Pat Swinton, Susan Saxe, the Lexington Six, and the New Haven lesbians—in political terms as victims of a patriarchal order that had unjustly persecuted them. Those who were imprisoned were seen as "political prisoners" (Hobson 2016, 62), and their defiance of the state celebrated as a political act.

Susan Saxe's fiery statement of defiance—not unlike Inez Garcia's unflinching refusal to repent—on her arrest in Philadelphia on March

27, 1975, fit into this narrative, but it also served to reignite the smoldering controversy surrounding Jane Alpert. Some came to see Saxe as the anti–Jane Alpert, one who instead of repudiating the male-dominated New Left, refused to do so, still implicitly maintaining that the violent actions taken in the antiwar struggle were justified, given the monstrous activities of the U.S. military in the Vietnam War and the repressive imperialistic policies of the U.S. government elsewhere. In many statements, Saxe linked lesbian-feminism with the overall struggle against U.S. imperialism and oppression. Today, the term *intersectionality* is used to convey the idea that people often hold more than one vilified identity, that these oppressions are linked, such that oppressed groups—women, LGBT people, racial and ethnic minorities, and Third World resistance groups—should work together to fight against their common oppressors.

In a statement later read at a fundraiser for African American activist Assata Shakur, Saxe amplified her intersectional theory: "I think it's so important to show that the white women's movement understands the connection between our liberation as women and the need to struggle against all forms of oppression. . . . Women everywhere are oppressed by sexism, but the vast majority of women in this world are also suffering under the burdens of racism, imperialism, and class oppression. There is no way we will ever be free by casting off just one of these oppressions" (Saxe 1976).

The term *Amazon* with which Saxe identified herself in her arrest statement referred to the legendary women warriors of ancient Greece. The term had become current in the early 1970s among American radical feminists; Ti-Grace Atkinson used it in the title of her 1974 collection of essays, *Amazon Odyssey,* and feminist theologian Mary Daly described a radical feminist as an "Amazon Voyager" in her *Gyn/Ecology: The Metaethics of Radical Feminism* (1978), the cover of which featured a labyris, the double-headed axe allegedly favored by ancient Amazons.

Saxe herself emphasized the contrast between herself and Jane Alpert in a lengthy statement issued on June 9, 1975, the day she pled guilty to federal charges connected to the Philadelphia bank robbery and theft of government documents (the Newburyport Armory job) in a plea deal. (The more serious felony-murder charge related to the Brighton robbery would be tried later in a Massachusetts state court.) In her statement, Saxe noted that "a deep and significant split has developed in the women's movement. On the one hand are women who like Jane Alpert feel that the Amerikan System can peacefully accommodate their feminist demands and that women as women have no obligation to support or protect any peoples' struggle that is not explicitly feminist in ideology or even separatist in practice. These women feel that it is permissible, even desirable, to collaborate with the state" (Saxe 1975b).

Saxe thus repudiated Alpert and appeared to reject those who advocated a separate women's movement apart from the New Left—as many radical feminists, including Roxanne Dunbar, Dana Densmore, Barbara Burris, Kate Millett, Robin Morgan, Susan Brownmiller, Shulamith Firestone, and many others—did (Donovan 2012, 139–45). It is misleading, however, to telescope feminists who repudiated the New Left, supporters of Jane Alpert, and so-called collaborators, implying thereby that anti–New-Left feminists or supporters of Alpert advocated collaboration. Most radical feminists, ironically, would have agreed with Saxe's underlying message that feminists in repudiating the New Left should not dissociate themselves from other liberation struggles. Lesbian separatism meant to most adherents separation from men, not from women in other oppressed groups. Many, if not most, feminists of the 1970s—whether "radical" or "socialist"—emerged out of the civil rights and antiwar movements and had been active therein. They were thus very cognizant of race and Third World oppressions and were sympathetic with and supportive of African American and Third World liberation movements, as recent works by Benita Roth (2004) and Becky Thompson (2001) have demonstrated.

To further point up the contrast with Alpert, Saxe proclaimed in her statement, "I am not and will never be a collaborator." Her recent emergence as "a feminist, a lesbian, a woman-identified woman" was not a "conversion" (as Alpert characterized her similar feminist awakening) but rather "a development, a natural process that followed my previous commitment as day follows night." Moreover, unlike Alpert, Saxe continued to remain unrepentant for the actions she took as a member of the New Left, still feeling, as she did in 1970 when she engaged in armed robbery for the cause, "that armed struggle against the Amerikan state was a valid and necessary escalation. . . . I understood at the time that the Amerikan Government was the most dangerous, powerful, organized violent opponent of peoples' liberation around the world." She refused, in short, "to repudiate our past" (Saxe 1975b).

The plea bargain that Saxe made with the Philadelphia court included an agreement by the government that she "will never testify against Kathy Power or give any information concerning anyone I have known or known about in the past five years." The government moreover "agreed to end the investigation in Philadelphia": "no grand juries, no harboring prosecutions, no legal torture of sisters who refuse to speak to the FBI" (Saxe 1975b). Under this deal Saxe was sentenced to ten or more years in prison, to be served concurrently with the likely much longer—possibly life without parole—sentence expected in the Boston case.

Saxe considered these concessions by the government, negotiated by her feminist lawyer Catherine Roraback, to be a "victory," the credit for which "goes to the feminist community here and to the sisters in New Haven, Connecticut, and Lexington, Kentucky, whose courage in the face of FBI and government harassment has been an example to us all." "Feminism," she concluded, in tribute to the New Haven women and the Lexington Six, "is not collaboration. Ellen Grusse, Terri Turgeon and Diana Perkins in New Haven, Gail Cohee, Debbie Hands, [Nancy Scott], Jill Raymond, Marla Seymour and . . . Carey Junkin in Lexington have shown us the way" (Saxe 1975b). Indeed, it was the resistance of the Lexington Six and the Connecticut women that helped to alert the Philadelphia community about the FBI's intrusive behavior and the need to stand up to it. Because of their example, circulated in a rapidly deployed information campaign, no one in the Philadelphia lesbian-feminist community cooperated.

In an interview published in the May–June 1975 issue of *off our backs* (but given before her January sentencing), Jane Alpert denied that she had collaborated or ratted on people in the movement. In the print edition of the journal the interview was placed adjacent to the reported grand jury testimony of Debbie Hands (Grimstad and Rennie 1975). As Hands had been, like Alpert, accused of collaboration (some even claimed, falsely, that her testimony had led to Saxe's arrest), an inadvertent and unfortunate guilt-by-association was operative in the layout.

Her "cooperation," Alpert specified in the interview, meant "simply supplying the Government with details of my *own* life as a fugitive, involving no one else at all, but merely demonstrating that my life underground had been legal and respectable." As she had in "Mother Right," Alpert continued to repudiate the Marxist ideology of the New Left as having little to offer women and the "Patriarchal" character of the movement: "The Left is hopelessly male in outlook. . . . So certainly . . . my conversion to radical feminism was a repudiation of men and the way they relate to women. But it was also, on a philosophical level, a repudiation of the Left and Marxism as an ideology. The Left does not deal with, cannot deal with the essential paradigm of power in human society, which is the sexual relationship between men and women. Until we break the back of that power relationship, as Shulamith Firestone pointed out . . . , there is not revolution worth talking about" (Grimstad and Rennie 1975). Alpert iterated here radical feminist theory—that the foundational oppression in the world is that of men over women, not capitalism, as held in the Marxist ideology of the New Left. Firestone had laid out this theory in her groundbreaking *Dialectic of Sex: The Case for Feminist Revolution* (1970).

In "Mother Right" Alpert also advanced what has come to be called "cultural feminist" theory—the idea that women have a culture of their own rooted in a feminine or maternal ethic that values "empathy, intuitiveness, adaptability . . . protective feelings toward others and a capacity to respond emotionally as well as rationally." More controversially, Alpert rooted women's different culture in *"female biology,"* which she defined as "the *capacity* to bear and nurture children." Alpert looked to ancient "gynocracies or women-ruled societies" as models, arguing that a feminist revolution "must be an affirmation of the power of female consciousness, of the Mother" (Alpert 1973, 92, 91, 94), which has been occluded, she amplified in the interview, "by wholesale burnings, persecutions, killings—and the thought of the Enlightenment. Socialist philosophy itself—Marx, Lenin, and the rest of them—grew directly out of this kind of super-rationalist misogyny" (Grimstad and Rennie 1975).

The contrasting positions of Saxe and Alpert have come to be seen by some historians, notably Alice Echols, as a split between radical feminism and cultural feminism with Saxe representing the former and Alpert the latter (Echols 1989, 262–65). However, this is incorrect: Alpert expressed *both* radical feminist *and* cultural feminist positions, and Saxe in her continuing endorsement of New Left ideology was a socialist or anti-imperialist feminist rather than a radical feminist.

Because they linked women's subjugation with the oppression of peoples in colonized countries, placing both in the context of Western imperialism, socialist feminists have in recent years been relabeled "anti-imperialist" feminists: "For white anti-imperialist feminists . . . the key was to put women's issues in the overall context of anti-imperialism . . . connect[ing] issues of racism and sexism at home with US's larger imperialist efforts to thwart self-determination for peoples of colour" (Berger 2016, 760). This vein of feminism incorporated Marxist-socialist critiques of capitalism but also condemned racism, which is largely ignored in Marxist theory. While these feminists repudiated the sexism and misogyny of male-dominated anti-imperialist groups, they remained willing to work with, if not in, them. This was Susan Saxe's position.

Saxe's insistence that her emergence as a feminist was not a "conversion"—unlike Alpert's—emphasized her allegiance to her socialist-Marxist ideological roots. The split between the Alpert supporters and the Saxe camp was thus a split between, on the one hand, radical and liberal feminists who were sympathetic to Alpert's position, and, on the other hand, what were called "politicos" at the time—those who endorsed Saxe's view, which remained that of the anti-imperialist, anticolonialist left, holding that economic domination—capitalism—was the root cause of all oppression, not male domination of women, patriarchy. Some socialist feminists endeavored to bridge the gap between the two theoretical positions but these attempts were not entirely successful (see Donovan 2012, 74–87).

A number of prominent lesbian feminists, notably Jill Johnston and Barbara Deming, were uncomfortable with Saxe's perceived linkage of lesbianism with past New Left violence. Johnston wrote a widely circulated piece on the subject in the April 28, 1975, issue of the *Village Voice*, "The Myth of Bonnies without Clydes: Lesbian Feminism and the Male Left" (Johnston 1975). Published in the center of the article's layout was an already iconic photo of Saxe being arrested. The reference to Bonnie and Clyde in the article's title referred to the popular 1960s film *Bonnie and Clyde* (1967) starring Faye Dunaway and Warren Beatty, in which they played highly romanticized versions of legendary 1930s bank robbers. The implicit characterization of Saxe and Power as "Bonnies without Clydes" was, however, inaccurate since there were three Clydes involved with Saxe and Power, the Bonnies, in the Brighton bank robbery.

In the article Johnston claimed that any linkage between lesbians and violence only fed into the FBI-fueled media narrative that a network of lesbian groups were harboring fugitives like Patty Hearst (still at large), as well as Saxe, Power, and others: "The isolated women here and there who've befriended them as fugitives become" in the media coverage "'lesbian communes' with overtones of violent revolution." Such "negative attention," Johnston claimed, tarred the lesbian and feminist movement and impeded progress (Johnston 1975).

New Left women who had recently become feminists but were once reportedly involved in various acts of violence, such as Saxe and Power, as well as Alpert and the Weatherwomen—Bernadine Dohrn, Kathy Boudin, and Diana Oughton—became "an interesting liability" to the feminist movement in that they reinforced in the public mind the association of feminism with violent revolution. In fact, she argued, lesbianism had nothing to do with the Brighton bank robbery; indeed, "there's no essential connection between sexual activity and political persuasion" (Johnston 1975)—here clearly rejecting any notion of linkage among oppressions and any assertion of lesbianism as a political identity. The latter position seems particularly naive given the obvious fact that gays and lesbians had been routinely persecuted for centuries because of their sexual identity.

In response, the Susan Saxe Defense Fund committee countered by insisting that being a lesbian is by definition to mark oneself as a political subject: "If not by our own identification, then by the actions of the FBI, the Department of Justice, and the news media, we have all become identified as 'dangerous women' because of our lifestyles, our private lives, and our politics" (Susan Saxe Defense Fund 1975).

Johnston concluded her Bonnie-and-Clyde piece by turning the term *cooperation* against those attacking Alpert and others for allegedly doing so. In reality, it was, she argued, the women in the male-dominated New Left who were the cooperators—cooperating with the sons against the fathers, "help[ing] the sons undo the fathers who in turn oppress the sisters. . . . This cooperation with the sons is as ancient as the origin of patriarchy." Violent revolution to overthrow the fathers is not what feminism is about, Johnston averred. Rather, a feminist revolution "is a glacial process of unknown cell structures that will evolve out of shared bits of profoundly internalized consciousness. . . . It's the feminism you never read about in the papers" (Johnston 1975).

Barbara Deming, another prominent lesbian feminist activist, defended Jane Alpert in an open letter published in *off our backs* to Susan Sherman, one of the signatories of the original attack on Alpert. The title of Deming's article—"To Fear Jane Alpert Is to Fear Ourselves"—sums up her thesis: that the huge outcry Alpert evoked in the women of the New Left suggested that she represented something they deeply feared. "Isn't Jane Alpert, too, there inside you, inside all of us?" Deming seems to imply that what the anti-Alpert women actually feared was to repudiate men, as Alpert had done. The claim that feminists should ally with all oppressed peoples obscures the fact, Deming maintained, that "women for centuries and centuries have been allowed to be *only* identified with, acknowledged as human being (the kind called 'real women') *only* in so far as we identified with others." The anger directed at Alpert was therefore misplaced "anger at men for treating us a mere extensions of themselves. Anger at ourselves—for allowing them to do this" (Deming 1975).

In her essay Deming pointed up the complexities of the New Left women's identities—part of which connected to their past "cooperation" (to reprise Johnston's use of the term) with sexist and misogynist men. In their confusion and anger about that past, she contended, they were lashing out at the purveyor of its truth, Jane Alpert. They feared the revelation of their own complicity. Instead, Deming argued, feminists needed to acknowledge that men had "invaded our being" (a point Ti-Grace Atkinson made in her article "Metaphysical Cannibalism"): "They stole from us our mother right." Deming concluded thus on a maternalist note, joining with Alpert in arguing that women needed "to remember . . . that we were born of . . . our mothers" and all "seek a communication with one another than can be learned . . . from that bond that existed with our mothers" (Deming 1975).

Another lesbian feminist who weighed in briefly on the question of lesbian feminism's relationship to the New Left was Rita Mae Brown, the author of a popular lesbian novel *Rubyfruit Jungle* (1973). Brown came down on the side of those feminists who advocated dissociation from the New Left. "We don't need them at all," she proclaimed. "They will drag us down into the pits with them. We need a strong and independent movement" (Brown 1975).

On Susan Saxe, Brown agreed with Jill Johnston that Saxe's lesbianism or feminism had nothing to do with her antiwar bank robbery: "These women, Susan Saxe, for example, did not commit their crimes as part of our movement. That was before feminism." Like Johnston, Brown feared that the powers-that-be "will try to incapacitate us" by draining the movement's energy in endless court battles and by establishing in the public mind a link between violence and feminism. "They will try to get us to identify with these women," she wrote. Still, Brown refused to "condemn" Saxe and others "for their crimes; it is difficult to call robbing a bank a crime when we pay Richard Nixon $60,000 a year to be a crook" (Brown 1975).

Upset about Jill Johnston's and Rita Mae Brown's pieces, Jill Raymond wrote a lengthy statement in support of Susan Saxe's position, published in the *Susan Saxe Defense Committee Newsletter,* in which she maintained that feminists should not deny their New Left radical roots "disclaiming our past." After all, back in 1965, she wrote, it was the rebellion of the women in the Students for a Democratic Society against the sexism of their male cohorts that gave birth to radical feminism. In accepting responsibility for her past actions, Saxe was challenging radicals to own their actions and thereby take their political beliefs seriously: "What we may be being asked [by Susan Saxe] to do is stare right down into the seriousness of all our political goals, and hopes, and struggles, and attempts, and understand that we are inevitably bound up to the fate of other people who share this seriousness" (Raymond 1976b).

Raymond thus favored Saxe's anti-imperialist position and rejected feminist separatism. She also, in refuting Jill Johnston, maintained that *lesbian* was inevitably a political identity: "Lesbianism does, by its existence in a patriarchal culture, do violence to the status quo," and the officials of the state and legal system — as guardians of the status quo — know this. Indeed, Raymond noted, governing authorities don't distinguish among the various challengers to the status quo — whether one is "a lesbian, a lesbian separatist, a hippie, a Black, a Trotskyist, a pacifist, a weatherman, a lost freshman English major at the University of Kentucky, Susan Saxe, or Alison Krause" (the latter an unarmed antiwar demonstrator killed by a National Guardsman at Kent State). All are lumped together as dangerous threats by governing authorities. So, "on that day back in September of 1970 when Saxe, Power,

Valeri, Gilday, and Bond allegedly pulled their bank job . . . if you think they were hunting Saxe, Power, Valeri, Gilday, and Bond . . . you have a dangerous case of tunnel vision. They were hunting for us" (Raymond 1976b).

Other members of the Lexington Six were more inclined toward a separatist radical feminist position. Nancy Scott wrote, "To me patriarchy *is* the root of all evil—more basic than economics as many socialist feminists would say" (letter to author, April 12, 1975). Many of the "radical women of leftist men" "cannot seem to shake the language and concepts of men" (letter to author, April 30, 1975). She claimed she would "relish . . . seeing in my lifetime" the "eventual crumble" of "patriarchal society." Her utopian state would be a matriarchy veering toward anarchy with a socialist economy (letter to author, March 29, 1975).

Marla Seymour resisted any kind of accommodationist or assimilationist feminism, which Saxe and others accused Alpert of: "Revolutionary womanhood and lesbianism seem so very much one to me. . . . I hate to see feminism become a civil-rightsy movement. . . . Asking the man who rapes our minds and bodies" to define us and allow us in is not acceptable (letter to author, March 29, 1975).

While all these heavy political debates were going on, the Lexington Six felt ambivalent at best about being used as symbolic icons in the discussion. Their more pressing concerns were those of survival—physically and mentally. Despite having been released, Debbie and Carey were still struggling with the aftereffects of their ordeal, which was, Carey recalled, "a psychic trauma" (Junkin 1987). Both felt they were still being followed weeks after their release (they probably were) and continued to feel anxieties and unease. "After your mail has been opened, your phone has been tapped and you've been railroaded through a corrupt judicial system, it's pretty easy to become paranoid," Carey commented. "I feel like I'm being followed wherever I go," Debbie said. "The idea seems to be to make you so paranoid you won't fight back" (Peterson 1975b). Neither was able to find a job, and Carey soon began having "horrible nightmares, screaming nightmares" about "concentration camps, about me being dragged off by the FBI, of Jill and Gail being tortured." For a time he turned to drugs, "a lot of pot," and tranquillizers (Junkin 1987). Only years later, with the help of a therapist and a committed relationship, did he begin to stabilize.

Sadly, though, after years of gay liberation activism, Carey Junkin died in 1993 of AIDS. Not long before he died, he told interviewer Pam Goldman that his principled stand as one of the Lexington Six was "one of the things I'm most proud of" (Junkin 1987).

Shortly after the Lexington Six were held in contempt on March 8, their attorneys Robert Sedler and Judith Peterson filed an appeal on March 11 to the Sixth U.S. Circuit Court of Appeals in Cincinnati. It was entitled "JAMES CAREY JUNKIN, MARLA SEYMOUR, JILL RAYMOND, GAIL COHEE, [NANCY SCOTT], and DEBORAH HANDS VS. UNITED STATES OF AMERICA"—a somewhat uneven match.

Hopes were raised at the end of April among the remaining four of the Lexington Six who continued to languish in their Kentucky county jail cells, having now served almost two months. On April 28, the federal appeals court sent the case back to the Kentucky federal district court (Judge Bernard Moynahan's court) for clarification, ordering the judge to determine whether, as Sedler and Peterson argued, the "sole or dominant" purpose of the grand jury had been to apprehend fugitives who had already been indicted (Ward 1975b). Such a purpose—to apprehend fugitives— would have been an improper use of the grand jury, nullifying the proceedings. In other words, Moynahan was ordered by the appeals court to justify the Lexington Six grand jury hearings, to provide a legitimate purpose for them, suggesting that it could not be to apprehend fugitives. The order read as follows: "It appearing to Court that issue in doubt is whether the sole or dominant purpose of subpoenaing witnesses before grand jury was to obtain information in apprehending already-indicted fugitives, case remanded to District Court for determination of this issue" (Order 1975).

The appeals court virtually echoed the Sedler-Peterson wording in its order, which suggested it might be susceptible to their argument. In their appeals reply brief, Sedler and Peterson contended that "in the case at bar there can be no serious contention that the sole or dominant purpose of subpoenaing the petitioners before the grand jury was anything other than to obtain information that the FBI believed would lead to the apprehension of two already-indicted fugitives" (Appeal A 1975b, 18).

Sedler said the remand ruling was a "small victory" in that the court "didn't confirm the contempt ruling." Even U.S. Attorney Eugene Siler admitted that the appeals court "sort of found in favor of the witnesses" in ordering Judge Moynahan to reexamine the purpose of the grand jury (Gatz, April 30, 1975). Ironically, the appeals court decision came on the day the Vietnam War officially ended, with the South Vietnamese government surrendering unconditionally to the Viet Cong—bringing to a close the original underlying historical backdrop to the Lexington Six's plight.

So Moynahan in essence was directed by the appeals court to certify that the sole and dominant purpose of the grand jury had *not* been to act as an arm of the FBI in apprehending fugitives. The appeals court also ordered that the four incarcerated women be freed on bail pending Moynahan's review of the case. Upon receiving the order that the women be released on bail, Sedler immediately filed a motion for their release. On April 29, Moynahan set the bond at $10,000 each—an unusually high amount.

In the intervening weeks between the contempt order on March 8 and the appeals court ruling on April 28, prominent Kentucky organizations had issued public statements in support of the Lexington Six and/or questioning whether the Lexington grand jury had indeed been improperly used and the six unjustly incarcerated. A lengthy editorial in the state's premier newspaper, the Louisville *Courier-Journal*, on April 7 held that civil liberties were being violated in the case: "Four young people face up to a year in jail because their private convictions clash with investigative impatience." Was the grand jury serving "simply to fatten the political intelligence files of the FBI?" The editorial writer's implied answer to the question was "Yes." The editorialist also made the point that the government's freewheeling deployment of "use immunity" "threatened the guarantee against self-incrimination under the Fifth Amendment" (Editorial 1975).

A moving letter to the editor by Jill Raymond's grandmother Dorothy Raymond published in the *Lexington Herald* may have intensified public sympathy for the plight of the Lexington Six. Regarding, she wrote,

> the case of the six young [people] now confined in Kentucky jails
> because of their stand against the grand jury as a tool of the FBI[,] I
> am the grandmother of one of these students and I am confident she
> is not guilty of harboring or assisting any refugee from FBI search. I
> hope [readers] will note that . . . recently one of the defendants, herself

under oath, declared that the defendants were unaware of the true identity of the young women with whom they became acquainted in the summer of 1974, nor do they know of their present whereabouts.

Mrs. Raymond ended by quoting philosopher George Santayana: "Every human reform . . . is the human reassertion of [people] against . . . [unfair] principles . . . which . . . obtain the idolatrous veneration of mankind." She concluded with the hope that "such a reform will come from the self-sacrifice of these prisoners so devoted to the cause of justice. . . . I hope others will join me in advocating for their freedom. Yours very truly, Mrs. Lowell W. Raymond" (D. Raymond 1975).

On April 18, the Louisville branch of the American Civil Liberties Union issued a strong condemnation, written by Anne Braden, of the FBI and federal authorities whose actions, it claimed, "violate basic human rights, as well as the U.S. Constitution." "We believe that the FBI behavior in Lexington is a gross abuse of power and a use of police state tactics that cannot be tolerated in a free society. . . . The historic function of the grand jury is being perverted. At the urging of the FBI, it is being turned into a tool of modern inquisition. . . . A grand jury used in this way is a vehicle for tyranny" (Louisville Civil Liberties Union 1975). Interestingly, this statement ended up in the FBI files of William Gilday. A delegation of four people, including Braden, from the Louisville CLU had met on March 26, 1975, with Thomas Hitchens, special agent in charge of the FBI operation against the Lexington Six. The group issued the above statement in conjunction with the meeting, which Hitchens characterized as a "propaganda stunt" (Finley 1975).

Although the women's release had been ordered on April 29, the money for the bail bond—$40,000—had to be raised and handed over to the court before they would actually be allowed their freedom. It happened to be the weekend of the Kentucky Derby, but the Lexington Grand Jury Defense Committee set about raising the money, which they were able to do by the following Monday, May 5. However, Moynahan ruled that the appeals court order only applied to the period between the order and his hearing on it, which was set for the following day, May 6. So the net effect was that the four were denied bail and not released, a huge disappointment for the women.

Nancy Scott recorded the emotional roller coaster the remaining four were undergoing: high hopes and crashing disappointments:

> *The hardest part of being in here is now becoming the constant prom-*
> *ises and hopes, always followed by disappointments. Each week we*
> *think—oh, it'll be by next Monday at the latest—but it never is. And*
> *now [April 30] that the "partial decision" is made—we still don't*
> *know anything. Yesterday, our hopes were really up; we thought for*
> *sure we'd get out on bond within a few days. But from the looks of*
> *today's paper—it could be 3 more weeks. Jesus! I'm beginning to doubt*
> *whether I could stand it that long or not. The woman I "live" with has*
> *held the same hopes. I don't know whether she could stand it either.*
> *(letter to author, April 30, 1975)*

The hearing in open court on May 6 once again pitted U.S. Attorney Eugene Siler for the government against Robert Sedler for the appellants, the four imprisoned resisters. Siler filed a sealed affidavit which apparently stated that the "sole or dominant" purpose of the federal grand jury was not to "obtain information on already-indicted fugitives." Sedler objected to this affidavit being sealed, arguing that it "force[s us] to fight with one hand behind our back. The government knows what's in there. Your Honor knows. The Court of Appeals will know," but he remained in the dark (Gatz, May 7, 1975). Sedler's objection was overruled.

Sedler then tried to present witnesses—namely, FBI agents—who could substantiate his now oft-repeated claim that the grand jury had in effect been but a subpoena-empowered arm of the FBI. Special Agent Wayne McDonald, one of the principal agents in the Lexington Six case, was called to the stand and asked by Sedler what he had told Siler when he "requested" Siler to order subpoenas for the six. Sedler also asked McDonald what kind of "background information" he had provided the grand jury before the six appeared before it, presumably prejudicing the jurors against them. Siler objected to these questions, and the judge sustained the objections. Sedler then roundly protested to the judge: "There is something fundamentally unfair in allowing the government to proceed in secret and not allowing us to present whatever evidence is available to us to show that there was abuse of the grand jury system" (Gatz, May 7, 1975).

Indeed, as in the original contempt decision, the judge's decision appeared to have been a foregone conclusion, no evidence needed. Relying solely on Siler's declaration (which Moynahan read for the first time in camera in the courtroom) that the grand jury's purpose was proper and within the law, the judge issued his ruling that the grand jury and the U.S. attorney in issuing subpoenas to the Lexington Six were "pursuing legitimate and bona fide subjects of inquiry. . . . It was not the sole or dominant purpose . . . to obtain information that would purportedly aid the Government in apprehending already indicted fugitives" (Moynahan 1975)—an assertion that was, of course, patently false. Any glance at the questions posed in the grand jury hearings showed that its perceived purpose was, as the foreperson, Ralph Agee, put it, "to find out where those two girls are" (Transcript 1975, DE 46–47, 271).

Moynahan's ruling was returned to the Sixth Circuit Court of Appeals to determine whether it was an adequate response. (Sedler's overall appeal was still pending there.) With the matter settled, Sedler asked that bail be continued for the remaining four until the final decision was rendered. But Moynahan refused to do so.

Three of the Lexington Six—Gail Cohee, Marla Seymour, and Nancy Scott—had determined beforehand that unless Moynahan granted them bail or, highly improbably, ruled that the grand jury had been improperly used, they would agree to testify and end their incarceration. They had had enough and saw no point in continuing to resist. Sedler informed the court at the end of the May 6 hearing that the three had agreed to testify. Judge Moynahan then released them on recognizance, so they were free to leave the courthouse, with their final grand jury appearance set for May 19. But Moynahan refused bail for still-defiant Jill Raymond, who was then carted back to jail alone.

Moynahan's decision to deny bail to Jill seemed to many to be unreasonably cruel and vindictive. He surely knew that she had no pertinent information for the grand jury. Her resistance seemed to have offended him personally: the stern father versus the rebellious daughter who needed to be taught a lesson. It was becoming a battle of wills.

The hearing itself seemed a travesty. The judge allowed no evidence or witnesses for the four appellants to make a case to support their claim of grand jury abuse, and the only evidence entered in support of the government's claim was the U.S. attorney's say-so, which itself was kept in secret so the appellants had no chance to rebut or challenge it. No one could claim that this was a fair procedure.

One virtue of the proceeding was that, as Jill pointed out, its unfairness was obvious to everyone: "The only saving grace is that Moynahan makes the true face of American justice clear for people, for reporters, for everyone. He sure is outrageous." But someday, she imagined, "people will prevail, and when we do we'll put people like Moynahan behind bars—if we have bars at all" (letter to author, May 7, 1975).

May 6 was an agonizing day for the four resisters, who were kept in a holding cell outside the courtroom while final decisions that would determine their fates were taking place in the main room. It was the first time lovers Marla Seymour and Gail Cohee had seen one another in two months. They had been allowed one phone call a week and otherwise connected only through letters since their incarceration. When they heard the judge's decision, Gail and Nancy Scott announced that they had decided to testify. It was clear that the courts were not going to rule in their favor, and they didn't see the point in staying on indefinitely. It was now up to Marla to make her decision. She and Gail had made a pact early in the FBI interrogations that they would do everything together, come what may. Gail had initially been reluctant to go along with the plan not to cooperate, but Marla eventually persuaded her to join the resistance action. So Marla felt she "owed one" to Gail. Consequently, when Gail said she was going to testify, Marla agreed to do so as well, so they "could be together." Marla was deathly afraid of having her relationship with Gail "taken away" and wondered how it could survive if she remained in jail. She also wondered if she could stand being alone in jail, since she presumed she and Jill would not be housed together (Seymour 1987a). Nevertheless, she like the others felt "really terrible" about testifying and finally cooperating, however reluctantly and minimally. "I felt I'd let Jill down. I'd let myself down" (Seymour 1987b).

Nancy Scott also agonized over the decision of whether to testify. She worried, "If I can't hold out, I'll be written off . . . like Jane Alpert was" (letter to author, April 30, 1975). "It seems that there are several women's groups throughout the country—mostly *socialist*-feminist groups—who do *not* support the remaining 4 of us *if* we testify after the Appeal (if lost). This split certainly doesn't help matters any. I must admit I won't be testifying without any feelings of guilt for succumbing (again as I often do) to patriarchal demands. But I realize that it's either that, or my own personal destruction" (letter to author, April 12, 1975).

Nancy noted that her internment could last years, if she were resubpoenaed at the end of the grand jury term "as Ellen G. and Terri T. in Connecticut" had been. She doubted whether "remaining in one 'room' for who knows how many years" would contribute much to the women's movement. "And once I'm out of here, I'll continue for the rest of my life to work for women—in whatever way I can" (letter to author, April 12, 1975).

At the time, I became concerned about the anguishing decision-making the four resisters were going through. It seemed cruelly unfair for people so young to have to face such an impossibly no-win situation: on the one hand, rotting away in jail indefinitely with incalculable effects on their mental and physical well-being; on the other hand, having to accept the fact that they had not lived up to their ideals and principles. No matter what decision they made, harm was going to be done—to their self-esteem, if they testified; to their minds, bodies, and relationships, if they remained in jail indefinitely. I felt angered by the pressure they were receiving from outside groups who didn't appreciate the complexities of their situation, and I wrote to each of the four saying she had my support, no matter what decision she made. I happen to have a copy of the letter I wrote to Nancy in response to her mid-April letter and, because it reflects the feelings of the day, I quote portions here:

> Dear [Nancy],
> I was very much moved by your letter, as I can see that you are going through . . . some difficult decision-making. I have to say that I have been very much angered by those who have criticized Debbie's and Carey's decision to testify. In my opinion these are personal decisions

*that clearly none of you has made lightly. It certainly is not fair for
those of us on the outside to judge in any way. I do hope that you will
not feel guilty . . . if you choose to testify. . . . You have done more than
any of us will probably ever be called upon to do. The sacrifice it has
involved has already been great. Moreover, I think that the whole case
has already been very effective in drawing attention to FBI behavior
as well as awakening lots of women in the movement to some realities
about the political world. . . .*

*The conflict between the personal and political commitment is a
difficult one to resolve. Naturally, I feel that political involvement is
important and that resistance like yours is very important, too. But I
also feel that personal relationships are equally, if not more, important. It is too easy to fall into the male trip of fighting for an abstract
Cause while losing touch with the beauty and love of a personal
relationship. . . . Any woman who chooses in favor of getting back
with the woman she loves has all my sympathy and support.*

In truth, I wrestled with the question of what I would do in their situation. I certainly felt that "collaboration" with manifest evil such as the
Nazi Gestapo was condemnable, and I hoped that I would have had the
stamina to resist in such a case or in any case where my testimony and
cooperation might have led to injury or death to friends and comrades.
However, I didn't feel the situation of the Lexington Six rose to that level.
And I felt that abstract commitment to a cause—however good—which
requires serious personal harm or violence to oneself or others is also ethically objectionable. All of the Lexington Six who agreed in the end to
cooperate did so either because they felt that prolonged incarceration would
irreparably harm them physically and mentally and/or because they feared
it would destroy a deep committed relationship with a lover.

After Marla made her decision in the holding cell to go ahead and testify,
she told Jill, who was devastated to realize she would now be alone. She
collapsed and began weeping (Seymour 1987a). It was terrible to see their
usually buoyant and spirited comrade reduced to such despair. "God, it
was painful for everybody," Jill exclaimed the day after the hearing. What a
"horrendous scene" it was (letter to author, May 7, 1975). "The courtroom

scene on Tuesday [May 6] was *really* grotesque and almost unbearably depressing for everybody (unlike March 8, when we had our own smug arrogance to get us through)" (Raymond, letter to Anne Rhodenbaugh, May 9, 1975).

As the only remaining prisoner, Jill was transferred on May 6 to the Franklin County Jail in Frankfort—to the cell previously occupied by Marla and Nancy. "It's very weird being alone in here. . . . The isolation is going to be the single most difficult thing—maybe *too* difficult in the end, but we'll see." Jill was so wracked the first day in the Franklin County Jail that she held hands with Robert Sedler through the bars the whole time he was there to bring her a copy of the bail motion submitted to the appeals court (Raymond, letter to Anne Rhodenbaugh, May 9, 1975). Knowing how painful the decision had been for Marla, Gail, and Nancy, Jill worried too about their states of mind: "I think that the next couple weeks are going to be extremely painful for them—especially Marla . . . and they'll probably need all the encouragement they can get" (letter to author, May 7, 1975).

Jill in fact had been sorely tempted to testify when the other three agreed to do so. She later noted, "There was a point at which I was about to testify, I'll be very frank. Two months after we went to jail, we were all trucked back to court for another hearing. The judge ruled that the grand jury's purpose was legitimate. At that point, the remaining three people agreed to testify. Now I was alone for the first time" (Raymond 1989, 299–300).

Once they were out of jail, Gail and Marla gave lengthy interviews to local newspapers detailing once again the FBI's offensive, intrusive behavior and explaining why they had resisted so long. "I don't think these people [the FBI] should have a right to come into our lives and totally disrupt them," Gail said. "We decided to fight it out in court and try to set a precedent so they can't intimidate people." As for her decision to testify, Gail explained, "I just got tired of waiting for the courts to do something. . . . We've fought them on their own grounds," now "we want to fight them on our grounds" (Ward 1975c).

Shortly after her release, Marla learned that she had been exposed to tuberculosis while in the Franklin County Jail. One of her cellmates, a woman who had been incarcerated for breaking and entering with her drug-addicted boyfriend, had active TB, and apparently Marla (and possibly

Nancy Scott) were thus exposed. Marla tested positive for the disease and a scar was detected in her lungs. She had to take a prophylactic drug (isoniazid [INH]) for a year following (Seymour, email to author, April 23, 2018; Gatz, July 28, 1975b).

I visited Jill in the Franklin County Jail on May 13, shortly after she had been transferred there. Jill was alone in the cell and seemed decidedly less exuberant than she had been when I visited her and Gail in Pineville. She wasn't sure where things were headed and had decided not to think in long-range terms but to take one day at a time. Each day, she said, she would decide whether she could stand to stay in jail for that day—not whether she could stand to stay for a week or a month or a year. That thought would have been unbearable. But to say to oneself, "I think I can make it through today but if tomorrow I can't hack it, I'll get out" made it easier psychologically to bear.

CHAPTER SEVEN

A Culture of Resistance

Although Jill was alone for the time being in her Kentucky county jail, she was not alone in resisting FBI and grand jury inquisitions that year. Across the country dozens refused to cooperate with federal authorities, were held in contempt of court, and landed in prison. One estimate is that approximately two hundred people refused to cooperate and suffered the consequences during the 1971–77 period, as opposed to thirty-five in the preceding twenty years (Gombe 1977). While the government's use of improper and in many cases illegal tactics was curtailed in the immediate wake of the Watergate revelations, it resumed shortly thereafter. In response, resistance to the abusive use of the federal grand jury also resumed, such that by the late 1970s, grand jury resistance had become a movement, largely inspired by the stands taken by the Lexington Six and the Connecticut women. This second wave of grand jury resistance came to include several minority communities connected by a supportive communicative network established by the New York Grand Jury Project in conjunction with the Center for Constitutional Rights and the National Lawyers Guild (as detailed in chapter 3), which circulated strategies and information about and among ongoing resistance cases.

The government's coercive use of grand juries started as part of an offensive against the antiwar movement initiated by the Nixon administration in the fall of 1971 in Tucson, Arizona, following the New York townhouse explosion of the Weather people in 1970. The Tucson case concerned the purchase of dynamite by a radical-looking (long-haired) young man. Five of his housemates—"the Tucson Five"—two of them women, were sub-poenaed *after* he had been indicted. These five refused to cooperate and were sent to jail for several months for contempt of court, a pattern that would be repeated hundreds of times in the next few years (Donner and Cerruti 1972). The case—and many succeeding cases—was orchestrated by Guy Goodwin, head of the Special Litigation Section of the Internal Security Division of the Department of Justice (DOJ). Goodwin became notorious among activists for his relentless, no-holds-barred campaign.

It is striking, as one reviews the cases in the later 1970s, how many of the resisters were women. One suspects that the FBI consciously or unconsciously targeted women, thinking they would be a weak link. It is also striking that an inordinate number of the attorneys and legal workers involved in grand jury resistance cases were women, among whom the most prominent were Rhonda Copelon, Susan B. Jordan, Nancy Stearns, Doris Peterson, and Linda Backiel. In addition, it is noteworthy that nearly all of these cases were in minority communities: lesbian, Native American, Chicano/a, Puerto Rican. Did the FBI consciously or unconsciously target these communities, perceived as *other* and dangerous, knowing that popular prejudices would support—or at least not object to—their harassment and repression? Quite probably that was the case.

In testimony submitted to a U.S. House of Representatives subcommittee investigating grand jury abuse in 1977, the Grand Jury Project reported that "the vast majority of those confined as recalcitrant witnesses in cases involv-ing political activities in recent years have been women." Linda Backiel, speaking to the subcommittee for the project, pointed out that potential witnesses were "singled out" according to "who was most vulnerable. . . . We [at the Grand Jury Project] think the singling out of women is symptomatic of the perception of the FBI that women are not particularly strong or [are] vulnerable to a lot of pressure and will be crushed under the pressure." But, as evidenced by Jill Raymond and others, "in recent years women in political movements have demonstrated that they are no more afraid of jail than men, and have gone to jail rather than testify despite conditions which have made their incarceration much more harsh than that of male civil contempt prisoners" (Eilberg Hearings 1977, 1:120, 91, 103)

In their May–June 1977 issue, the editors of the Grand Jury Project newsletter, *Quash*, included a special section on "Women and Grand Juries," which theorized as to why so many of the resisters jailed for contempt were women. In an article entitled "When Women Become Massively Political," they noted, "Many people have been puzzled by the fact that most of those jailed for contempt of political grand juries have been women. . . . Since the Justice Department reactivated its use of the federal grand jury as a political tool in early 1975 [the Lexington and New Haven cases], hundreds have refused to cooperate" (Anonymous 1977b).

The editors concluded that the FBI and Department of Justice were following a "sexist strategy," choosing to go after those "perceived as most 'vulnerable,'" with lesbians or others deemed socially deviant, such as unwed mothers, being especially vulnerable because of the fear of being outed and socially shamed. The government officials also likely entertained other sexist stereotypes, the editors theorized, such as that "women are gossips—therefore they can't keep from talking; they're obedient and submissive" (Anonymous 1977b).

But this strategy "backfired." The examples of the Lexington Six and others proved that women "*do not* fit the stereotypes. . . . They are strong and dedicated; not weak and submissive. They are aware of their own oppression as women and as members of oppressed groups, they are building cultures and networks of resistance." So the ironic result of the FBI/DOJ campaigns was that "instead of links being weakened, ties were strengthened" (Anonymous 1977b).

One of many salient examples of women's grand jury resistance occurred in a Native American community. On June 26, 1975, two FBI agents were killed in a shootout at the Pine Ridge Indian Reservation in southwest South Dakota. Joanna LeDeaux, a Cherokee Navaho who was working with the Wounded Knee Defense Committee, arrived on the scene of the shooting shortly after the agents were killed and attempted to negotiate a ceasefire between the police and the Indians. When that attempt failed, she left the scene. As reported later, "Several months after the incident FBI agents with sniper rifles stationed themselves around the house where Joanna lived with her parents and kept a vigil through the night. Early the next morning they broke into the house and dragged the young woman downtown to the federal courthouse in her nightgown. They . . . insisted that the danger that she would flee from the midst of these heavily armed men was such that she could not be given the time to change into street clothes" (Eilberg Hearings 1977, 1:21).

The perpetrators of the killings at Pine Ridge managed to escape the area; a massive FBI manhunt, called RESMURS in the FBI files, ensued, and a federal grand jury was empaneled on July 14. At least fifty Indians visited by the FBI refused to cooperate. Among them were June Little and Wanda Siers, "a small, delicate woman who pointedly shut her mouth and refused to open it every time she was approached by the FBI" (Matthiessen 1991 [1983], 214)—a gesture that recalls Debbie Hands's Bartleby-like silence before the Kentucky grand jury.

Angie Long Visitor and Ivis Long Visitor, who had fled the scene of the Pine Ridge shootout with their three young children while it was taking place, were subpoenaed before the grand jury on July 14. Because they had three children under the age of four and having no one to care for them should they be incarcerated, the Long Visitors partially cooperated but not enough apparently to satisfy the FBI, so they were subpoenaed and pled the Fifth.

When the grand jury term expired, a second grand jury was sworn in and the Long Visitors were resubpoenaed, along with Joanna LeDeaux, on August 24, 1975. All three refused to testify, were granted use immunity on September 2, held in contempt of court, and sent to prison on September 22. The District Court judge Andrew Bogue told LeDeaux, "The keys to the cell are in your mouth" (Matthiessen 1991 [1983], 214).

LeDeaux issued the following statement defending her resistance: "When the U.S. was born, dissent was called honorable. . . . As long as it was sanctified by the majority, the dominant social class, race, or group, it was condoned. Because I have not chosen to follow your ways but those of my native people, should this make my dissent less honorable, the following of my conscience and convictions less honorable?" (Grand Jury Project, 1976).

Joanna was several months pregnant. The baby was born while she was in the San Pedro federal prison in California. After serving eight months, LeDeaux was freed in May 1976 when a public outcry arose over prison officials' refusal to let her nurse the baby, forcing U.S. Attorney General Edward Levi to order her release.

Upon her release, LeDeaux proclaimed: "Throughout my incarceration I continued to reject every effort to break my spirit or compromise my beliefs regardless of the danger to my unborn child and myself. . . . When law attempts to maintain its validity through lies and deceits, such as those forced on Native peoples . . . , truth is buried. I can never be a part of such a system. And even though the United States government claimed jurisdiction over my body, it could [never] nor ever will, control my spirit" (Anonymous 1977b).

After three months in prison, Angie Long Visitor, unable to bear the separation from her kids, agreed to testify and was released in December. But her ordeal wasn't over. About a year after her release from the contempt imprisonment, "Angie was arrested by six heavily armed FBI agents who broke into her sister's bedroom while [Angie] slept" (Eilberg Hearings 1977, 1:20). She was then resubpoenaed and ultimately forced to testify in the 1977 trial of Leonard Peltier, though she gave no useful information (Churchill and VanderWall 1990, 398 n.157). Peltier, one of the leaders of the American Indian Movement, was eventually convicted of the Pine Ridge killings, many say unjustly.

In their appeals, both the Long Visitors and LeDeaux listed "fear of reprisals" as a reason for their refusal to testify, indicating that, like the Lexington Six, they were receiving considerable pressure from their community not to testify or cooperate. The Eighth Circuit Appeals Court turned down their appeal on October 6, 1975 (*In re Grand Jury, Ivis Long Visitor* 1975).

In November 1975, members of the Lakota Treaty Council, the governing body of Sioux elders at the Pine Ridge Reservation, met with President Gerald Ford to protest against abuses of the South Dakota grand jury system and the continued FBI harassment of their reservation (Brand 1993, 91–92). The egregiously aggressive FBI behavior in the Pine Ridge case attracted national attention and protest. On July 22, 1975, the U.S. Civil Rights Commission labeled the RESMURS investigation "an over-reaction which takes on aspects of a vendetta." In 1981, Amnesty International issued a report in which it condemned the FBI handling of the Pine Ridge investigation: "Amnesty International . . . wonders what conclusion should be drawn when a federal government agency (the FBI) . . . appears willing to fabricate evidence . . . and to withhold information. . . . It is . . . clear that the FBI have abused their power" (Matthiessen 1991 [1983], 209, 623 n.4).

On July 22, 1975, Veronica Vigil, a member of the Chicano Crusade for Justice in Colorado, was served with a subpoena to testify before a federal grand jury in Denver on August 19. She had refused to cooperate with FBI agents who tried to interrogate her on July 21. Like the other grand jury resisters, she refused to answer the grand jury questions (fifty in her case), was granted use immunity, continued to refuse, and was sent to prison for eleven months, the remainder of the grand jury term. At a hearing to vacate the contempt order, Veronica stated, "I have not testified and I will not testify. . . . I refuse to become an informer" (Anonymous 1976e).

Like the Lexington Six, Vigil in the course of her hearings attempted to address the grand jurors directly in hopes of educating and persuading them but to no avail. A Chicano newspaper, *El Gallo*, reported, "Veronica twice made personal appeals to the jurors (which does not include a single Chicano) to stop being pawns of the government, to end their investigation and to drop the subpoena. The only reply from the jurors was blank stares." Under a headline reading "FREE VERONICA VIGIL," the article concluded, "Veronica's refusal serves as an inspiration" (Anonymous 1975g).

The FBI was interrogating Vigil in connection with the car bombing of six Chicano/a students at the University of Colorado at Boulder in May 1974. Three were killed when a car bomb exploded on May 27, and three more when another bomb went off in a car two days later. All were activists involved in a nineteen-day sit-in to protest conditions for Hispanics at the university. They were called "Los Seis de Boulder"—the Boulder Six.

The perpetrators of the Boulder crimes were never brought to justice, and the case remains unsolved. Many Chicano/as thought that groups hostile to the Chicano/a cause had planted the bombs. Some thought the FBI was responsible or had fomented dissention—a COINTELPRO tactic—within the Chicano/a movement, causing one faction to turn violently against another. But the FBI seemed to think the detonations were, like the 1970 Weathermen New York townhouse explosion, accidently caused by the activists themselves (Taylor 2005; Dodge and Dyer 2014).

Following the bombings and apparently pursuing the townhouse analogy theory, the FBI launched a massive dragnet in the Chicano/a community, interrogating and harassing families and friends of "Los Seis." On July 11, 1975, four Chicanas—Frieda Bugarin, Lee Teran, Rita Montero, and

Guadaloupe Grenado—were among the first to be subpoenaed before a federal grand jury in connection with the Boulder Six (three of the women were wives of the activists killed in the bombings). "Knowing that the grand jury was not called to find those responsible for the attack and murder of the Boulder victims, the four women refused to answer the questions of the grand jury," *El Gallo* reported. The Chicanas' attorney, Federico Peña, filed a motion claiming racism in the jury selection, since there were no African Americans, Indians, or Chicano/as on the twenty-one-member panel. He also asked for a restraining order to get the federal officials "to stop intimidation and harassment against Chicanos that . . . agents have practiced in their investigation of the bombings" (Anonymous 1974). Perhaps because of community pressure—there were several hundred protestors outside the Denver courthouse on July 11—the U.S. attorney dropped the subpoena of the four Chicanas and they were let go.

Among those subpoenaed was an activist in the Crusade for Justice campaign, Ray Otero, who appeared before the federal grand jury in Denver in September and October 1974. Veronica Vigil had lived with Otero in Boulder during the period 1973–75. In December 1973, the two "became man and wife by mutual consent," according to an affidavit filed by Vigil in her contempt hearing. Vigil therefore claimed spousal immunity as one of the grounds for her refusal to testify, but the Tenth Circuit Court of Appeals rejected this claim as a "delaying tactic." Vigil also argued the FBI had engaged in electronic surveillance and that the hearing was invalid because "the investigation was not legitimate." As with the Lexington Six, Vigil presented substantial evidence that her phones were being bugged and that the grand jury questions were based on knowledge the FBI could only have gleaned from these overheard and illegally obtained phone conversations. But also, as in the Lexington case, the judges in Vigil's case accepted the FBI's and other government officials' say-so, that "to their best of their knowledge" no "court-ordered" eavesdropping had occurred (*In re Grand Jury, Veronica Vigil* 1975, 8, 1, 5).

The question of whether just relying on government officials' say-so is sufficient to prove that no surveillance occurred had been raised in several recent grand jury cases that reached appeals courts. In *United States v. Alter* (1973), the Ninth Circuit Court ruled that the government's affidavit of denial must be "responsive, factual, unambiguous and unequivocal," and not entail "ambivalent statements or loopholes" (*In re Grand Jury, Veronica Vigil* 1975, 6). Interestingly, the Colorado appeals court hearing relied in part on the Second Circuit decision in the Connecticut case of Ellen Grusse and Terri Turgeon, *United States v. Grusse*, issued on February 27, 1975. According to that ruling, while a "denial by affidavit" by the government is "insufficient," the testimony of an assistant U.S. attorney that he had personally checked with the FBI agent in charge of the case (who assured him that no wiretapping had occurred) was sufficient. In other words, sworn testimony in person as opposed to written affidavits was required. However, in the Grusse-Turgeon case, one of the Second Circuit Court judges, James Lowell Oakes, later chief judge of the court and a Nixon appointee, dissented, arguing that "the [government's] search to uncover electronic surveillance [in the Grusse-Turgeon case] was inadequate. . . . The failure of the prosecutor to make at the very least a so-called 'eight agency' search for possible electronic surveillance may be a result of an uneasiness about what the search might uncover. . . . The insufficient search for electronic surveillance leaves open the possibility that surveillance had taken place, thus potentially depriving appellants of their rights" (*United States of America v. Ellen Grusse and Maria Theresa Turgeon* 1975, 4–5). The "eight agency" search meant that several U.S. agencies should be contacted, not just the FBI. (This, of course, did not happen in the Lexington case where U.S. Attorney Siler conducted the search in a matter of hours.) In any event, the net result of the Tenth Circuit's denial of Veronica Vigil's appeal was that she remained in federal prison for seven more months until the grand jury term expired on April 5, 1976.

In the course of her incarceration, the Veronica Vigil Defense Committee sent a letter to *Quash*, the Grand Jury Project newsletter, indicating the extent of the communication network that had been established among the various grand jury resistance cases through the vehicle of the Grand Jury Project:

> *Companera[s], We are sending you information on Veronica Vigil's legal situation. . . . The information we have received from you has been very useful . . . [helping] the people realize, how our case, is*

not an isolated one. Also it has helped us very much . . . in making
ourselves see, how many of our struggling hermanos y hermanas are
confronting the same evil.

Saludo Fraternales y Solidaridad,
Nick Avila, Manuel Arcadia . . .
V. V. D. C. (use only initials) (V. V. D. C. 1976)

(The use of initials in the address presumed the mail was being intercepted
by the FBI.)

On December 29, 1975, J. Herbert Quinn, an Irish American former
mayor of Concord, New Hampshire, refused to answer a federal grand
jury's questions about "alleged gun-running to Northern Ireland" to aid
the Irish Republican Army (IRA). He was held in contempt of court and
sent to prison (Johnstone 1975). Quinn was recovering from hernia surgery
when held in contempt, and en route to prison under the escort of a federal
marshal he checked into a hospital to have his stitches removed. Quinn
served four months in prison. Earlier, several other Irish Americans had
been similarly subpoenaed in Fort Worth, Texas, regarding their alleged
connection to the Irish Northern Aid Society and illegal shipment of arms
to the IRA. Five of those subpoenaed — called the "Fort Worth Five" — were
granted use immunity, refused still to testify, were held in contempt on
June 20, 1972, and ended up spending a total of eleven months in a Texas
county jail.

During the proceedings in Texas, the district court judge, Leo Brewster,
revealed that a xenophobic animus motivated his contempt ruling: "All of
the witnesses are foreign born. . . . The thought occurs that they ought to
go back to where they came from if they cannot stomach the fundamental
principles upon which this country is founded" (Donner and Lavine 1973).
Since the witnesses were in fact invoking core U.S. constitutional rights,
the judge's statement is deeply ironic, suggesting again that government
stigmatizing of vulnerable minorities — whether Irish Americans, as in this
case, or lesbians and gays, Hispanics, or Native Americans — likely helped
legitimize their targeting by officials.

The Fort Worth Five were finally released in July 1973 when U.S.
Supreme Court justice William O. Douglas ruled they had been wrongly

held because of illegal government wiretapping. The U.S. attorney in that case actually admitted in the government's appeal brief that one of the attorneys for the Fort Worth Five had had his phones tapped by the FBI (Donner and Lavine 1973).

In response to the apparently unjust incarceration of the Fort Worth Five, Senator Edward Kennedy, himself of Irish descent, issued a scathing condemnation of the government's continuing abuse of the grand jury system: "Over the past four years under the [Nixon] administration, we have witnessed the birth of a new breed of political animal—the kangaroo grand jury . . . a dangerous form of Star Chamber secret inquisition that is trampling the rights of American citizens from coast to coast." In testimony before a House subcommittee hearing chaired by Representative Bella Abzug, Kennedy deplored the government's "small army of grand inquisitors barnstorming . . . across the country, . . . armed with dragnets of subpoenas and immunity grants. . . . These tactics are sufficient to terrify even the bravest and most recalcitrant witness, whose only crime may be a deep reluctance to become a government informer of his closest friends or relatives, or an equally deep belief that the nose of the United States Government has no business in the private life and views and political affiliations of its free citizens" (Donner and Lavine 1973).

In the spring of 1976, several women in Seattle, Washington, four of whom were single mothers with young children, were interrogated by the FBI and subpoenaed before a federal grand jury concerning the activities of the so-called George Jackson Brigade, a radical antiwar group that had engaged in several bank robberies and bombings. At one such incident at a Safeway grocery store on September 15, 1975, the perpetrator, Ralph Ford, although himself not a brigade member, was killed.

Several members of the George Jackson Brigade were lesbians: Rita Brown, Therese Coupez, and Janine Bertram. Brown dressed in drag for their bank-robbery jobs, reportedly influenced by the SLA lesbian couple Camilla Hall and Patricia Soltysik. Brown drove the switch car in a daring prison escape of John Sherman, one of the brigade members; police bulletins described her as a Black man. Earlier, Brown and Coupez, visiting in the East, had attended the trials of Pat Swinton and Assata Shakur (Burton-Rose 2010b, 175, 120, 131). All of these women—Brown, Coupez, and Bertram—were arrested in late 1977 and early 1978, convicted, and served several years in prison.

On International Women's Day in 1976, Rita and Janine issued a poem about their intersectional George Jackson Brigade philosophy:

> We are not all white and we're not all men . . .
> dykes niggers cons. . . .
> We are a collection
> of oppressed people . . .
> . . . break[ing]
> barriers of
> race class sex
> workers and lumpen
> all going together
> combating dull sameness
> corporations, government
> and the established rule of
> straight white cocks.

The poem concludes, "joining you sistah brother in freedom, Sue [Saxe], Assata [Shakur], George [Jackson], Jill [Raymond], Martin [Sostre]" (Burton-Rose 2010a, 92–93). (Martin Sostre was a Black activist imprisoned for many years on evidence believed to have been fabricated by the FBI.)

As in the case of the Lexington Six with respect to Susan Saxe and Kathy Power, those who were subpoenaed in Seattle in 1976 were innocent of the crimes committed by the George Jackson Brigade and knew little about its activities. On May 23, 1976, Jill Kray, a mother on welfare who had been romantically involved with one of the brigade's leaders, Ed Mead, was subpoenaed before a grand jury. At the hearing Kray's infant daughter was in the courtroom, and after initially refusing to cooperate, Kray did finally testify because of the child. Outside the courtroom demonstrators chanted, "Lexington, New Haven, Seattle, Sioux Falls: We Won't Talk When the Grand Jury Calls" (Burton-Rose 2010b, 183, 186)—revealing the extent to which earlier cases of grand jury resistance were providing motivational models for the Seattle activists. (Sioux Falls was the site of the Pine Ridge grand jury.) In a further example, Ellen Movescamp, a Native American woman who had recently moved to Seattle, reported to activists that "the same kind of patterns [of FBI harassment] were going on among Indian people at Pine Ridge" (Anonymous 1977c).

On May 18, 1976, several more single mothers, including Brenda Carter, Kathy Hubenet, and Katie Mitchell, were subpoenaed. Carter had been the girlfriend of Ralph Ford, who was killed in the Safeway bombing, and Hubenet and Mitchell were friends of hers. None of them had anything to do with the George Jackson Brigade or knew anything about it. Indeed, the underground brigade itself issued a public statement to this effect while the women were under subpoena (Burton-Rose 2010a, 255). Yet the police raided their house—for which they were evicted—and they were summoned before the federal grand jury. Each declared, "I will not talk." Carter laid out the bleak dilemma faced by those brought before a grand jury: "I have the choice . . . of being an informer—or going to jail" (Burton-Rose 2010b, 189, 192). Katie Mitchell commented, "We are virtually on trial for something that we never did" (Park and Ward 2010, 234). Both Katie and Kathy had young sons. Kathy's four-year-old in rallying to her defense made a demonstration sign that read,

> KILL THE DRAGONS
> POLICES [sic] DON'T PUT KATHY IN JAIL
> BREAK THE JAIL DOOR OPEN. *(Park and Ward 2010, 237)*

Both mothers worried about how they could endure being separated from their children if they ended up in prison. "That has been the most painful, the heaviest part for me," Kathy lamented. But, she added, "there is a line I will not cross in terms of my integrity. I will not testify about my friends, I will not . . . subject them to what I am going through, I will not do that" (Anonymous 1977b).

Brenda Carter summed up the underlying reason for her resistance in a passionate *cri de coeur:* "I do not want to testify [because] I want them to know there is a part of me that is myself, that they cannot touch, that they cannot have" (Park and Ward 2010, 235). Her words gave voice to the gut-level feelings of many grand jury resisters, including the Lexington Six. There is an inner core of self that is sacrosanct.

A crowd of a hundred or so protesters gathered outside the courtroom for the women's hearings, and their cases were eventually dismissed (Burton-Rose 2010b, 189, 192). However, further subpoenas ensued. Nancy "Michelle" Whitnack, a twenty-one-year-old activist, was subpoenaed several weeks later in the same case. Michelle had been a friend of Ralph Ford and was a housemate of Laurie Raymond, Jill Raymond's sister. At Whitnack's contempt hearing on June 29, 1976, Laurie Raymond burst out in the courtroom to her supporters, "Are you just going to sit politely by while they take us all away?" (Burton-Rose 2010b, 196). A marshal grabbed Laurie and Michelle and dragged them out of the courtroom (Laurie by the hair and Michelle by her handcuffs). For this Laurie was convicted on November 5 of assaulting an officer and served thirty days in jail (served concurrently with a sentence for trespassing on government property in pacifist protests at the Trident Nuclear Submarine Base and the Keyport Naval Torpedo Station). Michelle Whitnack was held in contempt and served six months in prison, released without explanation on December 20, 1976. In an article, "Michelle Whitnack: Beaten and Released," *Quash* reported that prior to her release, Michelle was "choked until she passed out and her fingerprints were taken while she was unconscious" (Anonymous 1977a). Laurie served her thirty days in November and December 1976, with her two young children taken care of by friends.

The mother of Therese Coupez, a member of the George Jackson Brigade, was subpoenaed at about the same time as Michelle Whitnack. Nancy Coupez refused to testify before the federal grand jury on August 25, 1976, and again on September 28. She made the following statement to the jurors: "I am shocked that a judicial body such as the grand jury would expect me to violate the very profound and sacred trust relationship that exists between parent and child." Nancy later commented to a reporter, "I thought I was living in the United States in 1976. But I feel like I'm in Germany in 1935" (Celarier 1976).

Puerto Ricans were another minority group targeted by the FBI, in particular anyone associated, however remotely, with the FALN (Fuerzas Armadas de Liberación Nacional Puertorriqueña, the Armed Forces of Puerto Rican National Liberation), a group fighting for Puerto Rican independence from the United States. The FALN was responsible for several bombings in New York City, notably a highly publicized bombing at Fraunces Tavern on January 24, 1975, in which four people were killed and fifty-five injured. Most of the blasts set off by the FALN were symbolic, however, without casualties, at places like banks, corporate headquarters, and large department stores.

The FBI dragnet of the Puerto Rican community began with Lureida Torres of the Bronx, New York, an out-of-work teacher and member of a Puerto Rican socialist group who wrote for a community newspaper. Subpoenaed along with five male activists in January 1976 before a federal grand jury regarding FALN activities, Torres refused to testify, was held in contempt on May 13, and jailed until the grand jury term ended in October. Significantly, it was only the woman in the group who was sent to jail. In August Torres issued a statement of resistance: "I state now . . . as I have stated since I was first subpoenaed . . . that I will not testify before this grand jury, and that no amount of jail will force me to change my mind" (Anonymous 1977b). She was not resubpoenaed.

In the next two years, at least nine Puerto Rican activists were jailed for refusing to cooperate with federal grand juries, creating a "climate of suppression" in those communities. The Puerto Rican resisters were motivated in part by a "spirit of non-collaboration"—termed *retraimiento*—established by the Puerto Rican Nationalist Party in the 1930s and 1940s (Starr 2010, 142–43, 146, 154 n.54).

On January 7, 1977, Marie Cueto, a Chicana, lay Episcopal minister, and director of the Episcopal National Commission on Hispanic Affairs, was subpoenaed, along with her secretary, Raisa Nemikin, a Venezuelan. The two women had been visited by the FBI at their Episcopal Church office in New York in November 1976. The two knew nothing about the FALN or its members, but the FBI insisted that they turn over church membership records, which they refused to do on privacy and confidentiality grounds. Both then refused to testify before a federal grand jury in New York, which asked the women for the names and files of members of the Hispanic Commission. Although Marie may have been involved in the church's ministry to FALN members, she knew nothing about the FALN per se or the bombings (Cueto, ca. 1978). Unfortunately for them, during their hearings, two bombs were detonated by the FALN in New York on February 19, 1977, one at the Gulf and Western Building and the other at a Texaco exhibit at the Chrysler Building with an accompanying message demanding *inter alia* a halt to "the FBI's harassment of the Puerto Rican people" and to "the illegal use of the grand jury" (Kihss 1977). Both women were jailed for contempt of court in February and March 1977 (Nemikin on February 26 and Cueto on March 8) and spent eleven months in the Metropolitan Correctional Center in New York. To publicize theirs and other Hispanic resistance cases, a defense committee published a two-page spread in Spanish in the Grand Jury Project newsletter *Quash:* "A La Represión del Gran Jurado/FBI" (El Comite 1978).

In their appeal, Cueto and Nemikin, designated as the "contemnors" in the document, maintained that their "refusal to testify" was "based upon moral and religious commitments" and is "irrevocable. . . . They will not betray their religious convictions by testifying" (*In re Cueto* 1978). They also contended that their ability to function as lay ministers would be destroyed if they betrayed the trust of the Puerto Rican community (New York Committee, ca. 1978).

Judge Robert L. Carter in ruling on the appeal interpreted the latter rationale as reflecting "a common-place view among the 'outs' in a social system[,] here the Hispanic poor among whom movants work[,] that one is being a traitor to one's group if she cooperates with law enforcement officials" (*In re Cueto* 1978). Carter, however, ruled in the appellants' favor, following an earlier decision, *In re Grumbles* (1973), in which it was held unconstitutional to keep grand jury witnesses incarcerated for "punitive" reasons when it became clear they had no pertinent information.

Regarding Marie Cueto and Raisa Nemikin, who had by then been in jail for over ten months, Carter wrote,

> *There has been no showing or indication in any of the papers presented to me that these women are other than what they appear to be persons legitimately engaged in the work of their Church. There has been no showing that they are themselves involved in criminal activities or engaged in crime. There has been no indication that they belong to FALN, or condone or espouse its terrorists' views. . . . Under these*

circumstances it does not appear to me that any legitimate purpose is being furthered in keeping the women in custody. . . . Humane considerations require their release. (In re Cueto 1978)

(Cueto was later held in criminal contempt on February 16, 1983, for refusing to testify regarding FALN and sentenced once again, this time to three years in prison.)

Humane considerations were not entertained, however, in the Kentucky case of Jill Raymond, nor the Connecticut case of Ellen Grusse and Terri Turgeon, in the summer of 1975. Jill remained in the Franklin County Jail awaiting a decision about her appeal and a further plea for bail, while in early June Ellen and Terri faced a second grand jury in New Haven.

Nevertheless, in retrospect, one may conclude that their and the other resisters' efforts had not been in vain. While none of these resisters—Joanna LeDeaux, Veronica Vigil, J. Herbert Quinn, Marie Cueto, the Seattle women—had known one another beforehand, in the process of their resistance they and their defense committees came into contact and began to network, creating a much more powerful public protest voice against grand jury abuse than any one single defense committee or resister would have. As Jill Raymond later noted, "We didn't know any of these people [the other resisters] before this happened, but we all got together. Our defense committee worked with their defense committees. It was as if the FBI had put together the very network that they claimed had already existed. Very literally, they created an alliance that lasted for many years" (1989, 301).

Because of their defiant stand in February and subsequent imprisonment, Ellen Grusse and Terri Turgeon had become celebrities in the Connecticut women's community—a status they did not relish. Ellen thought the public image of them as "superstrong," unflappable Amazons belied the reality that they were in fact "often confused and very frightened women. . . . People try to make us into leaders. We aren't leaders and we don't want to be," she lamented. "We're no longer private individuals. . . . We're public figures. All this has made it very hard for me to be me—just an ordinary person, which is what I am and what I want to be" (Harris 1976c, 76, 80).

Terri realized that such public apotheosis could go to one's head and felt the need to reexamine her motives in resisting the FBI and grand jury to make sure she wasn't cruising on an "ego-trip." "I'd never been one to analyze myself, but this time I had to. When I thought about it, I realized that the stand I was taking had nothing to do with my ego, because being a celebrity of any kind was the last thing I wanted. I just wanted and want to be left alone, to live in peace in my own way." In concluding her self-examination, she "decided . . . that I had to do what I was doing because it was right. . . . I knew that I was sincere in my decision to remain silent" (Harris 1976c, 76).

On May 6—the same day the fate of the Lexington Six was being determined by Judge Moynahan in Kentucky—the attorneys for Grusse and Turgeon, Michael Avery and Kristen Booth Glen, filed several motions before the Connecticut District Court, including one alleging that various government agencies had conducted illegal wiretapping of the phones of several persons connected to the case. As in the other grand jury contempt cases, affidavits were submitted that detailed evidence of probable surveillance. That same day, Grusse, Turgeon, and Diana Perkins were summoned before the newly empaneled grand jury—the second Grusse and Turgeon had faced. This time the questions (nineteen of them) seemed to focus on the women's community in Hartford, on "what they might have known about others who might have known Saxe and Power in Connecticut" (Harris 1976c, 81). All three refused to answer these questions; to do so would necessarily have implicated friends and acquaintances. Each was then granted use immunity.

The next day, appearing once again before the grand jury, Ellen Grusse delivered a plea directly to the jurors in which she asserted that the "sole, dominant purpose" of the grand jury had been to gather information on Saxe and Power, who had already been indicted by another grand jury. (Saxe's trial for the Philadelphia and Newburyport robberies was already on the verge of a plea-bargained conviction.) Grusse went on to say that the FBI had as one of its purposes "to harass and intimidate people, particularly women's groups." She concluded by asking the jurors "to take control of your own proceedings and refuse to be a party to the abuse of your historic function." As with similar exhortations by the Lexington Six and others, her plea likely fell on deaf ears. As attorney Avery later commented, grand jurors don't hear these admonitions because they "don't take their own function seriously. . . . They aren't even aware that they have both rights and the duty to assert them to protect the individual against the power of the state" (Harris 1976c, 81–82).

District Court Judge Jon O. Newman took under advisement the motion alleging illegal wiretapping, postponing the day of reckoning for Grusse and Turgeon until June 3. On May 12, Newman ordered the FBI to redetermine whether wiretapping had occurred. Once again, as in other cases, a sworn affidavit filed on June 6 from, in this case, William A. Harwood, a supervisor at the FBI Headquarters in Washington, that no "direct electronic surveillance" by the FBI or any other government agency had occurred in the Grusse-Turgeon case apparently sufficed to settle the issue. While acknowledging that "the Harwood affidavit does not absolutely foreclose the possibility of wiretapping in this matter . . . [and that] any central filing system may not be absolutely complete, and local filing may of course omit whatever entries are deliberately withheld," the judge nevertheless ruled that he was satisfied that government officials had complied with the court's request for a reexamination of the wiretapping allegation (*In re Marie Turgeon et al.* 1975). The equivocation in Newman's and Harwood's statements is glaring; both clearly leave open the possibility that wiretapping was going on. Indeed, a review of FBI files reveals that illegal actions do not seem to have been recorded by the FBI or, if recorded, filed, which doesn't mean that they didn't occur. Most of the records of illegal actions seem in fact to have been "filed" in what was termed a "DO NOT FILE" cache, that is, destroyed (Church Report 1976, 148). With the matter of alleged illegal wiretapping settled in the negative, Judge Newman ruled Grusse and Turgeon in civil contempt of court and ordered that they be "remanded to the custody of the United States Marshal" (*In re Marie Turgeon et al.* 1975) and escorted back to Niantic prison.

Meanwhile, considerable public support for the two women had been mounting. Approximately one hundred supporters were in the courtroom for the June 6 hearing. At one point they began chanting, "Silence is our right . . . with our sisters we will fight!" whereupon the judge threatened audience members with contempt of court (Harris 1976c, 90). The National Council of Churches—an umbrella group representing thirty-one churches with a combined membership of 40 million people—filed a friend-of-the-court brief in support of the women's resistance. In its brief the council pointed out that the coercive use of grand juries meant that those who held the moral conviction that personal connections are inviolate were most at risk of being imprisoned: "The greater the witness's moral commitment to silence, to confidentiality in human relations, the greater the possibility of perpetual incarceration." The brief concluded, "It is resoundingly offensive to the generally accepted sense of fairness of our society that a person who has committed no criminal act . . . can because of a moral commitment be placed in jail" (Harris 1976c, 86).

Perhaps because of this growing national attention and public pressure, Newman (who later became chief judge of the Second Circuit Court of Appeals, having been promoted to the court in 1978) began treating the case more respectfully. "At the start . . . Newman dismissed everything we said with utter contempt and treated us like lepers," one of the lawyers in the case commented. "But as support in the community and publicity in the media increased, he got more and more judicious and increasingly took pains to seem fair" (Harris 1976c, 86).

In order to counter Grusse's and Turgeon's claim that the grand jury had been used improperly, Newman took the surprising step of formally asking the grand jurors what they thought their purpose was. The nineteen sitting jurors were brought into the courtroom during the hearing on June 3, and the judge asked them to state what "their personal opinion of their actual purpose was." The judge then sent them out of the room to decide on their purpose, with the coaxing suggestion that it was to "investigate a possible violation of federal law that may have occurred in . . . Connecticut." This was basically to instruct the jurors that they were there to investigate possible accessory after the fact or harboring activity—not to abet the search for fugitives whose crimes had been committed in another jurisdiction.

Michael Avery asked the judge if the jurors could make their decision without the U.S. Attorney William Dow present, because he knew that Dow would further coach the jury how to answer the questions so as to sound legally correct. But Newman refused. (In fact, the grand jury itself has the right to determine who will be in the room with it; it even has the right to fire the U.S. attorney if it wishes. However, Judge Newman didn't inform the jurors of this.)

While the jury was out of the room deciding how to answer the judge's question, Ellen Grusse glanced at the word "Justice" that was carved above the judge's bench and thought what a travesty of the word these proceedings had been and what a charade the judge's interrogatory of the grand jury was. "This is the biggest farce I've ever seen," she reflected. "The Judge is covering himself . . . in case there's an appeal. First, he explained the grand jurors' duties to them, and then he asked their opinion . . . about what their purpose is. Of course, they're going to say that their purpose conforms to their duties to investigate crimes in . . . Connecticut. What else can they say? If they have any doubts about what they're supposed to say, Dow is there to help them out" (Harris 1976c, 87).

Another lawyer familiar with the case summed up the grand jury interrogatory as Newman "putting a gloss of fairness on his decision to lock up those women" (Harris 1976c, 88). Not surprisingly, the grand jury, after an hour's deliberation, told the judge what he wanted to hear and what they had been instructed to say—that they were investigating possible crimes committed in Connecticut. It is hard to escape the conclusion in this and other cases that judges and U.S. attorneys shamelessly manipulated grand jurors, and that they routinely and repeatedly exploited jurors' ignorance of the law and the Constitution.

After they were held in contempt on June 6, Ellen and Terri had a four-day reprieve before they were returned to prison. During that time they went to a women's retreat held in a woodland camp. They both found the support and understanding of the other women was vital to their own perseverance and psychological survival. "Without people who stood by us, I never would have made it," Terri later acknowledged. (Harris 1976c, 90).

On the morning of their incarceration, June 10, a rally in support of the two resisters took place in a park across from the federal building in New Haven. The crowd—about a hundred-strong—chanted,

Some of our sisters are subpoenaed
Bella ciao, bella ciao, bella ciao, ciao, ciao
Their silence makes us speak out
We want our revolution now.

The group escorted the two women to the federal building where the chant changed to "Silence is our right, is our right, is our right!" (Harris 1976c, 94). Ellen and Terri were then taken into custody by the federal marshal, handcuffed, chained together, and ferried back to prison.

Meanwhile, down in Kentucky, Jill Raymond continued to rattle around in the Franklin County Jail. The nearly two months she spent there turned out to be "one of the most terrifying times" of her entire ordeal, "a truly terrible time," Jill recently remembered. On the one hand, the physical conditions in the jail were intolerable; on the other, she was receiving increased, nearly unbearable pressure from outside political action groups not to testify. "I realized I'd been boxed into a terrible corner. . . . If I ended up testifying, I would never have any credibility ever again with anybody who did political work! I didn't plan to testify, but knowing I had no information that would help anybody find Kathy . . . had made it easier to face jail time as an 'undefined' period, in which we would try to free me with legal maneuvers, and I would stay in as long as I could, but which had this escape hatch if it became too much to bear." But this escape hatch was closed by the continued exhortations from left-wing groups that threatened expulsion from their ranks should she cooperate with the feds. "After I witnessed the rage that came from the left heaped on those of our group who did testify, I felt like I had a knife to my throat. . . . The state was squeezing me from one direction and the left from the other, and I was not doing well at that time at all" (email to author, March 22, 2018).

In addition, the psychological conditions in the jail were nearly unbearable. For days on end Jill was essentially in solitary confinement in the six-person cell. "Being alone," Jill came to realize, "is much worse than being with someone you know" (email to author, February 13, 2018). There was no radio or TV. Visitors were only granted fifteen minutes twice a week, and she was allowed only two phone calls a week. Except for the brief court appearance in May, she hadn't been outdoors since her incarceration in March.

One visitor to the jail, Janet Gallagher of the New York Grand Jury Project, thought Jill seemed "depressed and very physically worn." She was shocked at the abject conditions in which she found Jill. "I was freaked," Gallagher reported. The conditions were "so much worse than I expected," making her wonder whether resisters like Jill were being asked to pay too high a price by outside activists who were unaware of the "brutal physical" harshness such incarceration entailed, having instead a rather "romantic view of prison" (1987).

One of the worse aspects of Jill's situation was the lack of privacy. The front wall of the cell was completely open. The shower stall had no curtain. Male guards entertained themselves by watching her, as they had with Nancy Scott and Marla Seymour. In addition, Jill had to resist one guard's groping (Hixson 1977; *In re Jill Raymond* 1975).

In general, though, Jill felt relatively safe from guards' sexual assault, because of the high visibility of the cell and the publicity the case had attracted, as well as by her race and class privileges. However, the guards (all male and very right-wing) did taunt her about her lesbianism, telling her how "I 'need a man'!" Jill reported. "Jesus, If they only remembered how many women wind up in the slammer because of men . . . who forge checks and get their girl friends to cash them." Several of the women who were temporary cellmates of Jill in Franklin County had in fact "got [there] one way or another," she had discovered, "because of some goddamn man" (letter to author, June 16, 1975).

After an initial solitary stretch, Jill was joined by several others. She was glad for their company but most of these women were in jail for only a day or two. Even so, like Carey Junkin, Jill was surprised at how supportive her cellmates were for her case and also how indifferent they were when they learned that she was "one of those!"—a lesbian (Raymond, letter to author, June 16, 1975).

Soon after Jill arrived in the Frankfort jail, she was joined by a teenager named Beverly, who was half Native American and in for public drunkenness and resisting arrest. Although young, this was not Beverly's first time in jail. She was a regular who had decorated the cell wall with graffiti on previous stays. Beverly was tough; on one occasion she managed to break a jailor's thumb while resisting arrest. She and Jill played cards during her five-day stay, and they discussed lesbianism. Beverly was curious to know how Jill had come to figure out her sexuality, which suggested to Jill that she was wrestling with the question herself. Jill came to admire Beverly's toughness and her coolness about being in jail. Jill missed her when she left, though they corresponded once afterward (Raymond 1976a, 15).

A couple of days before Beverly left in mid-May, another woman, Connie, joined them, arrested for forging and stealing government checks. Unlike Beverly, Connie was a first-timer who freaked out about being in jail, as well as about being locked up with a lesbian (as forewarned by warden John Burke). The same warden also propositioned Connie; he would bail her out if she would sleep with him. Jill found Connie's fearfulness and inability to cope unsettling. She much preferred Beverly's nonchalance, which helped her to put her own situation in some perspective (Raymond 1976a, 13–17).

Judge Moynahan denied the Raymond plea for bail on June 3 after which Sedler filed a second appeal to the Sixth Circuit Court. (In mid-May, the appeals court had declared that their remand order had been misinterpreted and that a second appeal was required [Raymond, letter to author, May 29, 1975]). Since by law the court had to respond to the second appeal within thirty days, Jill had hopes that by early July she might be freed. A hearing was scheduled (but never held) for June 17, at which point bail was once again denied by the appeals court. As Susan Saxe wryly observed to Jill in a letter, "being a prisoner is such fun . . . full of surprises" (Raymond, letter to author, June 16, 1975).

Shortly after the bail plea was denied, Jill found herself with two new cellmates, Helen and Nanny. Jill had encountered Helen before on the night she had spent in the Madison County Jail with Gail Cohee before the remand hearing on May 6. Helen was "slightly insane" (Raymond 1976a, 6), so much so that the matron in the Madison County Jail, Katherine King, had locked Helen in a separate cell that night for Gail's and Jill's protection. But Jill had no such luck in the Frankfort jail; she had to live with Helen's hysterical laugh for ten days.

Nanny was an older African American woman who proved to be a steadying counterpoint to Helen. She followed an orderly routine, waking up early, showering, and reading the Bible. She was also caring and motherly toward Jill, sometimes even bringing breakfast to her bed. Like many succeeding cellmates, Nanny was supportive of Jill's case and loved the principled statement of resistance the Lexington Six had issued at the time of their contempt sentencing. Nanny had been married five times: "But no more!" She was afraid of being released to her most recent ex-husband because he beat her, and she hoped to be probated to her mother instead.

Jill was interested to see how Helen, a southern, working-class white, and Nanny, a Black, got along. She was surprised to find that their relationship was handled "totally casually," and she came to realize that "as a working-class white, Blacks were much more a part of [Helen's] everyday existence" than Jill's own middle-class world. "Nanny and Helen . . . had adapted to living with each other much more readily than I had adapted to either of them" (Raymond 1976a, 23).

Right after Helen and Nanny were released, Jill was joined by a seriously psychotic woman who was so crazy that Jill came close to agreeing to testify in order to get away from her. When the jailor introduced the woman into the cell, he said to Jill, "Make sure she doesn't hang herself" (Raymond, email to author, June 25, 2018). But then a new cellmate arrived, Kathy D., who helped Jill deal with the "crazy-lady" crisis, which only lasted a day or two, as it turned out.

Kathy D. was a classic hippie—"sort of the original hippie-check-sex-junkie-freak"—in for "growing weed" (possession and production of marijuana). Like Beverly, Kathy was a regular who had been busted several times for illegal drug-related activities. At a low point in her own ordeal, Jill found Kathy to be a great comfort, despite her hyped-up, talkative (nonstop) personality. But like Beverly's, Kathy's toughness and casual attitude toward incarceration—that it was "no big deal"—helped calm Jill's own shakiness and anxieties. Kathy was in fact "scornful of people who fell apart over things like [jail]" (Raymond 1976a, 26, 27). Indeed, she lectured Jill not to be too passive and submissive. On the other hand, she wasn't particularly supportive of Jill's principled resistance, since she herself didn't believe anything was worth making such a fuss over, an attitude typical of the apolitical, individualistic "drop-out turn-on" counterculture she belonged to.

In the last week of June and the first two weeks of July, Jill's cell became crowded, at times full to its six-person capacity, and the interpersonal relationships among the cellmates became increasingly complex. During the latter part of Kathy's week-long stay, a woman named Savage arrived. True to her name, she was a tough butch, in for armed robbery and aiding in a federal prison escape. Savage initially came on to Kathy aggressively, but she soon calmed down, and they all made their peace. Savage became an ally when three even more unsettling newcomers arrived: Judy, Vicki, and Missy, all in for trafficking or possession of drugs. Judy was an addict undergoing withdrawal traumas, and Missy and Vicki developed a strange "master-slave relationship" with Missy as Vicki's "whipping boy." Vicki herself, though, seemed to be "falling apart" and at the same time hostile, threatening violence, and with "a loser's instincts," Jill thought. But Judy, who after a night of "cold turkey" seemed to be back on her feet, was somehow able to manage Vicki, getting her under control. Jill watched all of this "like a sociologist" (Raymond 1976a, 34, 33, 32).

By late July there was still no decision forthcoming from the appeals court—despite the thirty-day deadline. A local newspaper headline referred to it as the "'Lost' Appeal" (Gatz, July 28, 1975a). Jill was getting desperate.

Reprieve came, however, from an unexpected source—a series of newspaper articles by Carolyn Gatz, a reporter for the *Lexington Herald-Leader*. (Gatz later went on to a distinguished career at the Louisville *Courier-Journal* as an investigative reporter and associate editor.) Although, according to the U.S. marshals' rule book, reporters were not allowed in the jail, Gatz managed to get inside as a "visitor" and interview Jill about the jail conditions. The two women huddled at the jail bars whispering, so that a surveillance guard couldn't hear what they were saying. It was very "cloak and dagger!" Jill recalled (Raymond, email to author, March 25, 2018).

"Jill Raymond's world," the Gatz article began, "consists for now of a six-bunk, barred cell. . . . Most of the last two months [have been] an experience in solitude" (Gatz, July 28, 1975a). The article went on to point out how inadequate the jail was in accommodating a woman prisoner; there was no matron, no women guards, and no privacy.

The article's exposé of the miserable jail conditions had a sensational, if unintended, result. The federal marshal, Sherman Hansford (under Judge Moynahan's direction), immediately transferred Jill to another jail, the Madison County Jail in Richmond, which Carey Junkin and Debbie Hands had found intolerable. Although in an interview with Gatz the marshal denied the move was punitive, it clearly appears to have been so. The Madison County Jail was known to be probably the worst in the state, graded "poor" on a scale of "very poor" to "very good" by the Kentucky

Bureau of Corrections, whereas the Franklin County Jail that Jill was leaving was rated "good." When asked why then the transfer, the marshal replied, "I don't have to have a reason." Further suggesting a punitive motive, officials imposed much stricter visiting regulations for Jill in Madison County, limiting visitors to her attorney and immediate family. The marshal acknowledged to Gatz that such restrictions were not the norm for federal prisoners (Gatz, July 30,1975).

As it turned out, in one of the ironies of the case, the conditions in the Richmond jail, though physically terrible, turned out to be psychologically much better for Jill than they had been in her previous locale. In part, this was because, as a backwater, quirky, family-run operation, the Madison County Jail was much laxer, more colorful, lively, and personality-driven than the austere, impersonal, bureaucratic drabness of the Franklin County pen. "When I got to Richmond," Jill recalled, "I immediately began to revive—emotionally, psychologically—and I felt like I could hang on a little longer" (Raymond, email to author, March 22, 2018).

CHAPTER EIGHT

Grand Jury Abuse: Growing Public Awareness

Richmond—the site of Madison County Jail, Jill Raymond's new home—is a town about an hour south of Lexington, on the margins of Appalachia to the east. Jefferson Davis, president of the Confederacy, once lived there. As is typical in rural America, the town centers around a square in which sits the county courthouse. Located behind the courthouse, in a flat, white-brick building, was the jail, housed together with the family quarters of the jailor, Frank King; his wife, Katherine, who served as the jail matron as well as its cook; and their thirteen children, the oldest sons of whom served as jail guards. Hanging over the entrance to the jail was a sign that read,

FRANK KING, JAILER

YOU-ALLS FRIEND.

Frank King was illiterate and had to rely on his wife to read court documents.

Jill was housed on the third floor of the jail but let out occasionally to visit with supporters in the lobby of the jail, which featured an assortment of spittoons, a Coke machine, and a torn vinyl couch that sat beneath a photo of Frank's parents, one of whom—his father—often ended up in jail himself on weekends due to intoxication. On the wall of the lobby was a calendar marked "Collins Funeral Home. Dependable Service."

Over the barred metal entrance door to the jail proper was a handmade sign with the following adaptation from Matthew 25:35–46:

> *For they were hungry, and ye*
> *gave them food. They were*
> *thirsty and ye gave them drink.*
> *They were naked and ye clothed*
> *them. . . . And they will go away into eternal punishment, but*
> *the righteous into eternal life. (Hixson 1977)*

This Christian message of compassion likely reflected the philosophy of Katherine King, who took a kindly maternal interest in Jill, to the point where the two became good friends. It was in large part because of Katherine's humane treatment that Jill was able to endure the remaining nine months of her ordeal.

Also helpful were the hundreds of letters of support Jill began receiving from around the country, as her case attracted national attention. Especially meaningful were the letters from Susan Saxe. The two began corresponding shortly after Susan was arrested in March. They exchanged the letters through their attorneys to avoid having them read and censored by prison authorities and the FBI. Reconnected with Susan, Jill felt "like I had her friendship back in my life and it helped me endure jail" (Raymond, email to author, February 13, 2018). Especially encouraging was Susan's assurance to Jill that she would continue to love and support her even if Jill in the end felt she had to testify.

In a letter dated May 30, 1975, shortly before Susan entered her Philadelphia plea deal on June 9—a letter apparently published by the Susan Saxe Defense Committee and widely circulated because of its lengthy explanation of her political position—Susan assured Jill of her continuing love and friendship: "I love you, Jill. . . . I'm damn proud to be known as your friend." Susan went on to express her continuing support for the others of the Lexington Six who had by then testified "They have done one fuck of a lot more for their principles than most people I know, and while I cannot support their talking, I love them and understand. It is not the nature of feminist justice to hold a person perpetually in the bad graces of the goddess for one weakness, especially an understandable one. . . . What's done is done . . . and understood . . . and forgiven. Now we move ahead" (Saxe, letter to Raymond, May 30, 1975).

Susan also asked Jill if she would write a response to the Jill Johnston piece that had criticized Saxe as a "Bonnie without Clyde." Saxe made the point that Johnston and those who agreed with her were misdirecting their attention: "We have to point the finger of guilt directly at the Man. The state alone is responsible for oppression, not the freedom fighters who dare to struggle against its unjust powers. It is incorrect," therefore, to claim that "repression is the fault of revolutionaries" (letter to Raymond, May 30, 1975). Jill agreed to write such a response, which appeared several months later, as noted previously.

Susan also recounted how the FBI tried to get her to inform on Kathy Power and others she had known while underground in exchange for reduced sentences—a proposal she roundly rejected: "It was made clear to me by the FBI on the first night [of her arrest] that they would give me all kinds of breaks in exchange for testimony against other people, and particularly information leading to the arrest and conviction of my dear sister Kathy. I don't think I have to tell you what my response is, was, and always will be to any such outrageous form of betrayal. Likewise to any notion of pulling Alpert's good-little-girl-led-astray-by-those-nasty-old-ex-cons-who-just-wants-to-go-home-to-daddy-and-be-peaceful-law-abiding-feminist–(??????!!!!!!) Bullshit." In short, Saxe concluded, "I will never cooperate, and will never never recant" (letter to Raymond, May 30, 1975).

An even more powerfully supportive letter pledging solidarity came from Susan Saxe in mid-July when Jill's spirits were reaching a low point in Franklin County. It was written in response to a despairing letter Jill had sent Susan in which she confessed her fears and anxieties, saying she didn't know whether she could continue to endure her jail confinement much longer. Susan, now in a county jail in Worcester, Massachusetts, awaiting her own trial in Boston, reassured Jill of her continuing love and support regardless of what Jill decided to do:

Dearest Jill, First things first—I love you, and I understand. There is nothing you could do that would make me lose faith in you as a person.

Nothing. . . . We are all ordinary women, and we can only do as much
as we are capable of doing. . . . We can struggle to our limits, give it
our best, know that we have tried, and go on from there, stronger and
wiser for the battle. As long as we are living, there is no such thing as
defeat. . . . And Jill, when and if you go into that room to hand over
your sword, as it were, go in with your head held high. . . . All I ask
is that you come back fighting. . . . I'll still be there, fighting by your
side. . . . Babe, if there is anything I can do or say or write to help you,
please let me do it. I have a lot of strength and that's what it's there
for. Lean on me. . . . I'll help you. . . . Hang on to me, babe—I'm
with you always. Love, Lena (Saxe, letter to Raymond, July 16, 1975)

A week after Jill's arrival in the Madison County Jail her hopes of winning release on appeal were dashed. On August 5, 1975, the Sixth Circuit Court of Appeals, sitting in Cincinnati, upheld Judge Moynahan's determination that the dominant purpose of the Lexington grand jury was not to apprehend fugitives but "to inquire into new matters constituting alleged violations of certain laws of the United States" (Appeal B 1975, 4). Those "new matters" were harboring fugitives and/or being an accessory after the fact. The decision was unanimous, issued by a three-judge panel consisting of Harry Phillips, a Kennedy appointee; John W. Peck II, a Johnson appointee; and William E. Miller, a Nixon appointee. The Sixth Circuit Court also determined that there had not been "an abuse of the grand jury process" and that for an FBI agent such as Wayne McDonald to give "background information" to the grand jury did not, as attorneys Robert Sedler and Judith Peterson had argued, in effect grant unauthorized subpoena power to the FBI (Gatz, August 6, 1975). Jill's attorneys said they intended to appeal the decision to the U.S. Supreme Court, a plan they later reconsidered.

Since the circuit court seems to have determined somewhat ex post facto that the principal purpose of the Lexington grand jury was to investigate the crime of harboring federal fugitives—and not, as grand jury foreperson Ralph Agee articulated, "to find out where those two girls [Saxe and Power] are"—one has to assume that U.S. Attorney Eugene Siler's sealed affidavit filed in the May 6 hearing must have presented some sort of evidence that would support the claim the grand jury was investigating the harboring charge. By then, however, Moynahan and Siler, as well as the FBI, must have known that the harboring charge was bogus because numerous informants and cooperating witnesses, such as the Enslings, had told them that Saxe and Power had no "pre-arranged contacts" in Lexington before their arrival (FBI, March 6, 1975), and that no one in Lexington knew of Lena's and May's true identities or histories at the time of their presence in the city. Indeed, one agent told Meredith Moore, an Alfalfa employee, as much, according to her March 8 testimony, cited previously. On February 5, she testified, Wayne McDonald "said no, he was sure that no one in Lexington know [sic] who they were when they were here" (Transcript 1975, DE 46–47, 504). McDonald denied having said this.

It seems likely that Siler in the sealed affidavit may have been relying on the incorrect or falsified FBI teletype issued, according to a cover memo, by the New Haven bureau on February 25, 1975, which described an April 12, 1974, collect phone call to Jill Raymond from the Hartford warehouse. As noted previously, the phone call in question did not occur until September 1974, *after* Kathy Power had left Lexington (and even at this date, Jill still did not know her as Kathy Power but as May Kelly, nor of her bank-robbing past). So there was no basis or uncontaminated evidence to support a harboring charge. It seems that the Sixth Circuit Court's remand order of April 28, 1975, forced Siler and Moynahan to come up with a legally justifiable cover for the whole grand jury operation, and the harboring charge served the purpose.

In his appeal of the May 6 decision, Robert Sedler pointed out that the timing of the entrance of the harboring charge into the picture was "indeed questionable," given that FBI Agent Wayne McDonald doesn't appear to have raised the harboring issue in the background information he gave the grand jury before the witnesses were called to testify. McDonald, Sedler and Peterson hypothesized, said "nothing about any FBI investigation into possible violation of the laws of the United States." But in the May 6 hearing on what the "sole and dominant" purpose of the grand jury was, Judge Moynahan didn't allow Sedler to present evidence in support of this claim or to cross-examine Agent McDonald under oath on the subject (Appeal B 1975, 4).

Had Sedler been allowed to see the FBI document in question, which alleged the April 12, 1974, phone call (the document was obtained only many years later under a FOIA request by Jill Raymond), or had it been presented in evidence, Sedler could have raised critical questions about its veracity by producing countervailing testimony and by reexamining phone company records, thereby challenging—perhaps fatally—the whole harboring charge. And, even if the prosecutor had had legitimate evidence that Jill Raymond had harbored Saxe and Power, that evidence could not have been used to indict her, because she had been granted use immunity.

While it is not implausible for federal officials to have considered the possibility at the start of their investigation in January 1975 that activists in Lexington had knowingly harbored Saxe and Power, it should have been clear to them after interviewing scores of members of the radical community that no one in Lexington knew at the time of the two fugitives' past or true identity. Virtually no one would have told them this—and indeed in the FBI files there are no reports of such testimony.

Indeed, in Jill Raymond's extant FBI files (not available to her attorneys in 1975 for their appeal), the designated classification number for the documents is 91, the FBI classification number for bank robbery, and not 150, the FBI classification number for harboring of federal fugitives. FBI file documents are designated by numbers such as, for example, 100–15375–17. The first number indicates the type of case; for example, 100 represents domestic security; 98, sabotage; 55, counterfeiting; 79, missing persons, and so forth. The second number designates the document's place in the file of a particular regional bureau. For example, the Lexington Six case is designated 91–5755: 91 for bank robbery and 5755 for the Louisville Bureau office, which oversaw the Lexington FBI operation. The FBI code name for the case was GILROB: OO:BS; GIL referring to William Gilday, one of the participants in the Brighton bank robbery, and ROB meaning robbery. OO means "Office of Origin," and BS signifies "Boston Field Office."

In the February 25, 1975, report issued by the New Haven FBI bureau, which includes the false information about an alleged April 12, 1974, collect phone call to Jill Raymond, the case is designated by the numbers 91 (bank robbery) and 98 (sabotage), as well as by the following FBI code terms: BR (Bank Robbery), UFAP-MURDER (Unlawful Flight to Avoid

Prosecution), REVACT-VIOLENCE (Revolutionary Act), TGP (Theft of Government Property), DGP (Destruction of Government Property), SABOTAGE, ESPIONAGE, and ITSMV (Interstate Transportation of Stolen Motor Vehicles).

At the bottom of the document a "FUG SUP" ("Fugitive Support") stamp was added at a later date by "FIVE," which means "Division Five," the intelligence or investigative division of the bureau, which dealt with domestic or internal security cases (Buitrago and Immerman 1981, 186). The date stamped next to FUG SUP is August 6, 1975, a suspicious date given that the Sixth Circuit Court ruling that the harboring charge legitimized the Lexington grand jury was issued on August 5. (It is, however, not entirely clear whether the August 6 date refers to the FUG SUP stamp.)

It is clear, though, from the principal classification (91) on the February 25 memo that the FBI's primary concern in the winter and spring of 1975 was with the Brighton bank robbery and the apprehension of its perpetrators, *not* collecting evidence for indictments on the charge of harboring fugitives. Only in the FBI documents concerning the Connecticut case of Ellen Grusse and Terri Turgeon do the files indicate a specific concern that said individuals "may be involved in possible harboring of SAXE and POWER or accessory after the fact of a felony" (FBI, January 28, 1975b). So it would seem that the grand jury interrogations of the Lexington Six were indeed what their attorneys claimed, namely, to aid in the collection of "apprehension information" (Appeal B 1975, 4) about already-indicted fugitives—to "find out where those two girls are"—an improper and unconstitutional purpose. It also appears that the introduction of the harboring charge issue was an attempt to provide legal cover for the grand jury and federal prosecution of the Lexington Six and especially for the continuing incarceration of Jill Raymond. Robert Sedler observed many years later, "There was no evidence that the six knew that Lena and May were Susan and Kathy," and "the FBI and the U.S. Attorney came to know this." For Judge Moynahan, "it became a matter . . . of defending the FBI and grand jury system" (Sedler 1986).

Had indeed—in one of the ironies of the case—the Lexington Six actually been indicted by the grand jury on charges of harboring federal fugitives and brought to trial, they would have been afforded much greater legal protections than they received as recalcitrant grand jury witnesses. They would have had the opportunity to present evidence to prove their innocence. They would have been judged by a jury of their peers, not by a vindictive judge. They would have had Bill of Rights protections, such as the First Amendment guarantee of freedom of association and the right to protest government injustice; the Fourth Amendment right to be "secure in one's person, houses, papers, and effects, against unreasonable search and seizure"; the Fifth Amendment protection against self-incrimination; the Sixth Amendment's right to a fair trial, "speedy and public"; the Seventh Amendment's guarantee of a "trial by jury"; and the Eight Amendment's ban on "cruel and unusual punishments." In fact, as Emmy Hixson, one of Jill's attorneys and later director of the Coalition to End Grand Jury Abuse in Washington, DC, testified before a House subcommittee in 1977, "Grand jury witnesses surrender their constitutional birthright when they enter the grand jury room" (Eilberg Hearings 1977, 1:890). Jill Raymond herself later ruefully noted, "Actually, if they had indicted us, we would have had the full protection that a trial by a jury of your peers provides, the right to cross-examine and present witnesses and the right to present more complete evidence. We probably would never have spent a day in jail. We certainly would have been granted bail. . . . The irony . . . is fantastic, because without ever being so much as charged with a crime, we spent a great deal of time in jail" (Raymond 1989, 301).

In testimony before the House subcommittee investigating grand jury abuse convened in 1977 by Joshua Eilberg, representative from Pennsylvania, Doris Peterson, an attorney for the Center for Constitutional Rights, pointed to the decisions in the Raymond, Grusse and Turgeon, and Fort Worth Five cases as examples where secret sealed affidavits filed by the government sufficed to condemn witnesses to months in jail without due process—an impropriety, she argued, that had become standard operating procedure in the federal judiciary. "It has become routine in grand jury cases," she stated, "for the government to submit *ex parte in camera* affidavits designed to justify the investigation. . . . The witness never has an opportunity to rebut the conclusions, facts or inferences contained in these submissions, yet they are the basis on which the witness' challenge to the legality of the grand jury subpoena is rejected . . . and that a person is ultimately . . . jailed for contempt" (Eilberg Hearings 1977, 1:42).

In the case of Jill Raymond, Peterson noted how "the Court accepted at face value the secret submission of the government alleging that harboring was the primary purpose of the grand jury and the witnesses' counsel [Sedler] was given no opportunity to examine either the agents or the prosecutors on this question." Significantly, Peterson continued, "After Ms. Raymond was jailed, the so-called 'harboring' investigation was halted" (Eilberg Hearings 1977, 1:42). Indeed, after Raymond was jailed, the Lexington grand jury and U.S. Attorney Siler conducted no further inquiries into the issue of whether anyone in Lexington had knowingly harbored Susan Saxe and Kathy Power. And no further subpoenas were issued.

A "similar pattern of abuse" occurred in the New Haven case of Ellen Grusse and Terri Turgeon and that of the Fort Worth Five. In the latter case, a Fifth Circuit Court judge, Griffin Bell, later a U.S. attorney general, rejected the witnesses' appeal on the basis of secret materials submitted by the government—materials that were later revealed to have included illegal FBI wiretaps of the witnesses' attorney. When this information was inadvertently disclosed, U.S. Supreme Court Justice William O. Douglas, as noted, ordered the witnesses' release. By this time, though, they had served ten months in Texas county jails.

As Peterson stated, "Such things would not happen at a criminal trial" (Eilberg Hearings 1977, 1:56) because fully indicted persons—unlike those held in civil contempt—would enjoy their full constitutional rights, including the right to cross-examine accusatory evidence, such as, in Jill Raymond's case, the FBI teletype report of February 25, 1975, as well as Wayne McDonald's "background information" and any other materials the FBI may have obtained, legally or illegally.

Upon hearing the Sixth Circuit's decision on August 5 upholding the legitimacy of the Lexington grand jury's rationale, Jill Raymond issued a statement in which she acknowledged she had never really "believe[d] that the courts would free us," despite the fact that "our case is a clear example of power abuse" and despite having a slim hope that her case was so blatant an example of the "contradictions in our system" that "even its own judges would have to confront them" and overturn Judge Moynahan's flawed decision (Raymond 1975b).

By this time Jill had spent, as she noted, five months in three Kentucky county jails, which had "taken a big, painful toll on me and the support community." But her hope was that her experience—however painful—would not have been in vain, having exposed to the public the unfairness and corruptness of the U.S. judicial system. In jail Jill had come to realize that her case was not unique: "People are regularly abused" by the system: "our most disgusting nightmares made routine" (Raymond 1975b). The Lexington Grand Jury Defense Committee succinctly summed up the situation in their response to the circuit court's decision: "Being in a Kentucky county jail at all is probably a cruel and unusual punishment because of their notoriously inhumane conditions. . . . For all prisoners in those jails the forced idleness of being kept in small cells, the lack of sunlight and proper ventilation, lack of recreation facilities constitutes a violation of basic human needs" (1975).

While all these court proceedings were occurring, Jill herself was getting established in her new surroundings in the Madison County Jail cell in Richmond, Kentucky, and becoming acquainted with her new cellmates. The cell itself was larger, lighter, and airier than the one she had left in Franklin County. She could actually look out the windows and see the townspeople in the streets below. It was very hot—at times unbearably so—and there was no air conditioning, but inmates did have a large fan before which they lay their mattresses on especially hot nights.

When Jill entered the cell with her belongings on July 29, 1975, there were three women in the cell to greet her: Paula, Marilyn, and Donna. While Marilyn welcomed Jill, the other two had "don't mess with me" expressions, and Jill wasn't sure what to expect. However, after a short chat with them, she felt a flood of relief: "These women were all right." Almost immediately, Jill felt a sense of confidence and security returning (Raymond 1976a, 42).

All three women were in their early twenties and were charged with cashing stolen checks. All three were in transition to the federal penitentiary in Alderson, West Virginia. Marilyn had been there before and said it was a "nice" place (presumably in comparison with Kentucky county jails), which planted the idea in Jill's mind of trying to get transferred there (Raymond 1976a, 43)—which, however, never happened.

Two more women soon joined them—one in briefly for public drunkenness and the other in for cashing cold checks and escaping from the

Federal Corrections Institute in Lexington. The latter, Jane, was an older woman who spent much of her time in jail crocheting a turquoise and white afghan. Jill's main relationships, though, were with Donna and Paula. It was Paula, a hippie type somewhat similar to Kathy D. in Frankfort, who provided Jill's main support during her first weeks in Madison County. Paula had been propositioned somewhat unceremoniously by an overnight transient whom they dubbed "Candy Man." This woman abruptly approached Paula soon after she arrived; shone a flashlight on her to appraise her looks, which apparently passed muster; and suggested sex. Paula, who was straight, was understandably unnerved by this episode, and Jill tried to reassure her that most lesbians "on the outside" didn't behave this way (Raymond 1976a, 46). Paula was another one, like Beverly and Kathy D., who seemed to be able to cope with jail conditions, which Jill found strengthening, so she was sorry to see Paula leave at the end of August.

Jill was beginning to appreciate how much these jail friends meant to her. They were like "life rafts," she felt, vital to her psychological survival. It seemed strange to her, though, that one would develop such strong relationships and such "psychological dependence on other people — people [one] hardly knew." Spaced apart, they were like isolated "sandbars" enabling her "to make it from one sandbar to another without going under" (Raymond 1976a, 51, 52).

But her relations with sister cellmates were necessarily short-lived, as the women were soon transferred elsewhere, leaving Jill alone again. One of the most difficult things about being in jail, Jill later came to realize, was the inevitably fleeting nature of relationships there. "The hardest thing," she told reporter Carolyn Gatz, "is having my life yanked around by people coming and going. It's easy to establish the kind of bond you develop with people in jail and then they get yanked out" (Gatz, March 8, 1976).

Despite the apparent flaws in the Sixth Circuit's decision, Jill Raymond and her attorneys decided not to appeal the ruling to the Supreme Court. Immediately following that decision, however, they did appeal for a stay of execution to the Supreme Court on August 6, which would have released Jill on bail, if granted. On August 21, however, Justice Thurgood Marshall denied *certiorari* to that plea. A similar appeal was addressed to the Court on September 26, but it too was denied by Justice William O. Douglas four days later. Jill thus remained in the Madison County Jail.

The reason Jill and attorneys Sedler and Peterson decided against appealing the case to the Supreme Court was that the conservative-leaning court had ruled against plaintiffs in similar cases, and they did not want to risk having the Court rule against her, thus "making bad law," as Rhonda Copelon of the Center for Constitutional Rights explained in her testimony on March 17, 1977, before the House Judiciary Subcommittee investigating grand jury abuse. The Supreme Court had in three recent cases—-*U.S. v. Mandugano* (1976), *U.S. v. Wong* (1977), and *U.S. v. Washington* (1977)—overturned "lower court rulings sustaining the rights of grand jury witnesses." In view of these decisions, and in view of the fact that the Court had denied *certiorari* to Jill's appeal, she and her attorneys determined that "the hostility of the Court was so great she didn't want them to take her case, even though there was an overwhelming factual showing [of wrongful use of the grand jury.] . . . [Raymond] felt that to do that would be a waste of time or would give the Court an opportunity . . . to make further bad law" (Eilberg Hearings 1977, 1:80).

The only legal remedy remaining for Jill Raymond was to file a "Grumbles motion" to claim that her incarceration was being maintained for purely punitive reasons—an unconstitutional purpose. Attorneys for Ellen Grusse and Terri Turgeon filed such a motion on September 26, in conjunction with which the Grand Jury Project organized a series of nationwide protest demonstrations demanding that the various grand jury resisters who remained in jail—including Joanna LeDeaux, Veronica Vigil, Ellen Grusse, Terri Turgeon, and Jill Raymond—be released. As part of this national protest, on September 23 the Lexington Grand Jury Defense Committee held a twenty-four-hour vigil in front of the federal courthouse in Lexington in hopes of intensifying public pressure for Jill's release (Gatz, September 27, 1975). A similar candlelight vigil was held in Louisville on September 20 with Emmy Hixson, Marla Seymour, and Nancy Scott as speakers (Creed 1975). And on September 27, a rally with approximately five hundred in attendance was held in New Haven in support of Grusse, Turgeon, and the others. Among the groups represented there were the New York Grand Jury Defense Committee, the Susan Saxe Defense Committee, the Puerto Rican Socialist Party, the American Indian Movement, the Martin Sostre Defense Committee, and the New York Black Liberation Army Defense Committee. The ethnic and cultural diversity of the groups indicates how the grand jury resistance movement had become a national, multiethnic, and multiracial campaign. None of these protest actions, however, yielded the desired results. All of the resisters remained in jail through the fall of 1975.

On September 18, 1975, Patty Hearst was captured in San Francisco, thus ending one of the largest FBI (wo)manhunts in history—codenamed HEARNAP in the FBI files. And on September 26, Pat Swinton, accused of conspiracy to bomb several corporate buildings in New York City as part of the antiwar movement, was acquitted, in part because her one-time accomplice Jane Alpert refused to testify against her, for which Alpert received an additional several months' prison sentence for contempt of court.

Meanwhile, on September 21, U.S. Attorney Eugene Siler, who had prosecuted the Lexington Six, was promoted to the U.S. District Court of Eastern Kentucky by President Gerald Ford; he thus joined Bernard Moynahan on the Kentucky bench. Siler was replaced by Eldon L. Webb as U.S. attorney for the district; he thus took over the Jill Raymond case. Siler eventually replaced Moynahan in 1984 as chief judge, and in 1991 was named to the Sixth Circuit Court of Appeals in Cincinnati.

On October 8, Jill's attorneys filed one more appeal to the Supreme Court. This time Justice Potter Stewart referred the matter to the full Court, but on October 20, 1975, that appeal was also rejected. In response Jill angrily told a reporter (in a front-page article in the Louisville *Courier-Journal*): "I am contemptuous. I am proud to be in jail on a charge that's labeled contempt, because that's exactly what I feel for the government" (Woolley 1975).

In a last-ditch attempt to get Jill released before the end of the grand jury term, that is, by May 1976, M. E. Hixson and William H. Allison, who had newly taken over as Jill's attorneys (Robert Sedler had left Kentucky to assume a position at Wayne State University in Detroit), filed a Grumbles motion with the district court on November 7, 1975. A Grumbles motion, which was later filed successfully, as noted, in the cases of Marie Cueto and Raisa Nemikin, referred to a New Jersey contempt case *In re Grumbles*

(1973) where grand jury resisters Patricia and Donald Grumbles were released early from their prison terms by the presiding judge because he felt that incarceration had become "punitive," which was not a proper purpose of a contempt citation. (The proper purpose is to coerce testimony.)

In the "Motion for Revocation of Order of Confinement," the Grumbles motion filed on behalf of Jill Raymond, much of which was prepared by Rhonda Copelon, Hixson argued that as Jill maintained in accompanying affidavits that she was determined to continue her defiance and refuse to testify, further "incarceration will not be effective in compelling her testimony." After all, Jill had already spent eight months in miserable conditions in Kentucky county jails without losing her resolve to resist and therefore further confinement was not likely to be effective. "Continued incarceration of the witness would [therefore] be punitive rather than coercive" (*In re Jill Raymond* 1975).

Hixson further argued that since the alleged purpose for which Raymond's grand jury testimony was being coerced—indictments on the crime of harboring federal fugitives—had apparently been dropped by federal law enforcement officials, her testimony should no longer be sought. No further subpoenas had been issued, despite the testimony of the other five of the Lexington Six, which presumably would have led to harboring indictments had any of them testified that any harboring had taken place. And the grand jury was no longer investigating the subject. So the issue appeared to be moot. The federal officials appeared to have concluded that no harboring took place. So what would be the purpose of Jill Raymond's testimony, which would only ratify what the other five had already stated under oath—that no harboring had occurred?

Even if the actual purpose of the grand jury were acknowledged—to help catch the two fugitives, Saxe and Power—any testimony Jill would have to offer about the whereabouts of Kathy Power (Saxe was already in custody)—information that in any event she didn't have—would have been useless. Power was long gone. Hixson, however, did not make this point, given that the search for the fugitives had, according to the government (the Siler May 6 affidavit), never been the official purpose of the grand jury.

"It seemed to me," Jill later wrote, "at that point the purpose [of] keeping me imprisoned was purely punitive. After I'd been in jail that long [nine months], any 'information' I had was useless. Susan Saxe had been caught and was already on her way to trial. The trail had to be fairly cold for Kathy Power. . . . By then . . . they had whatever information against me that was available. Obviously, it wasn't enough to come up with an indictment" (Raymond 1989, 301).

In her affidavits accompanying the Grumbles motion Jill declared emphatically, "I . . . continue to believe that the government's efforts to compel my testimony violate my constitutional and human rights. . . . I will not answer the government's questions . . . and will continue to suffer indefinitely deprivation of my freedom, rather than violate my own principles and conscience. . . . Jail is punishment, but not so great a punishment as would be the voluntary surrender of my . . . personal integrity" (*In re Jill Raymond* 1975).

In a supporting brief Hixson provided further pragmatic evidence as to why additional jail time would not coerce Raymond to testify. As compared with the other five of the Lexington Six, she did not have to worry about having her university education disrupted, since she had already graduated. Nor did she have to worry about losing her job—she had one waiting for her in Washington, DC, when she was released. Nor, since her parents were dead, did she have parental pressure to deal with. In short, there were few external influences pushing Jill to testify.

Hixson also cited previous legal decisions that supported her claim, in addition to the 1973 Grumbles decision. Certain of the conditions Jill was enduring had been adjudged by courts to be violations of the Eighth Amendment's prohibition of "cruel and unusual punishments." In *Battles v. Anderson* (1974), a court had ruled that "continual and enforced idleness," such as Jill was experiencing with no exercise, physical or mental, constituted cruel and unusual punishment. A lack of access to law books had also been adjudged cruel and unusual punishment in *Aikens v. Lash* (1974). But in the last analysis, it was Jill's resolve that precluded coercion being effective. Hixson summed up: "Ms. Raymond has in the past and will continue to firmly insist that she prefers physical incarceration to violating her conscience" (*In re Jill Raymond* 1975).

Within a matter of hours on November 7, the same day the Grumbles motion was filed, Judge Bernard Moynahan dismissed it as "patently frivolous and a blatant attempt to trifle with the court." Raymond "remains adamant in her defiance" in refusing "to comply with . . . a lawful Order of this Court." Moreover, she has stated that one of her purposes is that of "creating public awareness of the issues" (*In re Jill Raymond* 1975).

Moynahan did not address what would seem to have been the strongest legal argument laid out in the motion: that the harboring charge had been effectively dropped, so coercing her testimony would be to no end. The only possible reason for her continuing confinement seemed indeed to be to punish her for her audacity in defying the judge's order and in deliberately publicizing the case as an example of injustice. In her 1977 testimony before the House subcommittee investigating grand jury abuse, Linda Backiel for the Grand Jury Project characterized Moynahan as "vindictive" (Eilberg Hearings 1977, 1:103)—a characterization that seems warranted by the tone of his order dismissing the Grumbles motion.

As public awareness intensified of the illegal and improper activities of the FBI—thanks in part to the files revealed through the Media, Pennsylvania, break-in by antiwar activists in 1971, as well as by the publicity generated about FBI harassment and the misuse of the grand jury system by the grand jury resisters and their defense committees—the U.S. Congress began to investigate the issues. The most significant of these hearings were those begun in early 1975 by the U.S. Senate's Select Committee to Study Government Operations with Respect to Intelligence Activities, better known as the "Church Committee" after the name of the committee's chair, Senator Frank Church of Idaho, a Democrat. Most of the committee's hearings were closed, but sessions open to the public began in September 1975. The hearings concerning the FBI began on November 18, 1975, under the direction of committee member Senator Walter Mondale of Minnesota, also a Democrat and later vice president. After several months of hearings, the committee produced a scathing indictment of the bureau in its final report, issued April 29, 1976, as *Intelligence Activities and the Rights of Americans*.

In the opening statement of the report, Senator Church declared that "too often . . . constitutional principles were subordinated to a pragmatic course of permitting desired ends to dictate and justify improper means." Moreover, "Groups and individuals have been harassed and disrupted, because of their political views and their lifestyles" (Church Report 1976, iii, 5). Church's reference to lifestyles (a coded term for lesbians and gays) indicates the extent to which the Lexington Six and Connecticut cases had registered nationally.

The report highlighted how pragmatism often overrode legality. FBI officials, it noted, too often "did not regularly attach sufficient significance to questions of legality. The question was usually not whether a particular program was legal or ethical, but whether it worked" (Church Report 1976, 140). In his testimony on November 3, 1975, before the committee, FBI official George C. Moore testified as follows:

> Question. Did anybody at any time . . . discuss the Constitutionality
> or the legal authority [for illegal FBI programs]?
> Answer. No, we never gave it a thought. (Church Report 1976, 14 n.82)

W. Mark Felt, an assistant FBI director, testified in closed session on February 3, 1975, during the time the FBI dragnet was occurring in Lexington, that top-level FBI officials cared little about whether various operations were constitutional. "There was no instruction to me," he said, "that inspectors should be on the alert to see that constitutional values are being protected" (Church Report 1976, 155). Although he denied it vigorously at the time (Weiner 2012, 339), Felt was later revealed as Deep Throat, the leaker who supplied *Washington Post* reporters with information about Nixon officials' illegality, the scandal known as Watergate.

As Jill Raymond continued to fester forgotten in Kentucky's Madison County Jail, William C. Sullivan, a FBI assistant director for intelligence, testified on November 1, 1975, before the committee that "as far as legality is concerned, morals, or ethics, [it] was never raised by myself or anybody else" (Church Report 1976, 141). The Senate report concluded that lacking legal or ethical guidance from their superiors, agents in the field "rarely questioned the orders they received [and] frequently acted without concern for issues of law . . . at times assum[ing] that normal legal restraints and prohibitions did not apply to their activities" (Church Report 1976, 138–39).

However, although claiming to be oblivious to legal and constitutional restraints, FBI officials were sufficiently aware that many of their actions were illegal or improper that they covered them up by destroying evidence or by lying about them. A "special filing system" was set up "for memoranda written about illegal techniques . . . and highly questionable operations." This was the "DO NOT FILE" system whereby such materials were ultimately "systematically destroyed" (Church Report 1976, 148).

Beyond the obvious illegality and unconstitutionality of many FBI actions, the Senate committee also castigated the FBI for its failure to operate in terms of respect for basic human dignity. In its perhaps most damning indictment of the bureau from an ethical point of view, the committee decried how "a distressing number of programs and techniques developed by the intelligence community involved transgressions against human decency" (Church Report 1976, 140). In summary, "the most basic harm" done by offensive FBI behavior "was to the values of privacy and freedom which our constitution seeks to protect and which intelligence activity infringed on a broad scale" (Church Report 1976, 15). Thus, the Senate committee concluded by emphasizing the values that motivated Gail Cohee, Debbie Hands, Carey Junkin, Jill Raymond, Nancy Scott, Marla Seymour, Ellen Grusse, Terri Turgeon, and many other FBI and grand jury resisters in their determined and ongoing defiance—at great personal sacrifice—of political authority that would crush those values.

As Christmas 1975 drew near, the U.S. attorney in New Haven, William Dow, likely influenced by community pressure, apparently had a change of heart and suddenly on December 18 dropped the subpoena for Ellen Grusse and Terri Turgeon, who were then released from the Niantic prison the following day. The possibility of a resubpoena hung over their heads, but at least and at last they were free. Altogether they had served seven months and one week.

Jill decorated her cell for the holiday season with a small Christmas tree (eight inches tall) brought to her by her sister Dee and Mark Paster of the Lexington Grand Jury Defense Committee, and with ornaments and cards sent by many others. She continued to receive regular visits from other members of the Lexington Six. Nancy Scott brought her a Christmas present of Angela Davis's autobiography. But the biggest gift of the season was the news brought to her by Byrna Aronson, Susan Saxe's lover, who was in Kentucky in mid-December as the guest of Gail Cohee and Marla Seymour and visited Jill in jail several times. On December 19, Byrna told

Jill she had just received a phone call from Nancy Gertner, Susan Saxe's attorney, informing her of Ellen's and Terri's release.

"I can't tell you how excited that makes me," Jill wrote on December 21. "It's just gotta be true! Apparently the U.S. Attorney was struck with the Christmas Spirit or something—just dropped the subpoenas. . . . That's enough to make one believe in Santa Claus again!" (Raymond, letter to author, December 21, 1975).

The Christmas spirit did not, however, strike the federal officials in Kentucky, and Jill Raymond had to serve out the remaining four and a half months of her term—one of the longest in the history of contempt incarcerations. But even without early release, she was at least, as the New Year dawned in 1976, beginning to see light on the horizon.

As Jill continued to serve her term, various bills to curb grand jury abuse were introduced in the U.S. Congress. Public awareness—thanks in large part to the resistance of the Lexington Six and others—had intensified to the point where people had become cognizant of the more blatant misappropriations of the grand jury system and were demanding reform. During the period 1976–77, over fifty news articles and editorials supporting grand jury reform appeared in newspapers across the country from the *Christian Science Monitor, New York Times* (several), *Washington Post* (several), *Wall Street Journal, Boston Globe, Denver Post, St. Louis Post-Dispatch, Lexington Herald-Leader*, and many others.

Six major bills were introduced in 1977 by members of the 95th Congress, including John Conyers of Michigan (HR 3736), Barbara Jordan of Texas (HR 1830), and Elizabeth Holtzman of New York (HR 406)—all Democrats. The most important was HR 94, the Federal Grand Jury Reform Act of 1977, introduced by Joshua Eilberg, the Pennsylvania Democrat who chaired the Judiciary subcommittee hearings on the subject of grand jury reform from March to June 1977. Subcommittee members heard testimony from several members of or affiliated with the Lexington Six legal team, including Rhonda Copelon, Doris Peterson, and M. E. Hixson. The congressional representatives learned that "eight persons active in the women's and gay rights movement" were "jailed in 1975–76" as the result of FBI interrogation of "friends, employers . . . co-workers about political beliefs, activities and associations." The underlying offense, Hixson told the subcommittee, was that the current FBI/grand jury interrogation system violated "the sanctity of confidential relationships" (Eilberg Hearings 1977, 1:97, 891).

Representatives from various civic organizations offered testimony in favor of reform. The American Civil Liberties Union attorney stated, "Witnesses before grand juries in New Haven and Kentucky were asked specific questions about people they associated with in radical feminist groups. . . . These questions are clearly improper invasions into protected First Amendment protections" (Eilberg Hearings 1977, 1:547).

William P. Thompson, president of the National Council of Churches of Christ, also presented compelling testimony in favor of reform. Thompson had served as assistant prosecutor in the Tokyo War Crimes Trials following World War II regarding "crimes against humanity" committed by Japanese officials. In his testimony Thompson harked back to the early days of Christianity in which "thousands of Christians were imprisoned, exiled, or executed by Roman imperial authorities, often without benefit of 'due process of law' which Rome even then had developed to a high degree"—the implication being that U.S. authorities were replicating the Roman abuse of legal procedure in the persecution of Christians. "Jesus Christ fell afoul of the law—or at least of the authorities who purported to administer the law—and died upon a cross as the result of a gross miscarriage of justice, in which the authorities did not even follow their own canons of proper procedure" (Eilberg Hearings 1977, 1:679).

On May 5, 1977, Thompson reported, the governing board of the National Council of Churches adopted a "Resolution on Grand Jury Abuse" in which "the Board urged application of the principle of due process to the operation of the grand jury" (Eilberg Hearings 1977, 1:680). The American Bar Association, followed by the Kentucky Bar Association, also offered proposals for grand jury reform in resolutions passed in August 1977.

In general, these bar association recommendations and the congressional bills advocated the following reforms: (1) that incarceration for those convicted of contempt be limited to six to twelve months; (2) that the witness's counsel be permitted to accompany her or him into the grand jury room; (3) that the prosecutor should reveal exculpatory evidence; (4) that there should be no gathering of evidence for already-indicted defendants; (5) that the grand jury testimony should be recorded and available; and

(6) that no illegally obtained evidence, such as from FBI wiretapping, should be introduced to the grand jury. Some bills, notably those of Conyers and Eilberg, proposed that "use immunity" be replaced by "transactional immunity" whereby witnesses' Fifth Amendment guarantee against self-incrimination would obtain.

Despite the public and legal profession support for these reforms, the Department of Justice, represented in the 1977 Eilberg hearings by Assistant Attorney General Benjamin R. Civiletti, opposed most of them, saying they would impede law enforcement in the "War Against Crime." Representative Eilberg bluntly summed up Civiletti's and the DOJ's position: "You want to continue with a rubber stamp grand jury." Only "the prosecutorial establishment," M. E. Hixson concluded, wanted to maintain the system as it was (Eilberg Hearings 1977, 1:880, 738, 876).

Nevertheless, several states in following years reformed their state grand jury systems by admitting counsel into the grand jury room, following trial rules of evidence, and requiring formal recordings of the proceedings (Emerson 1983, 16–17, 108). The federal judiciary eventually adopted some of the advocated reforms, so that as of 2018, certain reforms proposed in response to the publicity generated by the grand jury resisters of the mid-1970s are now operative in the federal system. Under the *Federal Rules of Criminal Procedure* (2017), issued by the House Judiciary Committee, which lays out proper grand jury procedure, attorneys for the witnesses are still not allowed in the grand jury room, but the proceedings must be recorded (U.S. House of Representatives 2018, rule 6d, 6e [1]). The *U.S. Attorneys' Manual* currently issued by the Department of Justice, as amended in 2018, reveals that the DOJ has also incorporated several reforms derived from the grand jury cases of the mid-1970s. Indeed, it is striking that nearly all the legal decisions referenced in the manual date from that era; they thus established legal precedents that are still in effect.

One reform found in the manual that seems to stem directly from the case of the Lexington Six, as argued by Robert Sedler and Judith Peterson in their appeal, is that "the grand jury cannot be used solely to obtain additional evidence against a defendant who has already been indicted." Moreover, in a stipulation that also seems a direct response to the case of the Lexington Six and similar cases, the manual states, "It is improper to utilize the grand jury solely as an investigative aid in the search for a fugitive in whose testimony the grand jury has no interest," citing *inter alia In re Cueto* (1977). Only in cases where "the whereabouts of a fugitive is related to a legitimate grand jury investigation of offenses such as harboring . . . , misprision of a felony [or] accessory after the fact" may "the grand jury properly . . . inquire as to the fugitive's whereabouts," citing *In re Grusse* (1975). In summary, the manual concludes, "grand jury subpoenas should not be used to locate fugitives in investigations of unlawful flight to avoid prosecution" (U.S. Department of Justice 2018, 9–11, 120 [B]).

The manual further requires that persons called before a federal grand jury be clearly advised of their rights, including the Fifth Amendment ban on "compulsory self-incrimination." It recommends against resubpoenaing a recalcitrant witness who has served time in jail for contempt of court. Nor may a prosecutor present "illegally obtained evidence," as was likely the case with the Lexington Six and many others, and definitely the case with the Fort Worth Five. Finally, a prosecutor is required to present any "exculpatory evidence" to the grand jury regarding possible indictments (U.S. Department of Justice 2018, 9–11, 154, 160, 231, 233).

Insofar, therefore, as their resistance resulted in palpable reforms to the grand jury system, the sacrifices of the Lexington Six and the other grand jury resisters of the 1970s had positive results. It is also noteworthy that the current documents use nonsexist language ("foreperson," "his or her") unlike those of the 1970s, another result of feminist activism—seen, for example, in Gail Cohee's use of nonsexist language in her Lexington grand jury appearance. But these reforms were but a hope on the horizon in the spring of 1976 as Jill Raymond entered her final months in jail.

One of the first things Ellen Grusse and Terri Turgeon did after their release from prison in December 1975 was to make their way south to Kentucky in early January 1976 to visit their comrade Jill Raymond. They drove down on January 7 in Terri's Volkswagen, and were followed every step of the way by the FBI. "At each state line," Ellen recalled, "a different car, always with two men in it, would pick us up and keep us under surveillance" (Harris 1976c, 97). The three resisters had a joyous get-together in the lobby of the Madison County Jail, sharing their stories.

Not long after, Jill was joined in jail by a dynamic woman named Judy who was in transit to Alderson Federal Prison for interstate racketeering and prostitution. Judy was like no one Jill had ever met before. Hardened by "ten years of hustling and junk and moving around and watching lovers OD," her "system seemed purged" of "the ability to feel pain." Jill was entranced by Judy's ingrained hostility toward the system. She had never met anyone "so angry, so sarcastic." Despite her hardened numbness, Judy was incredibly "expressive and so gaddmmned alive," Jill thought, "in her hostility toward the criminal justice system" (Raymond 1976a, 80).

The first thing Judy asked Jill was whether she was an "urban guerrilla." At the time the trial of Patty Hearst was transpiring in California, and the term had become associated with her and the Symbionese Liberation Army. (Hearst was convicted on March 20, 1976, of bank robbery and sentenced to thirty-five years in prison—later reduced.) Jill was uncomfortable with the stereotyped images associated with Hearst and "urban guerrillas" and so demurred. Still, she herself was a "political prisoner" and believed in revolutionary action—to a point. But she resisted being characterized as an "urban guerrilla," or even a "radical," as if it were an occupation and the movement a profession where activists were the "specialists" with a "particular kind of expertise, like plumbers or electricians, which separates them from other people" (Raymond 1976a, 83). Jill struggled—unsuccessfully, she felt—to explain all this to Judy.

Jill was pleased, however, at Judy's reaction of outraged indignation to the "details of some of the atrocities of our case": "NO THEY DIDNT," "They had the NERVE." Judy's sympathy was heartfelt, being as she was "well acquainted with the FBI and their methods." "There wasn't a trace of upstanding citizen in her, she was 100% incorrigible," Jill concluded, "and it was fantastic" (Raymond 1976a, 80).

Judy told Jill the problem with the radical movement was that it didn't get its message out to ordinary people. She waved one of the political pamphlets Jill had on hand—"An Open Letter to the Movement"—and said, "If you mailed one of these to everybody in the country, then we would have a revolution" (Raymond 1976a, 81). When Jill asked her how they would fund such a mailing, Judy said you could hustle some "rich tricks" to raise the money.

One time Judy asked Jill, "What does sex have to do with politics?" Answer: "Power is the common denominator." But Judy didn't see the political aspects of sexual relations; for her power was an individual matter, what "a gutsy woman throws back in an obnoxious man's face." Jill became infatuated with Judy's militant defiance: "It was real easy for me to be crazy about her . . . over her special kind of deadpan rage. . . . It revived me and it was beautiful." Sometimes, Jill later reflected, "you want to hold someone because you have this desire to just make their whole world gentle for them for a while." In jail, "such a deprived and abnormal environment," some things "deplete" and others "recharge." Her relationship with Judy was one of the latter. "Being a lifeline sometimes for someone . . . recharges you." And apparently the effect was mutual. "Seeing what you're doing," Judy told her, "well, I know I can get through whatever I have to get through." "Being held in somebody's arms," Jill concluded, "is, maybe, sometimes, the ultimate affirmation of solidarity" (Raymond 1976a, 87, 85, 89, 90).

On March 8, 1976, the anniversary of the imprisonment of the Lexington Six, the Lexington Grand Jury Defense Committee held a mock "Peoples Grand Jury" hearing before the federal courthouse building in Lexington. It was part of a month-long, nationwide series of protest actions orchestrated by the New York Grand Jury Project—a campaign duly noted by the FBI as a "civil disturbance" and "anti-U.S. demonstration" (FBI, March 23, 1976).

The purpose of the Peoples Grand Jury was to "indict" federal political and judiciary authorities for "conspiring to overthrow the democratic rights of American people." Five "witnesses" were summoned before this grand jury. These included several who had been interrogated by the FBI in their Lexington sweep, such as Sally Kundert, as well as two of the original members of the Lexington Six, Gail Cohee and Marla Seymour. After hearing the "witnesses" describe how they were harassed and asked "personal, offensive questions" by the FBI, the fourteen "jurors" deliberated briefly before returning an "indictment." They charged the following suspects with "conspiracy against the American people": the FBI, U.S. Attorney Eugene Siler and the Department of Justice, the U.S. District Court, and, finally, "the rich and powerful hidden rulers of this country" (Peoples Grand Jury 1976).

In their "indictment," which was written by law students Barbara Sutherland and Dick Burr, the Peoples Grand Jury catalogued the offenses committed by each of these indicted figures. First, the FBI "unceasingly harassed, deceived and inflicted mental distress" on the Lexington Six and scores of others. No longer reflecting the interests of the people, the FBI in its coercive powers had brought the country "to the brink of tyranny." Second, the U.S. attorney was accused of enabling the grand jury to "do the FBI's dirty work." Third, the federal courts were indicted for standing "passively by" as these crimes against the American people were committed. Finally, the rich and powerful rulers who benefited from these crimes were indicted for encouraging their commission (Peoples Grand Jury 1976).

The Peoples Grand Jury performance was staged twice—once at noon and again at 5 p.m.—both before the courthouse steps. There appear to have been few spectators in attendance, but the occasion received local press coverage, notably in a front-page article on March 9 in the *Courier-Journal* (Ward 1976) and in the campus-based *Kentucky Kernel* (Ballinger 1976).

Similar enactments and demonstrations against grand jury abuse were held in several other cities in early April. In Washington, DC, a protest rally before the Justice Department transpired on April 5. Speakers included representatives from the Grand Jury Project, the Puerto Rican Socialist Party, the National Council of Churches, the Wounded Knee Legal Defense/ Offense Committee, and NOW. Emmy Hixson represented the Lexington Grand Jury Defense Committee. Protestors at the various demonstrations chanted repeatedly:

> *Grand Jury/FBI*
> *U.S. Justice Is A Lie*
>
> *(Anonymous 1976c)*

CHAPTER NINE

Jill Raymond Freed

Shortly before midnight on May 3, a large crowd gathered in the ground-floor lobby of the Madison County Jail: reporters, TV cameras, and supporters of Jill Raymond wearing "End Grand Jury Abuse" and "We Won't Talk" buttons. Dee, Jill's sister, was continuing her day-long vigil doing needlepoint while she waited. Katherine King, the jail matron, was sitting with her three-year-old son Frankie on her lap. The lad was singing "Amazing Grace" in a squeaky voice. At about 10 p.m. two men in business suits—U.S. marshals—approached Frank King, the warden, with a court document. As Frank was illiterate, he handed the paper to his wife to read. Katherine beamed as she read the words out loud: "ORDERED AND ADJUDGED that . . . Jill Raymond shall be discharged from the custody of the United States Marshal for the Eastern District of Kentucky at twelve midnight on the 3rd day of May, 1976" (Transcript 1975, Docket List, 5). Setting Frankie aside, Katherine drew a large ring of keys from her pocket and unlocked the barred door leading to the upstairs women's cell. A few minutes later she returned with the soon-to-be free Jill Raymond. The crowd burst into cheers.

Jill hadn't known for sure until that moment whether she would be released. She had actually gone to bed but, needless to say, couldn't sleep. In fact, when the federal courthouse in Lexington closed at 8 p.m., May 3, the release order still hadn't been filed. However, at some point between 8

Figure 4. Jill Raymond on her release from Madison County Jail, May 4, 1976.
Photograph by Mark Cantor Paster. Used by permission

and 10 p.m., Marshal Sherman Hansford received it and sent his deputies to Richmond to deliver the news.

After Jill arrived in the lobby she and her supporters settled down to wait out the remaining minutes with an eye on the clock. It was, Carolyn Gatz reported, "like a New Years Eve party" (Gatz, May 4, 1976). When the clock stuck midnight, more cheers, tears, and hugs. "It was quite a scene," Jill later recalled (Raymond 1989, 302).

Jill's sentence had been keyed to end when the grand jury's eighteen-month term expired—at midnight on May 3. But there remained the threat of a resubpoena by the next grand jury. The new U.S. attorney, Eldon Webb, had declined to say whether he would ask for a new subpoena, but Assistant U.S. Attorney Robert F. Trevey had earlier stated that he doubted she would be resubpoenaed (Gatz, March 8, 1976). In any event, for the time being at least, Jill was free and exhilarated to be so.

The only sad aspect about her liberation was that she had to leave behind alone in the cell one of her sister inmates, Ronnie Allen, an African American woman with whom she had become good friends. "So many times," Jill reflected wistfully to reporter Gatz, "I was there, watching everyone leave, and it was never my turn, and now suddenly it's my turn. But I hate to leave her alone" (Gatz, May 4, 1976).

The first thing Jill did on her release was to call her grandmother Dorothy Raymond from the lobby with the news. "Guess what?" Jill said. "That's wonderful," her grandmother replied. "But what's all this talk about your being a lesbian?" (Raymond 1987b). As Jill lit up a cigarette (she had become a chain smoker), her attorney Emmy Hixson asked her sarcastically, "Was it worth it!" "I don't know, Emmy," Jill echoed, "was it worth it?" (Gatz, May 4,1976).

"The first few days I was out were phenomenal," Jill later wrote. "I went to get my driver's license renewed and have my picture taken all over again. The people down at the motor vehicle department knew all about me and said, 'Oh, we're so glad you're out of jail'" (Raymond 1989, 302). Next, she went to the bank, getting back into regular everyday life again. The bank teller smiled when she heard Jill's name: "I'm so glad they let you out of jail. We were really behind you." Later that day, Jill and a friend dropped into a downtown bar. The cocktail waitress recognized Jill and brought them free drinks: "These are on the house!" she announced (Raymond 1987b).

The warm support Jill was receiving from apolitical strangers, who were unaffiliated with "the movement," was inspiring. She hadn't realized how her story had resonated beyond left-wing political circles. "God, this succeeded," she thought, "that's what this was for"—to reach people, to make them aware of the injustices and unfairness built into the system and thereby create a movement for change (Raymond 1989, 302). Maybe it had been worth it.

"I do believe time in jail has been 'worth it,'" Jill concluded in an article published that summer in the *Lesbian Tide* (Raymond 1976c). Worth it because of the growing movement to end grand jury abuse that emerged as a result of her and other resisters' stands. Worth it because of the various reform acts pending in Congress. Worth it because of the knowledge she had gained from hearing the searing stories of so many of her sister cellmates, from defiant teenaged Beverly to battle-scarred Judy. Upon Jill's release the Lexington Grand Jury Defense Committee issued its commentary: "The government may have been able to hold our sister Jill for fourteen months, but it was totally unable to hide its spiteful, repressive, police-state tactics from the view of the people" (1976).

Coincidentally, four days after Jill's release, Clarence Kelly, the director of the FBI, in response to the just-published Church Committee Report, "acknowledged" on May 8 "that the FBI had engaged in operations that were indefensible . . . and would never be repeated" (Weiner 2012, 336). An internal investigation was begun at the FBI to look into charges of illegal activities. Several agents were indicted for such illegalities as unwarranted wiretapping, mail-opening, and others. One agent, John Kearney, ironically, refused to testify in the spring of 1977 when subpoenaed before a federal grand jury in New York. Hundreds of FBI agents gathered in a protest demonstration before the courthouse. Bryan Burrough in his recent work on the FBI and the antiwar movement noted the irony: "Here were the men . . . of the FBI—the agency that for a decade had been the bane of student protesters, whose undercover agents had secretly circulated through thousands of antiwar rallies, who had bugged and wire-tapped long-haired activists . . . turning to the very tactics they had been trying to stop for years" (Burrough 2015, 378).

On August 26, 1976, former FBI deputy director Mark Felt and former FBI chief of intelligence Ed Miller were subpoenaed before a federal grand jury. And on April 10, 1978, the former head of the FBI L. Patrick Gray was charged in a thirty-two-count indictment of "conspiracy to injure and oppress citizens," a wording that could have been lifted from the mock Lexington Peoples Grand Jury indictment of 1976. All three of these men — Felt, Miller, and Gray — were found guilty on November 6, 1980, but were pardoned by the newly elected president, Republican Ronald Reagan, on March 30, 1981 (Weiner 2012, 340, 345, 349).

Throughout the summer of 1976 preparations were underway for the trial of Susan Saxe for the 1970 Brighton bank robbery, scheduled to begin on September 15 in the Suffolk County Courthouse in Boston. A Susan Saxe Defense Committee was set up. It issued statements and occasional newsletters in an attempt to rally support and to counter the intensely negative publicity Susan Saxe was receiving in the press.

Media coverage of Saxe in the Boston area had been for the most part highly sensationalized, with Susan demonized as a "revolutionary lesbian cop-killer," the defense committee noted, linked in the public mind to the Weather Underground women Kathy Boudin, Cathy Wilkerson, and Bernadine Dohrn — not to mention Patty Hearst (Susan Saxe Defense Committee 1975).

In her transfer to the Boston venue from Philadelphia, Susan had engaged a new lawyer, Nancy Gertner, a young, recent (1971) graduate of Yale Law School. This was to be her first criminal trial. She took the case, despite her feelings that it was "likely a loser" (Gertner 2011, 8), because she felt some identification with Susan and was sympathetic to her feminism and her antiwar militancy. In time, the two became close friends.

Gertner realized that the lynch-mob atmosphere that had developed boded against a successful defense. "The publicity," she later noted, "was anti-student, anti-Semitic, anti-lesbian. And it was unrelenting. . . . Susan was a caricature of everything that the public had grown to fear during the years of Nixon/Agnew — a feminist, radical revolutionary, and a lesbian to boot" (Gertner 2011, 9). The pretrial publicity was indeed so hostile that Gertner filed a motion to dismiss the charges on the contention that a fair trial was impossible. This motion, along with several others, was dismissed by Judge Walter McLaughlin. And so Saxe remained charged with "felony murder," which had a "mandatory punishment of life in prison, without parole" (Gertner 2011, 9).

Saxe was determined to have the defense reflect her feminist values. Therefore, the legal team would be comprised largely of women. There would be no defense based on sexist stereotypes, such as "the 'poor vulnerable woman' approach," which depicted her as an innocent victim of more worldly-wise male co-conspirators. Nor would she place the blame on anyone else. "She would not be painted as anything other than the architect of her own fate," Gertner said (2011, 30). At the same time, while willingly claiming responsibility to Gertner for her acts, Saxe did not want to plead guilty to felony murder. Gertner was therefore uncertain how to proceed when the trial opened on September 15.

The courtroom was filled to capacity. Among the hundred or so in attendance that day were Susan Saxe's parents. Her mother had told Gertner, "We'll stick by her through this mess, and then I'll kick her teeth out for being such a damned fool when it's over" (Gertner 2011, 15). The first week of the twenty-seven-day trial was devoted to a rigorous examination of potential jurors in an attempt by Gertner and her team to screen out jurors who were already convinced of Saxe's guilt. Presentation of evidence by the prosecution, headed by John Gaffney, began on September 23, coincidentally the sixth anniversary of the robbery itself.

As it turned out, the evidence linking Saxe to the robbery, much less to the killing of police officer Walter Schroeder, was slim. There were no eyewitness identifications, no fingerprints, no bank photos, no guns. Two of her former co-conspirators, Robert Valeri and Michael Fletcher (the latter did not actually participate in the robbery), identified Saxe as having taken part in the operation but both also testified that Susan was "very upset" when she learned of Officer Schroeder's death (Gertner 2011, 39). While the prosecution did have damning evidence—letters Susan had written to her father and rabbi admitting her participation in the bank robbery—for some reason it was never produced in the trial.

With the evidence against Susan thus so weak, Gertner ventured a daring move: she would present no defense but simply argue that the proof was insufficient for a conviction. Her strategy worked. After a week's deliberation, the jury could not reach an agreement. The result was a hung jury, and a mistrial was declared.

The prosecution immediately moved for a retrial, however, and in succeeding months Saxe, Gertner, and the prosecutors worked out a plea deal to avoid a second trial. On January 17, 1977, Susan pled guilty to two counts of armed robbery and one count of manslaughter in exchange for a twelve-to-fourteen-year sentence, less the two years already in custody, to be served concomitantly with her ten-year federal sentence. Saxe eventually served six years in prison. "You saved my life," Susan told Nancy Gertner (Gertner 2011, 51).

Gertner, however, had come to have second thoughts. She observed, "The plea, and the relatively light sentence, was a victory for Susan and me. Was it a victory for truth? . . . Or had I just learned crass manipulation, the trade of the hired gun? What about the principles that had prompted me to be a lawyer?" But in thinking it through, Gertner came to realize that truth in a legal setting has to be conceived within its terms. After all, the truth was that Susan had not killed or conspired to kill Officer Schroeder. But under the legal concept of felony-murder, anyone involved in a crime where a murder is committed is charged with the murder, regardless of who pulled the trigger. So Susan was in fact innocent of the murder though guilty of the robbery. In the end, Gertner felt that truth was in fact served, even if the means to the end—implying in the trial that, because of the lack of evidence, Susan had not verifiably participated in the robbery—was questionable. A lawyer's obligation, Gertner finally concluded after this soul-searching, was to "make the system . . . be fair" for her client (Gertner 2011, 49, 50). Gertner went on to a highly successful legal career and in 1997 was appointed a judge on the U.S. District Court for the District of Massachusetts by President Bill Clinton.

Meanwhile, following all this from afar was Kathy Power, still on the loose but now on the West Coast, after working a few years incognito in the New York City area (after she left Lexington). In 1977, Power obtained the birth certificate of an Alice Louise Metzinger, who had died as in infant, and from that was able to get further identification cards. Under that name she moved to Oregon and established a new life there with, eventually, a child, a partner, and as a restauranteur. In 1984, Katherine Ann Power was dropped from the FBI's "most wanted" list—the longest time any woman had enjoyed that distinction.

But despite her successes, Kathy remained conscience-stricken about the death of Officer Schroeder and felt the need to pay some sort of recompense. "I vowed I would make my life as an act of contrition for my wrong to the Schroeder family," she later reflected (Franks 1994). An Act of Contrition in Catholic doctrine (Power was brought up a Catholic) is a statement of acknowledgment and regret for wrong-doing and a resolution to amend one's ways. ("I firmly resolve with the help of Thy grace to sin no more and to avoid the near occasion of sin" is one version of the litany repeated in the confessional.)

Feelings of remorse and depression intensified in the early 1990s, and Kathy consulted a psychotherapist, under whose treatment she decided to turn herself in. On September 15, 1993, Kathy Power, shackled in handcuffs, pleaded guilty in Boston's Suffolk County Courthouse to manslaughter and armed robbery. On October 6, she was sentenced to eight to twelve years, with eligibility for parole in five. At her parole hearing, members of Officer Schroeder's family testified vehemently against her release. Upon hearing them, Kathy felt she had not done enough penance for the wrong she had done to the Schroeder family and withdrew her bid for parole, agreeing to continue serving her term for another year and a half. "His death was shocking to me," she said in a statement issued at the time of her plea. "In response I have lived my life as something of a penitent, ever seeking to grow as a person of peace" (Lambert 1993).

In her parole statement, Power wholly recanted her participation in the Brighton bank robbery, expressing abject remorse for the pain it had caused: "In the summer and fall of 1970 I was guilty of a series of ethical failures, compulsive rebelliousness, and wrong thinking that resulted in the robbery . . . and the murder of Walter Schroeder. . . . We were arrogant in our confidence of our moral rightness. . . . We were drenched with dangerous romanticism and saw ourselves as noble warriors. . . . We thought there was glamour in gun-toting violence." All of these actions and attitudes Power says she now regrets: "I was wrong. I was wrong all along. Before God I am sorry. I will always be so sorry" (Power 2010).

In her life as a fugitive, while she had dedicated herself to peniten-
tial peace, Power came to appreciate that her duplicitous life necessarily
involved lying to and deceiving everyone she encountered or knew—
including her son. Thus she realized the potential harm she was continuously inflicting on others. By turning herself in and publicly acknowledging
these injuries and wrongs, Power hoped to begin to atone for them.

Susan Saxe remained true to her vow never to recant her past actions;
however, although she remained defiant in public (and private) statements,
she admitted in a letter to Jill Raymond in the summer of 1975 that she
regretted the disruption she had caused in the lives of people she knew while
underground in Lexington and New Haven, effectively causing so many to
end up in jail. "I've been going through some pretty heavy changes in my
head lately," she wrote. "Part of it . . . is the people who are in jail because
I walked into their lives. Now . . . I know exactly what you're going to say,
and I agree . . . it's on the Man. But knowing that is never going to stop it
from weighing very heavily on me" (Saxe, letter to Raymond, July 31, 1975).

Saxe also regretted the necessarily transitory nature of those
relationships—that she had to deceive people and continuously move on.
"I have been going into relationships for the past few years without thinking
about the responsibility I have to be around to support the people I get
involved with," she reflected. And now, as she faced years in prison, perhaps
her entire life, she realized that "pain is built into [any future] relationships
from the start . . . just assuredly as it was when I was underground" (Saxe,
letter to Raymond, July 31, 1975).

In August 1978, the FBI reopened its search for Kathy Power and began
another series of interrogations of people connected to the case throughout
the country. On August 23, 1978, Jill Raymond testified before a subcommittee of the U.S. Senate's Judiciary Committee, chaired by Senator James
Abourezk, a Democrat from South Dakota, which was holding hearings
on grand jury reform legislation. She reported that the FBI had visited
Ellen Grusse and Terri Turgeon again on August 16 and the following day
contacted Gail Cohee in Lexington, threatening her with another grand
jury subpoena if she didn't cooperate (Nelson 1978). She and several others in Lexington were offered a $10,000 reward for information leading

to Power's capture. The agent in charge of the operation was once again Wayne McDonald, "who believe[d] that Kathy Power [was] in Lexington" (Anonymous 1978). A former faculty member at the University of Kentucky, Suzanne Howard, who had chaired the Women's Studies Committee, was also interrogated by the FBI at that time in Washington, DC, about the Saxe-Power case. She told them she knew nothing about it or them.

The renewed investigation seemed especially intense in Boston, where hundreds were contacted by the FBI and several offices and apartment broken into with files ransacked. The FBI agent in charge of the Boston dragnet, Richard Bates, vowed "to penetrate that curtain of silence" which remained invincible, he said, in lesbian-feminist and gay communities (Anonymous 1978). On August 17, the greater Boston TV stations ran information about the reward with photos of Kathy Power, followed the next day with articles on the reward in the *Boston Globe* and the Boston *Herald-American*. Several phone records were subpoenaed, including those of Dorothy Raymond, Jill's stalwart grandmother, who wrote the U.S. attorney in Boston in protest: "I am an 82-year-old widow. I know of no reason why my out-of-town phone records should be made available to anyone. . . . I demand an explanation" (Anonymous 1978).

Others connected to the grand jury resistance movement, including Judy Peluso in New York and Byrna Aronson, found their belongings ransacked (Judy in her car, Byrna her apartment). Relatives of Emmy Hixson, Jill's attorney, were also contacted by the FBI in the fall of 1978, including her eighty-year-old grandmother living alone in Oklahoma. And one of the Lexington Six, Nancy Scott, lost her job in 1979 when the FBI informed her employer about the case (Hixson 1986).

I was visited by an FBI agent in mid-November 1978 at my new home in Portsmouth, New Hampshire. "Hi, I'm your friendly local FBI agent," he said when I opened the front door. I froze in dread, knowing what could come next. He held up a photo of Kathy Power (I recognized it, of course, from countless news photos). "We were wondering if you know this individual." I shook my head and said, "I have nothing to say." "Have you seen her recently?" he persisted. I repeated, "No, I have nothing to say." He turned then and left. I had been well primed, of course, by then not to cooperate with the FBI and in any case had no idea where Kathy Power was. Happily for me, I never heard from the FBI again, though I lived in fear of it for some time after.

The Grand Jury Project issued a warning to feminist and gay groups on August 21, 1978, that the FBI had renewed its search for Kathy Power, citing the incidents Jill mentioned in her testimony. It also noted that phone company records of 1977–78 had been subpoenaed by the FBI of people on the Susan Saxe Defense Committee (Grand Jury Project 1978). In response, Senator Abourezk, sponsor of one of the grand jury reform bills in Congress, "The Grand Jury Reform Act of 1978," wrote to Assistant Attorney General Philip Heymann asking why the FBI was renewing its Kathy Power investigation (Coalition to End Grand Jury Abuse 1979). But it remained unclear what had retriggered the Power investigation. The Grand Jury Project editors concluded, "This latest siege seems targeted mainly against people who originally met each other while fighting FBI/ grand jury harassment back in 1975. . . . The feds are going after a network *they* pulled together" (Anonymous 1978).

In response to the renewed FBI campaign in 1978, the Grand Jury Project set up a "Harassment Hotline." A formal protest letter was sent to the head of the FBI, William Webster, in which over a hundred individuals representing over forty-five organizations protested the renewed onslaught against feminist and gay communities, which they characterized as a "witch hunt." The letter-writers deplored "the long-standing tendency of the FBI to act as [a] . . . thought-police agency which is more dedicated to rooting out dissent than injustice" (Anonymous 1978). The lead signatory was Jill Raymond.

As late as 1984, Marla Seymour once again faced that dreaded visit. This time two men in trench-coats came to the bakery where she was working in Baltimore. At first she froze, feeling helpless before the prospect of another jail term. But a sudden surge of strength buoyed her up, and she turned to face the agents. She said no, she wouldn't cooperate. The agents threatened her: "Well, then we'll have to take further measures." She told them she thought they already had. Marla suspected they had entered her apartment illegally a few days previously, leaving mud traces on the hardwood floor. She asked the manager if any maintenance people had been there. He said no. "I was furious," she said, "I knew it was them" (Seymour 1987a).

After Kathy Power's name was removed from the FBI "most wanted" list in 1984, the FBI seems to have abandoned their search, and, of course, once she surrendered in 1993, the case was closed.

Grand jury abuse and resistance continued, however, in other cases, notably those connected to African American protest movements. Many in the Republic of New Afrika and the Black Liberation Movement refused to cooperate with grand juries following Assata Shakur's escape from prison on November 2, 1979, and the Brinks robbery at Nyack, New York, on October 20, 1981, in which a guard and two police officers were killed. As a result, "dozens served time for refusing to cooperate with grand-jury investigations" (Berger and Dunbar-Ortiz 2010, 69; see also Berger 2006, 245–64). In more recent years, grand jury resistance has continued in reaction to the "Green Scare," in which the FBI targeted eco-warriors and animal liberationists (see Potter 2011).

Concluding Summary and Commentary

The FBI went into Lexington, Kentucky, in the winter of 1974–75 hoping to find fugitives Katherine Power and Susan Saxe. Frustrated and embarrassed by the bureau's lack of success in capturing Patty Hearst and other women fugitives such as Kathy Boudin and Cathy Wilkerson, FBI agents were highly motivated to find the Brighton pair. Operating apparently under a theory that a nationwide network of subversive lesbians was providing a haven for these women fugitives, they intensified their investigation into the perceived hubs of this alleged network, Lexington and Hartford, Connecticut. The FBI hoped through the threat of subpoena, grand jury inquisition, and jail to coerce recalcitrant members of those communities to tell agents where Saxe and Power were or at least to give them information that would lead to their capture.

While many of the tactics the FBI used in this phase of the investigation were objectionable, such as informing Sally Kundert's mother that she was pregnant, badgering Jill Raymond's grandmother, and relentlessly questioning lesbians about their private lives and relationships, in general the agents were engaged in a legitimate purpose, that of capturing fugitives suspected of major crimes. Where the case veered off the rails, so to speak, in terms of proper and legal procedure was in the use of the grand jury as a coercive arm of the FBI investigation. The fact that an FBI agent actually acted as bailiff in the Lexington grand jury proceedings indicates how intertwined the two government agencies had become. And the grand jury itself clearly saw its role as that of helping the FBI "find out where those two girls are," as the foreperson put it. At the time of the grand jury hearings, none of the Lexington Six was under consideration for indictment for any crime, and the principal subjects in the case, Saxe and Power, had long since been indicted in other jurisdictions. The idea that the Lexington Six might be indictable for harboring fugitives was introduced during the appeals arguments when the federal attorney and judge realized that they had to come up with a legitimate reason for the grand jury interrogation of the Lexington Six, because the actual reason—that they hoped thereby to elicit information leading to the capture of fugitives—was an illegitimate use of a grand jury. The federal Appeals Court of the Sixth District accepted this trumped-up rationale, which meant that the contempt decision held and that Jill Raymond had to remain in jail until she cooperated or until the grand jury term ended.

What is disturbing about the case, and what invites speculation about underlying and perhaps unconscious motives, is that after interrogating dozens of members of the Lexington community (many of whom fully cooperated with the FBI), federal authorities must have known that no one in Lexington knew where Saxe and Power were, and, moreover, no one had known who they were while they were in Lexington, so no one could have knowingly harbored them. And certainly, once two of the Lexington Six testified before the grand jury that no one had known Saxe's and Power's identities or where they were, it must have been clear to all concerned that there was no "there" there.

Still, federal authorities persisted. It is at this point that the mythic aspects of the case took hold. As his contempt ruling makes clear, the federal judge handling the case had come to see the Lexington Six as threats to the "natural," patriarchal order who needed to be taught a lesson. Their jailing was conceived as a punishment for their obstreperous defiance of his orders and more broadly for their defiance of societal norms in being who they were, in their "deviant" sexuality. For this, their lives were violently disrupted and they suffered serious physical, psychological, and moral injury, which lasted long beyond the time they spent in jail.

For their part—to return to my opening question—why then did the Lexington Six resist so long in the face of nearly unbearable pressure and pain? Certainly, their reasons varied. For one, it was principally a matter of loyalty to and solidarity with beloved friends and comrades. For at least two others, however, ironically, it was the same feeling of loyalty and bonding—but with lovers on the outside—that moved them to cooperate with authorities, so they could be reunited with their partners. But overall the resistance of the six may best be understood within the context of the 1960s and 1970s American political world. That government authorities were capable of deceit, fraud, and illegal behavior had become clear in the wake of the Vietnam War deceptions and the Watergate revelations. And that the justice system was not a neutral arbiter that treated all groups and peoples equally but rather was infected with ideological biases which determined judicial decisions had also become patently clear from the McCarthy-era persecution of alleged communists to the Vietnam-era persecution of antiwar activists. The collusion of the FBI in such persecutions through COINTELPRO and other programs was by then well known, thanks to the publication of the Media, Pennsylvania, burglary documents. Their awareness of these ideological biases made the Lexington Six from the outset distrustful of governmental authorities and reluctant to cooperate, seeing them—as it turned out, correctly—as the enemy. Informed as well by newly formulated second-wave feminist theory, the Lexington resisters saw federal officials as representing a patriarchal order and reflecting its values of female subordination and LGBT stigmatization. The six were motivated by a desire to protect and stand up for their lesbian feminist community against "the Man" who would destroy it. Yet underneath all of their determinations to resist lay an even more fundamental feeling—that in this country one has a right to live one's life in peace without unjustified invasive and coercive interference by the state, that such freedom is a fundamental requisite of human dignity.

Lawyers for the Center for Constitutional Rights and the National Lawyers Guild clearly used the Lexington Six case as a means of publicizing and organizing a national movement against grand jury abuse, a campaign that largely succeeded. But while the six themselves agreed with the center's position and willingly played out the legal strategies it promoted, their primary issue remained that of lesbian feminist and gay resistance to patriarchal domination expressed in the FBI's and federal officials' intrusion into and violation of their private lives.

Although it was not clear to anyone involved in the case at the time, when regarded from the vantage point of forty-five years hence and placed in historical perspective, the resistance of the Lexington Six may be seen as a decisive moment in lesbian, feminist, and gay history comparable perhaps, if not in scope at least in impetus, to the more celebrated gay uprising in June 1969 known as Stonewall. On both occasions resistance to unjust intrusiveness and harassment by government authorities arose spontaneously. A breaking point had been reached. The bullying presumption of entitlement on the part of the authorities had simply become intolerable. Because of their stigmatized identity, lesbians and gays—like other minority groups— were in essence fair game. Mythologized on the one hand by officials as monstrously powerful, they were, on the other hand, seen as beings of lesser status who did not have to be treated with equal respect and dignity. The fact that of those in Lexington who refused to cooperate with the FBI only lesbians and a gay man ended up in jail suggests as much.

The defiant stand of the Lexington Six was not in vain. It helped set in motion a nationwide culture of resistance wherein many in other minority communities, such as the Hispanic and Native American described in chapter 7, were inspired to resist. Through the offices of the Grand Jury Project and other groups, a widespread FBI/grand jury resistance movement emerged, creating a remarkable, multiethnic network of solidarity.

The publicity surrounding the cases helped to raise awareness of these governmental abuses and garnered public sympathy and support for the resisters, which led to at least some legislative and judicial reforms. Even in the short run, the grand jury resistance movement and the publicity it engendered meant that FBI excesses were curtailed (many high-level FBI officials were, as noted, convicted of these illegalities) and careerist prosecutorial zeal was muted, such that some resisters, such as Ellen Grusse and Terri Turgeon, were released early and none were repeatedly resubpoenaed to face endless incarceration. None of this would likely have happened without the intensive movement mobilization that followed on the resistance of the Lexington Six.

There is an unconscious climate of opinion that legitimizes and shapes public acts. While the FBI agents, U.S. attorneys, and federal judges would probably not have consciously admitted being biased against lesbians, gays, and other minority groups, they were undoubtedly guided by their knowledge that the public at large held these groups as alien and of lesser status than straight whites. It is for this reason that virtually all of the attorneys—from Robert Sedler and M. E. Hixson to Michael Avery and Nancy Gertner—thought their cases were hopeless. When the public holds stigmatizing prejudices against minority groups, fair treatment for them becomes extremely difficult, if not hopeless.

In addition, as men, government prosecutors were also likely unconsciously alarmed and threatened by the rising women's liberation movement, which they didn't understand and which they exaggerated in potency and danger, further motivating their animus against the Lexington Six.

All of the resisters in this book—from Ellen and Terri in Connecticut, to Jill, Carey, Debbie, Nancy, Gail, and Marla in Kentucky—seem to have reacted in a strong, visceral way to the violation of their personal lives by the FBI agents' intrusive questions. Their responses reflected an indignant outrage that official authorities should presume to invade their lives in this manner: indignation arising from deep-rooted feelings about the sanctity of personal relationships and the inviolability of personal dignity. An important part of that dignity involved affirming and protecting their identity as lesbian or gay and not accepting to be treated as an unworthy inferior. What is remarkable is how these women (and one man), despite their terror and the devastating onslaught their lives and communities suffered, held true to these feelings with grit, tenacity, and determination and remained firm in these beliefs.

Many ethical issues surround this case. There is, for one, the basic question of the actions of Susan Saxe and Kathy Power back in 1970, which resulted in the tragic death of Officer Schroeder. I personally feel and felt (and stated) at the time that violence committed by antiwar activists was ethically indefensible. However, it is important to understand the historical context of their actions. The atrocities being committed in Vietnam by the U.S. military and the haunting memory of analogous evils committed in and by Nazi Germany, enabled by "good Germans," weighed heavily on activists at the time and created the feeling of desperation, the desire to do anything to stop that war. These were undoubtedly motivations for Saxe and Power.

Other ethical questions pertain to the issue of collaboration or non-collaboration with unjust or evil authority. While the abstract principled position that one should never collaborate with evil is admirable, in practice the situation is usually more complex. When it becomes a matter of sacrificing one's own life, health, and sanity to the principle of noncollaborative resistance, equal weight must be given to that too. One's own life and well-being also have value, and it is at least arguable that they should not be automatically sacrificed to abstract principle. At the very least, it is an individual's own decision to make, depending on the circumstances, and not for outsiders to judge, condemn, or coerce.

Finally, there is the ethical question of the purpose of a grand jury. It is patently clear from this and other cases that grand juries were badly misused and manipulated in the postwar years to be instruments of persecution by the government. While at least some of these improprieties have been corrected and reformed, the larger ethical question of the use of the grand jury and the contempt sentence to coerce testimony remains. While it is not torture per se, the deprivation of a person's liberty and confinement in often miserable conditions does involve the infliction of pain on the resisting "witness." And the purpose of that pain is to force the witness to divulge desired information. This is the rationale behind the use of torture, which is forbidden implicitly by the U.S. Constitution and explicitly by the United Nations Convention against Torture and other international covenants. Therefore, the abiding question remains whether the continuing use of the grand jury in this way constitutes a violation of human rights. I think it does.

As for the Lexington Six, it is always heartening, I believe, to see people stand up—unprompted and unrewarded—for human rights and dignity and against injustice. I wanted, therefore, to tell their story—and in so doing, to bear witness.

AFTERWORD AND ACKNOWLEDGMENTS

I was on the faculty of the Honors Program at the University of Kentucky as an assistant professor from 1971 to 1976. I served as the founding chair of the Women's Studies Committee and was otherwise active in feminist activities on campus. Before the Lexington Six case developed, I knew some of its future members—notably, Jill Raymond and Gail Cohee—through these activities. I met Marla Seymour later and corresponded with Nancy Scott and the others when they were in jail. I was also on the fringe of the group that lived at the "Off Hand Manor" collective, many of whom I knew in varying degrees.

I happened to be away on a sabbatical leave in Cambridge, Massachusetts, for the fall semester of 1974 and therefore not in Lexington while Susan Saxe and Kathy Power were there. I was in the Boston area with my new partner/lover Anne Rhodenbaugh (later Barrett) in early January 1975 when the startling news broke that Saxe and Power had lived for a while in Lexington. I read the famous John Wood article in the *Boston Globe* when it first appeared, and the local Boston-area television stations were consumed with the story at the time.

So when I returned to Lexington in mid-January to resume teaching at UK for the spring 1975 semester, I was aware that fugitives Saxe and Power had been there and somewhat familiar with their stories but unaware that they had been involved with any of the students or friends that I knew.

Gradually, however, I discovered that the FBI was questioning many of these people and, as the case intensified, became mindful of the fear and dread that was spreading through the community. I did not feel personally threatened, because I had had no contact with the fugitives, but as the dragnet spread, it became clear that all known feminists were at some risk of hearing that dreaded knock on the door.

In a somewhat odd coincidence, Anne Rhodenbaugh had known Kathy Power and Susan Saxe when they were students at Brandeis. (Anne had been Kathy's dorm mother.) She'd had no further contact with them, but she was in Lexington (on the UK administrative staff) at the time the two were there in 1974 and had seen them, she realized retrospectively, at some feminist gatherings. But, as they were in some disguise, and as it had been a matter of years since Anne had seen them, she didn't recognize them—and apparently they didn't recognize her. If they had, Kathy Power recently told me, they might have left town immediately (email to author, October 8, 2018).

Anne, meanwhile, had by early 1975 moved to New England, living on a farm in Kittery, Maine. At some point in late spring she found herself being tailed everyday by a car with two men in suits—the usual FBI attire—when she left for work at her new position at the University of New Hampshire. Someone had evidently informed the FBI about her connection to Kathy Power. At about the same time as the Lexington Six contempt hearing in mid-March, my mail from Anne began being opened—and not very subtly: the envelopes were torn and officially resealed with Scotch tape and stamped by the U.S. Post Office. My mail carrier in Lexington even commented on it at one point, disapprovingly: "I don't care what you're doing," he said, "but no one has the right to open your mail."

As noted in the text, I attended the contempt hearings of the Lexington Six on March 6 and 8 and visited the Bell and Franklin County Jails thereafter. After Jill's release, she came up to Boston to speak at a Gay Pride parade and rally on June 28, 1976. Anne and I attended the rally, and we met up with Jill afterward for dinner at the then-trendy Orson Welles restaurant in Cambridge. I was later visited by the FBI agent, as noted, in Portsmouth, New Hampshire, in 1978.

I have long wanted to write up the story of the Lexington Six, but until the audiotapes of the Pam Goldman interviews became available, I didn't feel the project was feasible. Those interviews—thirty-two in all—were recorded by Goldman in 1986–89 with most of the principal people involved in the case. These were later deposited by Goldman in the Louis B. Nunn Center for Oral History in the University of Kentucky Libraries but remained closed until recently. The restrictions on several have, however, been lifted, so that only the permission of the interviewee is now required. I have thus, with those permissions granted, as well as those granted by Pam Goldman, been able to access fourteen of the most important of these interviews. Three of the principals are now deceased: Letty Ritter, Carey Junkin, and Sue Ann Salmon. Those interviews are accessible without restriction. There were no restrictions placed on the interviews of Robert Sedler and Sally Kundert. In 2019, Pam Goldman granted me permission to access the hitherto restricted tapes of M. E. Hixson, Judith Peterson, and Mark Paster. The following graciously gave me permission to access their recorded interviews: Jill Raymond, Judy Martone Peluso, Peter J. Taylor, Barbara Sutherland, Marla Seymour, Edwin Hackney, Janet Gallagher, and Mark Paster. I want to express my thanks and gratitude to all these individuals whose cooperation made the book possible. A huge debt of gratitude is also owed to Pam Goldman, who spent countless hours and traveled many miles to record these interviews, which provide invaluable insights into the personal experiences of the participants in the Lexington Six drama.

I also want to give my heartfelt thanks to Jill Raymond, who fully cooperated with this project from the beginning, providing me with scores of documents about the case from her personal collection, including her valuable "Jail Notes," an unpublished manuscript, and her FBI file, as well as that of William Gilday, which she happens to have (both obtained through FOIA requests). Jill has also provided me with much additional information through a stream of emails. Also my thanks to Marla Seymour, who likewise gave me important information and perspectives in a series of emails in 2017–18; Katherine Power, who graciously shared with me parts of her unpublished memoir, *Surrender*, as well as other recollections about her stay in Lexington; and Susan Saxe, for granting me permission to cite from her letters to Jill Raymond.

Others who in the past several months have kindly provided me with clarifying and enlightening material include Ellen Grusse and Mary Anna Palmer, who filled me in on aspects of the Connecticut case; Sally Kundert, who gave me further fresh information about her encounters with the FBI in 1975; Janet Gallagher and Julie Schwarzberg about the New York Grand Jury Project; Laurie Raymond about the Seattle resistance; Barbara Sutherland; Mark Paster; Jonathan Coleman; Nancy Gertner; M. Hardy Griffith; and Ann Devigne Donovan. My thanks to them all.

Also helpful were Desiree Wallen, archives technician at the National Archives at Atlanta, which holds the transcripts of the contempt hearings in the U.S. District Court of Eastern Kentucky, as well as the "Grumbles" motion; Robert Beebe, archivist at the National Archives at Kansas City, which holds the appeals documents related to the case; H. Neil Reid, archives librarian, Sixth Circuit Court of Appeals in Cincinnati; Judy Hackett, oral history librarian, and Jeff Suchanek, senior archivist, University of Kentucky Libraries; the research and general library staffs of the Wisconsin Historical Society in Madison; the University of Illinois Libraries staff in Champaign-Urbana; the Interlibrary Loan staff at Fogler Library at the University of Maine; the Freedom of Information Act staff at the FBI, who provided me with over eight hundred pages of redacted files; Margaret A. Hogan, copyeditor; and at the University of Massachusetts Press, Brian Halley, senior editor; Sally Nichols, production director; Rachael DeShano, production editor, and the press's editing staff, board, and readers. Unless otherwise noted, all letters to me and to Anne Rhodenbaugh (now deceased) are in my possession. All emails and unpublished materials are published by permission of the sender (when obtainable) and the author.

REFERENCES

Audiotaped Interviews

All interviews are located in the Bluegrass Music Hall of Fame and Museum Oral History Project, Louis B. Nunn Center for Oral History, University of Kentucky Libraries, Lexington. Copyright © University of Kentucky, all rights reserved. Published by permission.

Gallagher, Janet. 1987. Interview with Pam Goldman, September 16, 1987.

Hackney, Edwin. 1989. Interview with Pam Goldman, June 19, 1989.

Hixson, M. E. 1986. Interview with Pam Goldman, October 27, 1986.

Junkin, J. Carey. 1987. Interview with Pam Goldman, October 15, 1987.

Kundert, Sally. 1986. Interview with Pam Goldman, October 25, 1986.

Paster, Mark. 1987. Interview with Pam Goldman, January 18, 1987.

Peluso, Judy Martone. 1987. Interview with Pam Goldman, September 18, 1987.

Peterson, Judith. 1987. Interview with Pam Goldman, September 25, 1987.

Raymond, Jill. 1987a. Interview with Pam Goldman, January 24, 1987.

———. 1987b. Interview with Pam Goldman, September 11, 1987.

Ritter, Letitia Ann. 1987. Interview with Pam Goldman, August 30, 1987.

Salmon, Sue Ann. 1987. Interview with Pam Goldman, March 9, 1987.

Sedler, Robert. 1986. Interview with Pam Goldman, October 6, 1986.

Seymour, Marla. 1987a. Interview with Pam Goldman, January 16, 1987.

———. 1987b. Interview with Pam Goldman, January 17, 1987.

Sutherland, Barbara. 1986. Interview with Pam Goldman, December 22, 1986.

———. 1987. Interview with Pam Goldman, January 3, 1987.

Taylor, Peter J. 1987. Interview with Pam Goldman, October 30, 1987.

Articles

Abbott, Sidney, et al. 1975. "Petition #3: Vindication of the Rights of Feminists." *Majority Report*, March 8, 1975.

Alpert, Jane. 1973. "Mother Right: A New Feminist Theory." *Ms.*, August 1973.

Anonymous. 1974. "Chicanos Win." *El Gallo*, July–August 1974.

———. 1975a. "FBI Misuse of Grand Jury Alleged by Lawyers in Fugitive Case." *New York Times*, February 23, 1975.

———. 1975b. "Agent Watching." *Majority Report*, April 19, 1975.

———. 1975c. "I Was a Lesbian for the FBI." *Majority Report*, April 19, 1975.

———. 1975d. "Saxe Arrested: Lesbians Harassed." *off our backs*, April–May 1975.

———. 1975e. "FBI Defines Harassment." *Majority Report*, June 14, 1975.

———. 1975f. Editorial. *Quash*, October 1975.

———. 1975g. "Free Veronica Vigil." *El Gallo*, October–November 1975.

———. 1976a. "Ellen Grusse and Terry Turgeon." *Majority Report*, January 24–February 17, 1976.

———. 1976b. "Grand Juries: A History of Repression." *Quash*, January 1976.

———. 1976c. "Counter-Attack. April 8th." *Quash*, May 1976.

———. 1976d. "Jill Raymond Is Free." *Quash*, May 1976.

———. 1976e. "Veronica Vigil Out!" *Quash*, May 1976.

———. 1977a. "Michelle Whitnack: Beaten and Released." *Quash*, January–February 1977.

———. 1977b. "When Women Become Massively Political." *Quash*, May–June 1977.

———. 1977c. "Women Resist." *Quash*, May–June 1977.

———. 1978. "FBI Returns." *Quash*, November–December 1978.

Asbury, Edith Evans. 1975. "Bomb Jury Frees Patricia Swinton." *New York Times*, September 27, 1975.

Atkinson, Ti-Grace. 1974. "Metaphysical Cannibalism." In *Amazon Odyssey*, 56–63. New York: Links Books.

Bailey, Rex. 1975a. "Judge Cites Grand Jury Witnesses." *Courier-Journal*, March 7, 1975.

———. 1975b. "Six Are Ruled in Contempt, Ordered Jailed in Lexington." *Courier-Journal*, March 9, 1975.

Ballinger, Scott. 1976. "Jill Raymond Supporters Stage People's Grand Jury, Indict 4."*Kentucky Kernel*, March 10, 1976.

Berger, Dan, with Roxanne Dunbar-Ortiz. 2010. "'This Struggle Is for Land!': Race, Territory, and National Liberation." In *The Hidden 1970s: Histories of Radicalism,* edited by Dan Berger, 57–76. New Brunswick, NJ: Rutgers University Press.

Berger, Say. 2016. "White Women, Anti-Imperialist Feminism and the Story of Race within the US Women's Liberation Movement." *Women's History Review* 25, no. 5: 756–70.

Bernikow, Louise. 2008. "1974 Rape Trial Spurred Women's Quest for Justice." *We.News,* September 30, 2008.

Blum, Patty. 1975. Typescript Notes. Freedom Archives, www.freedomarchives.org, April 1975.

Boston Gay Collective. 1973. "In Amerika They Call Us Dykes." In *Our Bodies, Ourselves,* by Boston Women's Health Book Collective, 56–73. New York: Simon and Schuster.

Boudin, Cathy [Kathy], and Brian Glick. 1975. "Civics Lesson." *Majority Report,* April 19, 1975.

Braden, Anne. 1975. "The 50s and Now." *Quash,* October 1975.

Brown, Rita Mae. 1975. "Rita Mae Brown on Everything." *Gay Community News,* May 24, 1975.

Celarier, Michelle. 1976. "Mother of Seattle Activist Resists Grand Jury Probe." *Liberation News Services,* September 25, 1976.

"Chicanos Win." 1974. *El Gallo,* July–August 1974.

Clark, Judy, et al. 1975. "Petition #1: Loyalties in Face of the State." *Majority Report,* March 8, 1975.

Coalition to End Grand Jury Abuse. 1979. Untitled Notice. *Grand Jury Washington Bulletin,* April 1979. Carl and Anne Braden Papers, box 125, folder 23, Wisconsin Historical Society Archives, Madison.

Cohee, Gail, et al. 1975a. "Statement of Witnesses Subpoenaed by Lexington Federal Grand Jury." March 8, 1975. Carl and Anne Braden Papers, box 143, folder 2, Wisconsin Historical Society Archives, Madison.

———. 1975b. "Commentary: Grand Jury Defense Committees." *off our backs,* April–May 1975.

Cooper, Janet. 1975. "Saxe's Companion in Bust Speaks to GCN." *Gay Community News,* April 12, 1975.

Cordova, Jeanne, and Ann Doczi. 1975. "Power or Paralysis." *Lesbian Tide,* May–June 1975.

Creed, David. 1975. "Vigil Protests." *Courier-Journal,* September 21, 1975.

Cueto, Marie. Ca. 1978. Video Interview with Michael Deutsch. mediabarn.org.

Daly, Nancy, and Joel Zakem. 1975. "Jill Raymond in Jail." *Kentucky Kernel,* October 17, 1975.

Davis, Angela. 1975. "Jo Anne Little: The Dialectics of Rape." *Ms.,* June 1975.

Deming, Barbara. 1975. "To Fear Jane Alpert Is to Fear Ourselves." *off our backs*, May–June 1975.

Deutsch, Michael E. 1984. "The Improper Use of the Federal Grand Jury: An Instrument for the Internment of Political Activists." *Journal of Law and Criminology* 75, no. 4: 1159–96.

Dodge, Jefferson, and Joel Dyer. 2014. "Los Seis de Boulder." *Boulder Weekly*, May 29, 2014.

Donner, Frank J., and Eugene Cerruti. 1972. "The Grand Jury Network." *Nation*, January 3, 1972.

Donner, Frank J., and Richard I. Lavine. 1973. "Kangaroo Grand Juries." *Nation*, November 19, 1973.

Dunbar, Roxanne. 1970. "Female Liberation as the Basis for Social Revolution." *Notes from the Second Year: Radical Feminism*, edited by Shulamith Firestone and Anne Koedt, 48–56. New York: N.p.

Editorial. 1975. *Courier-Journal*, April 7, 1975.

El Comite de Nueva York Contra la Represión. 1978. "A La Represión del Gran Jurado/FBI." *Quash*, November–December 1978.

Finley, John. 1975. "Group Meets with FBI to Protest Probe." *Courier-Journal*, March 27, 1975.

Flower, Rose. 1975a. "Woman Picked Up in Philly Police Panic." *Gay Community News*, April 12, 1975.

———. 1975b. "Saxe Arraigned." *Gay Community News*, April 19, 1975.

Fosburgh, Lacey. 1975. "Trial Raises Questions on Rape Victims' Rights." *New York Times*, October 30, 1975.

Fox, Tina. 1975. "I Was a Feminist for the FBI." *Majority Report*, May 3, 1975.

Franks, Lucinda. 1994. "Annals of Crime: Return of the Fugitive." *New Yorker*, June 13, 1994.

Gatz, Carolyn. February 19, 1975. "Local FBI Probe Sparks Court Fight." *Lexington Herald*.

———. March 8, 1975. "Six Face Jail Terms in Contempt Hearing." *Lexington Saturday Herald-Leader*.

———. March 9, 1975. "Six Are Jailed for Contempt." *Lexington Sunday Herald-Leader*.

———. April 30, 1975. "Victory, 'Sort Of.'" *Lexington Herald*.

———. May 7, 1975. "3 Agree to Talk for Freedom." *Lexington Herald*.

———. July 28, 1975a. "'I'm Surviving' . . . Raymond Awaits Outcome of 'Lost' Appeal." *Lexington Herald*.

———. July 28, 1975b. "Jails Made to Hold Men Are Problems for Women." *Lexington Herald*.

———. July 30, 1975. "Prisoner Transferred after News Interview." *Lexington Herald.*

———. August 6, 1975. "Local Court Backed in Contempt Hearing." *Lexington Herald.*

———. September 27, 1975. "Jill Raymond Supporters Hold 24-Hour Vigil Here." *Lexington Herald.*

———. March 8, 1976. "Jill Raymond Says Jail Has Taken Its Toll." *Louisville Times.*

———. May 4, 1976. "Jill Raymond Ends Jail Term of 14 Months for Contempt." *Louisville Times.*

Goldman, Pam E. 1998. "'I Am Kathy Power': Expressions of Radicalism in a Counterculture Community." In *No Middle Ground: Women and Radical Protest,* edited by Kathleen M. Blee, 19–37. New York: New York University Press.

Gombe, Harry. 1977. "Grand Juries: The New American Inquisitions." *Open Road,* Spring 1977.

Grand Jury Project. 1975. Statement. *Quash,* October 1975.

———. 1976. "FBI/Grand Jury Jail Four." Pamphlet. Author's Collection.

———. 1978. Letter/Flyer. August 21, 1978. Carl and Anne Braden Papers, box 125, folder 23, Wisconsin Historical Society Archives, Madison.

Grimstad, Kristen, and Susan Rennie. 1975. "Interview." *off our backs,* May–June 1975.

Grusse, Ellen, and Terri Turgeon. 1975. "The FBI and Grand Juries." *off our backs,* February 1975.

———. 1977. "Warning." *Quash,* May–June 1977.

Hands, Debbie. 1975. "q. and a." *off our backs,* May–June 1975.

Hanover, Renee C. 1975. Letter to Paul Alpert. April 10, 1975. Freedom Archives, freedomarchives.org.

Harris, Richard. 1976a. "Annals of the Law; Taking the Fifth—I." *New Yorker,* April 5, 1976.

———. 1976b. "Annals of the Law; Taking the Fifth—II." *New Yorker,* April 12, 1976.

———. 1976c. "Annals of the Law; Taking the Fifth—III." *New Yorker,* April 19, 1976.

Hixson, M. E. 1977. "Grand Jury Abuse: A Case in Point." *AAUW Journal,* April 1977.

———. 1978. "Bringing Down the Curtain on the Absurd Drama of Entrances and Exits—Witness Representation in the Grand Jury Room." *American Criminal Law Review* 15, no. 4 (Spring): 307–35.

Homer, Julia. 1975. "Prosecutor: 'Are You Trying to Show Contempt for This Court?' Mae West: 'I'm Trying My Best to Hide It.'" *Second Wave,* Spring 1975.

Horan, Jean. 1975. "Feminism Is Not Collaboration." *off our backs*, July 1975.

Johnston, Jill. 1975. "The Myth of Bonnies without Clydes: Lesbian Feminism and the Male Left." *Village Voice*, April 28, 1975.

Johnstone, Laurie. 1975. "Notes on People." *New York Times*, December 30, 1975.

Jones, Arthur. 1975. "For 4½ Years FBI Pursued a Trail That Went Nowhere." *Boston Globe*, March 29, 1975.

Jordan, Susan. 2000. "The Case of Inez Garcia" (1977). In *Dear Sisters: Dispatches from the Women's Liberation Movement*, edited by Rosalyn Baxandall and Linda Gordon, 201–3. New York: Basic Books.

Junkin, Carey. 1975. "A View from the Madison County Jail." *Kentucky Kernel*, April 7, 1975.

Kennedy, Florynce, et al. 1975. "Petition #2: The Crisis in Feminism." *Majority Report*, March 8, 1975.

Kihss, Peter. 1977. "Bomb Note Asks End to U.S. Investigation." *New York Times*, February 20, 1977.

Kirkharn, Michael J. 1976. "Jill Raymond Waits It Out." *Nation*, February 28, 1976.

Koedt, Anne. 1971. "Loving Another Woman." In *Notes from the Third Year: Women's Liberation*, edited by Anne Koedt and Shulamith Firestone, 25–29. New York: Notes from the Third Year.

Lafferty, Elaine. 1975a. "The Saxe Case: Feds Fantasize 'Huge Lesbian Underground.'" *Majority Report*, April 19, 1975.

———. 1975b. "Saxe Pleads Not Guilty." *Majority Report*, April 19, 1975.

Lambert, Pam. 1993. "Alice Doesn't Live Here Anymore." *People*, October 4, 1993.

Lee, Julie. 1975. Letter. *Majority Report*, April 19, 1975.

Lexington Grand Jury Defense Committee. 1975. Statement. August 19, 1975. Author's Collection.

———. 1976. Statement. May 6, 1976. Carl and Anne Braden Papers, box 143, folder 2, Wisconsin Historical Society Archives, Madison.

Louisville Civil Liberties Union. 1975. Flyer. April 18, 1975. Author's Collection and Gilday FBI Files, Private Collection.

Millett, Kate. 1970. "Sexual Politics: A Manifesto for Revolution." In *Notes from the Second Year: Radical Feminism*, edited by Shulamith Firestone and Anne Koedt, 111–12. New York: N.p.

Mitchell, Ron. 1975a. "Moynahan Grants Immunity to Witnesses." *Kentucky Kernel*, February 24, 1975.

———. 1975b. "Grand Jury Witnesses Cited for Contempt." *Kentucky Kernel*, March 7, 1975.

Morgan, Robin. 1970a. "Good-Bye to All That." *Rat*, February 9–23, 1970.

Morrison, Mathew M. 2001. "Currents in the Stream: The Evolving Legal Status of Gay and Lesbian Persons in Kentucky." *Kentucky Law Journal* 89, no. 4: 1159–1202.

Nelson, W. Dale. 1978. [no title]. Associated Press, August 24, 1978. http://www .lexisnexis.com.

New York Committee against Grand Jury Repression. Ca. 1978. "The Political Grand Jury." Author's Collection.

Park, Roxanne, and Emmett Ward. 2010. "Grand Jury: Three Who Refused to Speak" (1976). In *Creating a Movement with Teeth: A Documentary History of the George Jackson Brigade*, edited by Daniel Burton-Rose, 231–39. Oakland, CA: PM Press.

Peoples Grand Jury. 1976. Report. March 8, 1976. Author's Collection.

Peterson, Bill. 1975a. "Fugitives . . . Two of FBI's Most Wanted Fit into Lexington Subculture." *Courier-Journal*, May 11, 1975.

———. 1975b. "Lexington Gays Shaken by Case" *Courier-Journal*, May 11, 1975.

Power, Katherine. 2010. "My Journey to Non-Violence." Practical Peace. www .practicalpeace.com.

Power, Kathy, and Susan Saxe. 1971. "Underground in America." *off our backs*, April 15, 1971.

Radicalesbians. 1971. "The Woman Identified Woman." In *Notes from the Third Year: Women's Liberation*, edited by Anne Koedt and Shulamith Firestone, 81–83. New York: Notes from the Third Year.

Raymond, Dorothy. 1975. Letter to the Editor [of the *Lexington Herald*]. April 14, 1974. Private Collection.

Raymond, Jill. 1975a. "Complexities." *off our backs*, May–June 1975.

———. 1975b. Statement. August 8, 1975. Author's Collection.

———. 1976a. "Jail Notes." Unpublished manuscript. Private Collection.

———. 1976b. Statement. *Susan Saxe Defense Committee Newsletter*, March 1976. Author's Collection. Also published in *Gay Community News*, November 22, 1975.

———. 1976c. "Raymond, Freed: Says 'It Was Worth It.'" *Lesbian Tide*, July–August 1976.

———. 1989. "The Grand Jury: An Extension of FBI Authority." In *It Did Happen Here: Recollections of Political Repression in America*, edited by Bud Schultz and Ruth Schultz, 290–302. Berkeley: University of California Press.

Saxe, Susan. 1975a. Statement. *Majority Report*, April 5, 1975.

———. 1975b. Statement. June 9, 1975. Author's Collection.

———. 1976. Statement. *Susan Saxe Defense Committee Newsletter*, March 1976. Author's Collection.

Segal, Mark. 2019. "From *And Then I Danced.*" In *The Stonewall Reader*, edited by Jason Baumann, 119–27. New York: Penguin.

Seymour, Marla, et al. 1975. "Statement from Five Imprisoned Witnesses." March 19, 1975. Private Collection.

Shinell, Grace. 1975. "Pat Swinton: Jane Taught Me Feminism." *Majority Report*, April 19, 1975.

Shoshana. 1975. "'What You Do Matters.'" *off our backs*, July 1975.

Smith-Rosenberg, Carroll. 1975. "The Female World of Love and Ritual: Relations between Women in Nineteenth-Century America." *Signs* 1, no. 1 (Autumn): 1–29.

Starr, Meg. 2010. "'Hit Them Harder': Leadership, Solidarity, and the Puerto Rican Independence Movement." In *The Hidden 1970s: Histories of Radicalism*, edited by Dan Berger, 135–54. New Brunswick, NJ: Rutgers University Press.

Susan Saxe Defense Committee. 1975. Statement. June 11, 1975. Author's Collection.

Taylor, Carol. 2005. "'Los Seis de Boulder' Died in '74 Car Bombings." *Boulder Daily Camera*, May 15, 2005.

V. V. D. C. [Veronica Vigil Defense Committee]. 1976. Letter. *Quash*, January 1976.

Von Hoffman, Nicholas. 1975. "Even If They're Not Guilty, They Still Could Be of Some Help." *Washington Post*, March 19, 1975.

Ward, Joe. 1975a. "Woman Answers Grand Jury Questions about Fugitives." *Courier-Journal*, March 21, 1975.

———. 1975b. "Lexington Women Jailed in FBI Case May Be Freed." *Courier-Journal*, April 30, 1975.

———. 1975c. "Two Women in Grand Jury Case Say Roles as Political Activists New." *Courier-Journal*, May 8, 1975.

———. 1976. "Jill Raymond's Backers Hold Grand Jury." *Courier-Journal*, March 9, 1976.

Whitehorn, Laura, and Ginger Ryan. 1975. Letter to the Editor. *Real Paper*, February 2, 1975.

Wiseman, Devie. 1975. "Rights and Rungs." *Kentucky Kernel*, March 16, 1975.

Women of the Weather Underground. 1975. "Did Jane Talk? The View from Women Underground." *Majority Report*, April 19, 1975.

Wood, John B. 1975a. "Were Susan Saxe and Kathy Power Living in Kentucky?" *Boston Sunday Globe,* January 12, 1975.

———. 1975b. "Capture of Saxe: Lucky Break or Setup?" *Boston Globe,* March 30, 1975.

Wood, John B., and Robert J. Anglin. 1975. "Saxe Bail $350,000, Power Hunt Intensified." *Boston Globe,* March 28, 1975.

Woolley, Bryan. 1975. "'I Am Contemptuous.'" *Courier-Journal,* October 25, 1975.

Books

Abbott, Sidney, and Barbara Love. 1972. *Sappho Was a Right-On Woman.* New York: Stein and Day.

Atkinson, Ti-Grace. 1974. *Amazon Odyssey.* New York: Links Books.

Berger, Dan. 2006. *Outlaws in America: The Weather Underground and the Politics of Solidarity.* Oakland, CA: AK Press.

———, ed. 2010. *The Hidden 1970s: Histories of Radicalism.* New Brunswick, NJ: Rutgers University Press.

Berman, Harold J. 1983. *Law and Revolution: The Formation of the Western Legal Tradition.* Cambridge, MA: Harvard University Press.

Brand, Johanna. 1993. *The Life and Death of Anna Mae Aquash.* Toronto: Lorimer.

Brownmiller, Susan. 1999. *In Our Time: Memoir of a Revolution.* New York: Dial.

Buitrago, Ann Mari, and Leon Andrew Immerman. 1981. *Are You Now or Have You Ever Been in the FBI Files? How to Secure and Interpret Your FBI Files.* New York: Grove.

Burrough, Bryan. 2015. *Days of Rage: America's Radical Underground, the FBI and the Forgotten Age of Revolutionary Violence.* New York: Penguin.

Burton-Rose, Daniel, ed. 2010a. *Creating a Movement with Teeth: A Documentary History of the George Jackson Brigade.* Oakland, CA: PM Press.

———. 2010b. *Guerrilla USA: The George Jackson Brigade and the Anticapitalist Underground of the 1970s.* Berkeley: University of California Press.

Churchill, Ward, and Jim VanderWall, eds. 1990. *The COINTELPRO Papers.* Boston: South End.

Daly, Mary. 1978. *Gyn/Ecology: The Metaethics of Radical Feminism.* Boston: Beacon Press.

Davis, James Kirkpatrick. 1997. *Assault on the Left: The FBI and the Sixties.* Westport, CT: Praeger.

Donovan, Josephine. 2012 (1985). *Feminist Theory: The Intellectual Traditions.* New York: Bloomsbury.

Echols, Alice. 1989. *Daring to Be Bad: Radical Feminism in America, 1967–1975.* Minneapolis: University of Minnesota Press.

Emerson, Deborah Day. 1983. *Grand Jury Reform: A Review of Key Issues.* Washington, DC: U.S. Department of Justice.

Faderman, Lillian. 2015. *The Gay Revolution: The Story of the Struggle.* New York: Simon and Schuster.

Firestone, Shulamith. 1971 (1970). *The Dialectic of Sex: The Case for Feminist Revolution.* New York: Bantam.

Fosl, Catherine. 2002. *Subversive Southerner: Anne Braden and the Struggle for Racial Justice in the Cold War South.* New York: Palgrave Macmillan.

Gertner, Nancy. 2011. *In Defense of Women: Memoirs of an Unrepentant Advocate.* Boston: Beacon Press.

Gilligan, Carol. 1982. *In a Different Voice: Psychological Theory and Women's Development.* Cambridge, MA: Harvard University Press.

Hobson, Emily K. 2016. *Lavender and Red: Liberation and Solidarity in the Gay and Lesbian Left.* Berkeley: University of California Press.

Johnson, David K. 2004. *The Lavender Scare: The Cold War Persecution of Gays and Lesbians in the Federal Government.* Chicago: University of Chicago Press.

Marcuse, Herbert. 1962 (1955). *Eros and Civilization: A Philosophical Inquiry into Freud.* New York: Vintage.

Martin, Del, and Phyllis Lyon. 1972. *Lesbian/Woman.* New York: Bantam.

Matthiessen, Peter. 1991 (1983). *In the Spirit of Crazy Horse.* New York: Vintage.

McSweeney, Anne. 2008. "'Highjacking the Movement': The Saxe-Alpert Controversy and the Making of Radical Feminism in the United States, 1974–76." B.A. thesis. Wesleyan University, Middletown, CT.

Medsger, Betty. 2014. *The Burglary: The Discovery of J. Edgar Hoover's Secret FBI.* New York: Knopf.

Morgan, Robin, ed. 1970b. *Sisterhood Is Powerful: An Anthology of Writings from the Women's Liberation Movement.* New York: Vintage.

National Lawyers Guild. 1974. *Representation of Witnesses before Federal Grand Juries: A Manual for Attorneys.* San Francisco: Fits Printing.

Potter, Will. 2011. *Green Is the New Red: An Insider's Account of a Social Movement under Siege.* San Francisco: City Lights Books.

Power, Katherine. N.d. *Surrender: A Journey from Guerrilla to Grandmother.* Unpublished manuscript. Private Collection.

Rosen, Ruth. 2000. *The World Split Open: How the Modern Women's Movement Changed America.* New York: Penguin.

Roth, Benita. 2004. *Separate Roads to Feminism: Black, Chicano, and White Feminist Movements in America's Second Wave.* Cambridge: Cambridge University Press.

Ruben, Albert. 2011. *The People's Lawyer: The Center for Constitutional Rights and the Fight for Social Justice from Civil Rights to Guantánamo.* New York: Monthly Review Press.

Sears, James T. 2001. *Rebels, Rubyfruit, and Rhinestones: Queering Space in the Stonewall South.* New Brunswick, NJ: Rutgers University Press.

Thompson, Becky. 2001. *A Promise and A Way of Life: White Antiracist Activism.* Minneapolis: University of Minnesota Press.

Weiner, Ted. 2012. *Enemies: A History of the FBI.* New York: Random House.

Wortman, Marlene Stein, ed. 1985. *Women in American Law: From Colonial Times to the New Deal.* New York: Holmes and Meier.

Legal and Congressional Documents

Appeal A. March 11, 1975a. *James Carey Junkin, Marla Seymour, Jill Raymond, Gail Cohee, [Nancy Scott], and Deborah Hands vs. United States of America.* Case no. 75–8045. U.S. Court of Appeals for the Sixth Circuit, Cincinnati. Record Group 276, Case Files, 1924–1994. National Archives–Chicago.

Appeal A. April 15, 1975b. Reply Brief for Petitioners-Appellants. *James Carey Junkin, Marla Seymour, Jill Raymond, Gail Cohee, [Nancy Scott], and Deborah Hands vs. United States of America.* Case no. 75–8045. U.S. Court of Appeals for the Sixth Circuit, Cincinnati. Record Group 276, Case Files, 1924–94. National Archives–Chicago.

Appeal B. June 5, August 5, 1975. *Jill Raymond vs. United States of America.* Case no. 75–1622. U.S. Court of Appeals for the Sixth Circuit, Cincinnati. Record Group 276, Case Files, 1924–94. National Archives–Chicago.

Church Report. 1976. U.S. Senate. *Intelligence Activities and the Rights of Americans. Final Report of the Select Committee to Study Governmental Operations with Respect to Intelligence Activities.* Book 2. Washington, DC: U.S. Government Printing Office.

Eilberg Hearings. 1977. U.S. House of Representatives. *Hearings before the Subcommittee on Immigration, Citizenship, and International Law of the Committee of the Judiciary.* 95th Congress, 1st session on HR 94, Grand Jury Reform. 2 vols. Washington, DC: U.S. Government Printing Office.

In re Cueto. 1978. 443 F.Supp. 857 (S.D.N.Y. 1978). https://law.justia.com.

In re Ellen Grusse and Marie Theresa Turgeon. February 19, 1975. Case no. 75–42. U.S. District Court D Connecticut, New Haven. 402 F.Supp. 1232 (D. Conn. 1975). http://scholar.google.com.

In re Grand Jury, Ivis Long Visitor, Angie Long Visitor, Joanna Ledeaux. 1975. 523 F.2d. 443 (8th Cir. 1975). https://law.justia.com.

In re Grand Jury, Veronica Vigil. 1975. 524 F.2d. 209 (10th Cir. 1975). https://law.justia.com.

In re Jill Raymond. November 7, 1975. Case no. 75–26. U.S. District Court, Eastern District of Kentucky, Lexington. Records of the District Courts of the United States, Record Group 21, Civil Case Files, 1974–75. National Archives–Atlanta.

In re Marie T. Turgeon et al. June 3, 6, 1975. 402 F.Supp. 1239 (D. Conn. 1975). http://scholar.google.com.

Moynahan, Bernard T., Jr. May 6, 1975. Findings of Fact and Order. *In re Grand Jury Proceedings, James Carey Junkin, Marla Seymour, Jill Raymond, Gail Cohee, [Nancy Scott], and Deborah Hands vs. United States of America.* Case no. 75–8045. U.S. District Court, Eastern District of Kentucky, Lexington. Record Group 276, Case Files, 1924–94. National Archives–Chicago.

Order. April 28, 1975. *In re Grand Jury Proceedings, James Carey Junkin, Marla Seymour, Jill Raymond, Gail Cohee, [Nancy Scott], and Deborah Hands vs. United States of America.* Case no. 75–8045. U.S. Court of Appeals for the Sixth Circuit, Cincinnati. Record Group 276, Case Files, 1924–94. National Archives-Chicago.

Transcript. March 7–8, 1975. Contempt Hearing. *In re Grand Jury Proceedings, Jill Raymond, Marla Seymour, Gail Cohee, Cary [sic] Junkin, Debbie Hands and [Nancy Scott].* Case no. 75–26. Docket entries [DE] 1–49. U.S. District Court, Eastern District of Kentucky, Lexington. Records of the District Courts of the United States, Record Group 21, Civil Case Files, 1974–75. National Archives–Atlanta.

United States of America v. Ellen Grusse and Marie Theresa Turgeon. 1975. 515 F.2d 157 (2d Cir. 1975). https://law.justia.com.

U.S. House of Representatives. 2018. *Federal Rules of Criminal Procedure.* Washington, DC: U.S. Government Printing Office.

U.S. Department of Justice. 2018. *U.S. Attorneys' Manual.* www.justice.gov.

FBI Documents

(Unless otherwise noted, all obtained through Freedom of Information Act requests.)

FBI. July 26, 1972. Memorandum. Louisville Bureau. Raymond FBI File. Private Collection.

FBI. September 9, 1974. Memorandum. https://vault.fbi.gov.

FBI. January 13, 1975. Teletype. Louisville Bureau. Author's Collection.

FBI. January 16, 1975. Teletype. From Director. Author's Collection.

FBI. January 22, 1975. Teletype. Louisville Bureau. Author's Collection.

FBI. January 23, 1975a. Louisville Bureau. Author's Collection.

FBI. January 23, 1975b. Teletype. New Haven Bureau. Author's Collection.

FBI. January 25, 1975. Night Teletype. New York Bureau. Author's Collection.

FBI. January 28, 1975a. Teletype. Honolulu Bureau. Author's Collection.

FBI. January 28, 1975b. Teletype. New Haven Bureau. Gilday FBI File. Private Collection.

FBI. January 29, 1975. Teletype. From Director. Author's Collection.

FBI. February 1, 1975. Teletype. Cincinnati Bureau. Author's Collection.

FBI. February 3, 1975. Report. Seattle Bureau. Raymond FBI File. Private Collection.

FBI. February 4, 1975. Teletype. Boston Bureau. Author's Collection.

FBI. February 5, 1975. Teletype. New Haven Bureau. Author's Collection.

FBI. February 7, 1975. Teletype. Louisville Bureau. Author's Collection.

FBI. February 8, 1975. Teletype. New York Bureau. Author's Collection.

FBI. February 20, 1975. Teletype. Louisville Bureau. Gilday FBI File. Private Collection.

FBI. February 25, 1975. Teletype Report. New Haven Bureau. Raymond FBI File. Private Collection.

FBI, March 6, 1975. Teletype. Louisville Bureau. Author's Collection.

FBI. March 11, 1975. Memorandum from Director. Gilday FBI File. Private Collection.

FBI. March 27, 1975. Teletype. From Director. Gilday FBI File. Private Collection.

FBI. March 28, 1975. Teletype. From Director. Gilday FBI File. Private Collection.

FBI. April 1, 1975. Night teletype. Louisville Bureau. Authors' Collection.

FBI. May 13, 1975. Memorandum. Philadelphia Bureau. Gilday FBI File. Private Collection.

FBI. March 23, 1976. Form Letter from Director. Raymond FBI File. Private Collection.

INDEX

JOSEPHINE DONOVAN is Professor Emerita of English at the University of Maine. She is the author of eleven books and fifty articles and editor of five collections. Her most recent books include *The Aesthetics of Care: On the Literary Treatment of Animals*; *European Local-Color Literature: National Tales, Dorfgeschichten, Romans Champêtres*; and *The Feminist Care Tradition in Animal Ethics*, co-edited with Carol J. Adams. *Feminist Theory: The Intellectual Traditions* (4th edition) and *Women and the Rise of the Novel* were named Outstanding Academic Books of the Year by *Choice*. Her work has been translated into eight languages. Born in Manila, Donovan earned her B.A. degree, *cum laude*, at Bryn Mawr College and her M.A. and Ph.D. in Comparative Literature at the University of Wisconsin–Madison.